W9-BCT-141

Doctrines of Imperialism

NEW DIMENSIONS IN HISTORY

Essays in Comparative History

Series Editor: Norman F. Cantor

John Wiley & Sons, Inc., New York • London • Sydney

DOCTRINES OF IMPERIALISM

A. P. THORNTON

WINGATE COLLEGE LIBRARY
WINGATE, N. C.

Copyright © 1965 by John Wiley & Sons, Inc.

All Rights Reserved
This book or any part thereof
must not be reproduced in any form
without the written permission of the publisher.

Library of Congress Catalog Card Number: 65-27652
Printed in the United States of America

For J.J.T.

34971

PREFACE

There will be no end to the books on imperialism, no last word issued concerning it, since there is no limit to the emotions it can arouse.

To say, however (as has been said), that the historian should stay out of this dangerous country is to deny both humanity to him and any power of illumination to his craft. Emotion owns a formidable record, as long as that of man himself. Any "proper study of mankind" has therefore to include it; and the historian must grapple with its problems with what equipment he can find. I do not doubt that a bias is to be found in this book: if this were not so, it would say even less than I hope it does about the nature, and fascination, of its subject.

Accordingly my thanks are owed to Professor Norman Cantor for suggesting that I do what I can with it.

A.P.T.

The University of Toronto,
September 1965

CONTENTS

"Our intentions are pure and noble,
our cause is just; the future
cannot fail us."

Louis Faidherbe, 1865.

ONE

Overtones

What is a doctrine?

That which is laid down, says the *Shorter Oxford English Dictionary*, as true concerning a particular department of knowledge. It is, says *Webster's*, a principle or position, or the body of principles, in any branch of knowledge.

A use of the word argues the presence of doctrinaires. These are the people who make the rules and act as the managers of that particular department, that special branch, of knowledge. They are busy men, and very ready to quarrel, since they are committed to taking a business to its end, however bitter. Lenin himself, a prince of this intellectual captivity, roughly handles the *bourgeois* scholars and publicists who say they are analyzing society,[1] but who in fact are only excusing it—for how could they do otherwise, since they are such ornaments of it? They continue to explain their case while not admitting they have a case to explain: for a need for reassurance, it seems, weighs on each successive generation of these persons. They must justify what their predecessors have done. But the Marxist concept of history (they are told) is not subjective at all. It describes what is true. It needs no justification. Once men have opened their eyes to see it, the misconceptions they have carried fall away. Whenever this doctrine, this body of true principle, is applied to modern problems, it illuminates their essence. At once they relate to one another, to the past, and to the pattern which the future must take. In a word, they make sense.

Part of the doctrine demands that sense is. there to be made.

[1] He calls them the hired coolies of the pen of imperialism.

1

Life encompasses a series of problems which can be resolved if the human intelligence is rationally used. Bred to this optimism, the committed have sometimes the best of the argument—and often enough its last word, for the "age of progress" complacently popularized by the nineteenth century's industrialists, the pattern-spinners of their time, has been sorely hammered by the twentieth century's events. The *bourgeois* has refused to claim the nearby ruins as his own, but he is now as aware of the Marxist as the latter always was of him. All argument has to pass, or at least to meet, a double test.

It is thus in a baleful atmosphere, in a context less of measured criticism than of sharp reproof, that imperialism in its theory and practice must, in this second half of the twentieth century, be examined. It comes before a court whose adverse verdict has already been handed down.

And what is imperialism?

The Emperor Napoleon I's own name for those who did not agree with him, who did not make sense as he understood it, was *idéologues:* and no one touches on this matter of imperialism without at once finding out how various are the ideologues who crowd at his elbow, ready to applaud or to ridicule, with equally misplaced vehemence, his definition. The many books that discuss it have a different point and purpose from those that deal with the history of empires and with the working methods of colonization—and for a good reason. Colonization, even when passing under the name of culture-shock, deals with the tangible. There are matters in evidence, ready for examination: the processes of settlement, the extension of the ring of government, the building of a colonial society secure in the support of its metropolis. These elements can be studied, compared, and contrasted from one century to another—in Turkestan and in the Americas, in Australia and in the Polish marches, in Dutch and in British South Africa, in Roman North Africa and in the Arab society which replaced it.

But imperialism is less a fact than a thought. At its heart is the image of dominance, of power asserted; and power is neither used nor witnessed without emotion. The colonizer who triumphed over nature and circumstance takes his place in the national story as a hero of his time; but the imperialist, forever using others for ends of his own, has bequeathed to his posterity the controversies that pursued him through life. Imperialism is therefore more often the name of the emotion that reacts to a series of events than a definition of the events themselves. Where colonization finds its analysts and analogists, imperialism must contend with crusaders, for and against. Books that set out to analyze it cast a net as wide as their authors' imaginations. "Is not the hatred of women so characteristic of Euripides," asks Emil Reich in his *Imperialism* (1905), "a consequence of the imperialization of the women of Athens?" Such a question either makes one think again about women, Euripides, empire, and Athens—or else close his book. Equating imperialism, especially in its English manifestations, with the context of national life, this tilter of lances goes on to discuss why English speech is so laconic and English music so sterile, why the Englishman is so addicted to irony and so proud of his sense of humor (for if his life were truly satisfying he would need neither), why he rates character above intellect, and why his women are so cold—if compared, say, to "the volatile daughters of Erin."[2]

In this view, imperialism is something for men only. It molds an entirely masculine world, whose keynote is stridency. In it the aggressive instinct holds, and must keep, pride of place. When not in the imperialist mood, the French developed their arts, the Americans their democracy, the Germans their thought, the Russians their literature and their soul. But imperialism is a sentiment that allows no rival. Before Republican Rome could become Imperial, declared H. T. Buckle in a once-famous *History of Civilisation* (1857–61),

it had to be eviscerated of its ancient core and filled with a servile population, to whom the old convictions were figures of speech.[3]

Wherever it arises, the aggressive instinct is sooner recognized than explained. It is found even in men who profess entire rationality. Adam Smith's fame is not that of an imperialist, since in his *Wealth of Nations* (1776) he adduces all manner of argument

[2] Emil Reich, *Imperialism* (London, 1905), pp. 49, 117; and see also his *Success among Nations* (London, 1904), p. 99.
[3] Henry T. Buckle, *A History of Civilisation in England* (London, 1857), I, p. 130.

why the British Empire of his day was such a wasteful, ill-managed institution, based on fallacious principle. Yet he also says, in a moment of penetration of quite another kind, that

It is a sort of instinctive feeling to us all, that the destiny of our name and nation is not here, in this narrow island which we occupy; that the spirit of England is volatile, not fixed.[4]

And from this mood of perception, from this recognition by a gentle soul of immortal longings, it is no distance at all to the roar of the lion. In 1911 it was Lloyd George, then notorious as a radical pacifist, the enemy of the *ethos* of the governing class, who was chosen to "speak for England," the better to make the Germans pause. He did it with a verve no contemporary "imperialist" could have matched. If a situation were to be forced upon us, he cried,

. . . in which peace could only be preserved by the surrender of what Britain has won by centuries of heroism and achievement, by allowing Britain to be treated where her interests were vitally affected as if she were of no account in the Cabinet of Nations, then I say emphatically that peace at that price would be a humiliation intolerable for a great country like ours to endure.[5]

To trace such instincts, with their deep historical roots, was the intention of the Austrian scholar Joseph Schumpeter. In his brilliant essay "The Sociology of Imperialisms" (1919) he explains national aggression by relating it to the concept of "interests"—such as Russia's drive for "warm water," or the United States' drive for "the west"—since only an appeal to images of security can arouse "the dark powers of the subconscious." But this concept has its own mysteries. It describes the growth of an attitude towards the world rather than the world itself. It severely tests men's qualities of perception. The ideas of any one generation, Schumpeter argues, spring less from the circumstances of its present than from its assessment of the past. The past holds a greater empire over men's minds than many men ever know, dis-

[4] Adam Smith, ed. E. Cannan, *An Inquiry into the Nature and Causes of the Wealth of Nations* (London, 1904), Bk. IV, vii, p. 238.
[5] Speech at the Mansion House, as reported in *The Times*, London, 22 July 1911.

cover, or admit. That significance, like memory, fades we do not easily believe. And, since ideas on national interest are so slow to change, events may overlay or contradict them. The last prop left to a bewildered patriot may only be the same sense of rectitude that supported his more fortunate forebears, for

the very word "imperialism" is applied only to the enemy, in a reproachful sense, being carefully avoided with reference to the speaker's own policies.[6]

In 1935 a distinguished student of the matter, Professor W. L. Langer, confessed his irritation at this state of affairs:

If imperialism is to mean any vague interference of traders and bankers in the affairs of other countries, you may as well extend it to cover any form of influence. You will have to admit cultural imperialism, religious imperialism, and what not. Personally I prefer to stick by a measurable, manageable concept.[7]

But in the thirty years that have passed others have not shown this preference; and even by 1935 it was a beleaguered position, for there were then as there are now many who did not and who do not share Professor Langer's attachment to manageable concepts, if only because the necessary powers of management are uncommon. To consider imperialism as the direct control of one area and its inhabitants by the government of another is certainly to deal in a manageable idea, but to do this at all asks for a detachment neither found nor wanted on the hustings, or in the basement rooms where conspirators gather. There, the sense of grievance and wrong is too heavy. These dissenters fight against not only their own subordinate status but against all the factors that have combined to fasten it upon them. They campaign against Professor Langer's "what not," which in fact makes up the context of their lives. Accordingly we find Indonesia's President Sukarno, at the first Afro-Asian conference held in Bandung in 1955, exhorting his willing listeners to change their style in myth. They should no longer think of imperialism, and of colonialism,

[6] Joseph Schumpeter, "The Sociology of Imperialisms," as reprinted and translated in *Imperialism and Social Classes,* ed. Bert Hoselitz (New York, Meridian Books, 1955), pp. 11, 71.
[7] William L. Langer, "A Critique of Imperialism," *Foreign Affairs,* xiv (October 1935), p. 103.

only in the classic form. . . . It has also its modern dress in the form of economic control, intellectual control, and actual physical control by a small but alien community within the nation.[8]

Even those who dislike these unclassic forms cannot doubt that they hold the field, ready to challenge all comers, and equipped in advance with a formidable weapon—the sense of rectitude itself.

Sukarno's reference to colonialism suggests that it, too, has a classic form. If so, no one has succeeded in defining it. It is a concept that has been unable to shake free of the bitterness that bred it. It is therefore not a "manageable" idea. It contains a recognition of one's own weakness, which acts as a corrosive, burning out the possibility that a dependent relationship can hold anything of value. Colonialism is only imperialism seen from below. It is that view of the controllers which is held by the controlled. The view is conditioned by attitude, latitude, altitude, and angle. What is being looked at is power—power itself, not its use; since the only point sensibly to be made about a benevolent despot is not that he is benevolent but that he is a despot. Power is always in the wrong hands. The European nations, in the past, were powerful. The Americans and the Russians are seen to have inherited their power today. Being powerful, they own empires; and, having empires, they will want them to extend, or at least will not want them to diminish, which is a wish that generates policies of extension. Their spheres of influence will not be called empires, for empire and any admission of imperialism, for reasons here to be examined, stand in the public pillory. But it does not matter and it will not matter what they are called, since imperialists are congenitally incapable of giving things their right names. Even their euphemism, a "sphere of influence," summons up the Svengali who rules it and casts him as the villain of the piece. "Colonialism," then, has been invented to describe not the status of the subordinate but the state of mind in which he lives. It represents the context of existence for the men whom other men move on the international chessboard. It categorizes those who are not agents, but patients.

The resentment goes deep. Never to initiate, always to react;

[8] *The Times,* London, 27 May 1955.

never to move, always to be moved; always to wait to see how a distant foreign capital (Rome or London in their era, Moscow or Washington in theirs) is going to deal with a local situation: people who have not had this experience cannot know how galling it can be. (Not that there are many now who do not know this in part at least: for the Russo-American confrontation in Cuba in October 1962 brought home to every bystander the innate indignity of his own position.) It is the shared sense of weakness that has drawn together the Afro-Asian *bloc*, which in political terms is less a *bloc* than a zone of protest. The same experience explains the degree of admiration that is accorded to Nasser in the United Arab Republic and, to a lesser extent (as he is so plainly a lesser man), to Castro in Cuba. These are charismatic heroes, who have successfully asserted themselves against great powers. What else it is that they have to assert is of secondary importance. Tunisia's President Bourguiba has cheerfully admitted this: "To show how truly independent one is, one insults the former colonial Power."[9] China's President Mao Tse-tung once remarked to a delegation of nationalists from a still-French Algeria, "The bond that unites us is that we have both been humiliated."[10] That is a bond indeed.

"Colonialism," evoking the awareness of men for their masters, of Friday for Crusoe, is thus of more recent coinage than "imperialism," which was used to dignify Crusoe's protection of Friday. The coinage itself is baser. In imperialism was invested as much emotion as money. It had friends as well as enemies; indeed it would never have made so many enemies had it not been able to claim so many friends. There have been many men who admitted willingly to the title of imperialist, insisting on their sense of mission, declaring their faith in the future, so long as that future was controlled by their own kind. They saw themselves as the trustees of civilization. They reckoned it their duty to see to it that civilization was disseminated among as many beneficiaries as could be contrived. They wanted to leave the world better than they found it, "to drive forward the blade a little further in our

[9] Habib Bourguiba, "The Outlook for Africa," *International Affairs,* vol. 37, no. 4 (October 1961), p. 428.
[10] *The Times,* London, 4 March 1958.

time,"[11] and it has yet to be proved that they did not succeed. In this school of thought and action such men as Hubert Lyautey in France and Alfred Milner in England were bred. They died unashamed of it, nor are their countries ashamed of them now, even in an age that has made rubbish of their plans.

But no one admits to the title of colonialist. It is too plainly abusive. If colonialism ever had a school, its alumni have taken care to conceal its whereabouts. To be a colonialist is to be, ineluctably, an exploiter. In the propaganda issued by the Soviet Union for Afro-Asian consumption, the bloated capitalist in top hat and limousine has been replaced by the man in topee and riding boots, cracking a rhinoceros-hide whip. (Topees are as out of fashion in the tropics as top hats on Wall Street; but to Soviet propaganda there is always an antiquarian tinge.) The point of the caricature is underlined when Russian and American dictionaries are compared. *Webster's* defines colonialism as

the system in which a country maintains foreign colonies for their economic exploitation.

(In parenthesis, it is worth remark that the *Oxford English Dictionary* does not contain the word at all—and that an English mind avoids framing such a notion as a "foreign colony," since a colony can hardly be foreign if it legally belongs to the colonizer's country.)

The Russian definition is more robustly expressed than the American, but stands at no great distance from it. The Russian language has no separate word for "colonialism": the same word serves for "colonization," and even that is carefully identified as a foreign importation. In the *Soviet Dictionary of Foreign Words* we find "kolonizatsiya" defined as

the seizure of a country or region by imperialists, accompanied by the subjection, brutal exploitation, and sometimes annihilation of the local population.

[11] A phrase from Lord Curzon's farewell speech as Viceroy of India, delivered to the exclusive (white) Byculla Club in Calcutta, 16 November 1905; ed. Sir T. Raleigh, *Lord Curzon in India, 1898–1905; being a Selection from his Speeches as Governor-General and Viceroy of India* (London, 1906), II, p. 332.

In the Soviet world imperialism, colonialism, and colonization are aspects of one and the same thing. They are all of them tentacles of the octopus it knows as international capitalism. When the world's Communist parties met in Moscow in November 1960, they issued a statement declaring that "the mainstay of colonialism today is the United States of America."[12] Radio stations throughout Africa and Asia, taking their lead from Moscow and Cairo, still hammer this home. For, in Lenin's definition which has long been accepted as the classic form, imperialism is the last phase of capitalism. Since the United States, also by classic definition, is nothing if not capitalist, that nation inevitably pursues an imperialist policy. It is equally obligatory on the Soviet Union, and on all freedom-loving peoples under totalitarian governments, to oppose it.

But here there is a common view. The fact that both antagonists level the same accusation at one another shows how offensive the implications of imperialism have become. Even Adolf Hitler, this century's principal freebooter to date, never admitted to it. Imperialism was plainly immoral, and thus a policy impossible to the Third Reich. In continuing so to think of it, the Russians, like the Germans, are only following an American lead; since the Americans, whose nation is the product of a rebellion against imperial control, could never consistently have thought of it as anything else. Many Americans long looked on governmental authority, even when not an outright usurpation, as suspect: and on the existence of a "foreign policy," a polite name for interference in other peoples' business, as something basically un-American.

In this century, those who have power must fortify themselves with moral sanction for its use. In the "western" democratic system, those who do not hold power but want to must claim that they will handle it better—that is to say, for the greater good of more people—than those now in office. In the totalitarian system, the dissenter is classified as a deviationist, an enemy of the people (and probably in someone else's pay) by those who claim to rule in the interests of the general will. Authority, knowing it must justify itself, does so by fulfilling and by being seen to fulfill a service to the community. But what justification can anyone show for the system of authority known as imperialism, which by its

[12] *The Times,* London, 16 November 1960.

nature cannot include any pattern of a community (since alien rule is of its essence) and which is designed from the outset to profit a few at the expense of the many? It is this lack of a moral center that, in the eyes of our own time, has so condemned it.

Yet, if the durable forms of governance are those that fulfill a social need, imperialism itself has been able to make just this claim. In the nineteenth century, American ideas of manifest destiny were reflected in Russian zeal for Pan-Slavism. Both were based on the conviction of a civilizing mission. Both saw it as a duty to proselytize. Both appealed less to man-made than to providential authority. Both, under that agency, carried with them the concepts and the apparatus of a superior society: before their force, the Indian in North America, the Turkoman in Central Asia, met a similar fate. The superior society crushed, absorbed, or segregated him. Whatever his destiny, it was not thereafter visible. His history, like that of the "displaced person" in twentieth-century Europe, remains a matter of guesswork. Those who do not find a way of asserting an identity, who make no mark on their own time, often escape the historian's notice. Who can know the woe and hope of Wends, Kurds, Armenians—save a Wend, a Kurd, or an Armenian? These are peoples which, never having caught the world's attention, do not stir its conscience; for even resentment has to find a context and a frame.

Accordingly, the process of *overland* expansion has been awarded an acceptance and favor of a kind denied to the spectacular, far-flung depredations of the sea powers, fanning out from continental beachheads and bridgeheads to which they had clearly no "right" in the first place. Climbing a range of hills or crossing a river in order to command the farther horizon seem natural, almost involuntary acts: but taking ship has always been an adventure, a conscious act of will, one that expects to impinge on someone else's world, to pass within someone else's horizon. Opposition is likely; and its very likelihood often produces it.

Moreover, the sea-power imperialists brought to their areas of conquest in Asia and in Africa only their apparatus of government. Forever in the minority, a wary handful among the million, they could not transfer and implant the creed of the societies from which they came. They had the power to police the great native communities, but they could not and did not expect them to assimilate European ways. The "loyalty" of native levies to an alien ruler was a loyalty to a superior technique of control. As the secrets of this technique were discovered, the loyalty naturally diminished; and what in its latter days is respectfully known as a "nationalist movement" normally begins its career as the protest of a lobby of educated men, denied scope for their talents in professions which are the perquisites of the ruling group.

Since the alien ruler could not absorb the ruled, since it was militarily impossible and economically undesirable for him to crush them, and since what segregation took place isolated the white expatriate himself far more effectively than the subordinate native, there was no way of stifling this protest, which grew stronger as the ruled found out through the channel of their alien education the precise type of argument by which their masters could be convinced.

The Spaniards who in the sixteenth century organized their empire in Mexico and South America were never inhibited by any doctrine of the rights of man. When Las Casas pleaded for better treatment for the Indian, he did so on the ground that it was virtue in the Spaniard to accord it, not the right of the Indian to demand it. But in the age that was penetrated throughout by the principles of the American and French Revolutions, Spain's Dutch, French, and English successors had to seek justification both for the presence and the use of their imperial mastery. This was hard to do. They could not appeal to divine right, or to Papal blessing, or to that simpler doctrine, honored indeed by time but not now by anything else, of "to the victor, the spoils." A morality had entered public affairs, which was never to leave them. Those humanitarians who first busied themselves with the task of abolishing the traffic in human beings found that they had to take the next, logical step: towards a similar abolition of slavery as a status. And when slavery was condemned, how could mastery survive? That the doctrine of a social contract kept odd company with every doctrine of imperial control, was a lesson easily learned by the subordinate. The European concept of the rights of man was one that made an explosive appeal to men who had never before had any opportunity of approaching a tribunal where such a claim would not have been dismissed as a piece of preposterousness. European officials under the distant sun might mute this doctrine, since they did not doubt that its consequences would prove as inimical to the maintenance of "law and order" as they had so often done in Europe itself; but, since they themselves were a product of it, they were never able entirely to conceal it from the perceptive among those they ruled. The protest the latter made had thus a permissive context. The dissenters, while pushing at this open door, came to look on imperialism as the agent of their oppression; forgetting that it was also the means of their rescue.

In contrast to Asia and Africa, in North America lived no great native population, able to obstruct the westward march and the growing optimism of the United States. In India the British could extend only their ring of government, not a way of life: but in America the republican government was free to take its demo- cratic creed wherever it went. Although there is little "consent of the governed" in evidence in the circumstances of the Louisiana Purchase, or of the attachment of Florida and California to the Union, it could be (and was) argued that the opening of these areas to the American way of life rescued them from the stagnation which was inseparable from their status as adjuncts of European imperial power. At the same time they provided new ground for the exercise, and consequent strengthening, of beneficial American ideas. It was in this fortunate context that the doctrine of manifest destiny, morally binding the citizens of the United States to establish the principles of their republic from the Atlantic to the Pacific, was confidently evolved. A significant myth soon attached to all its practices. The image of "the Frontier," whether evoked by television's unflinching heroes or by President John F. Kennedy, has never lost its potency and attraction. It conjures up a race- memory of pioneering effort, of courage, morality, and democ- racy. If and when American historians deal with imperialism in the national context they are referring only to the anti-Spanish adventure of the era of President William McKinley; and the only aspect of exploitation that is recognized in the image of expan- sion and in the story of the frontier is the physical exploitation of natural resources, placed there by God for Americans to use.

It was so in Russia also. There, destiny had always to be weighed in the same balance as policy. Successive Caesars or Tsars of Russia saw themselves as heirs of Byzantium, the Roman

Empire in the East, gone down to darkness and the Turk in the catastrophe of 1453. Russia held up a beacon light for civilization, was warden of the eastern marches, keeper of the imperial flame. The revolution of 1917 did not remove the vision. The moralities of the Tsardom were only overlaid by something even more sweeping, for there is no remarkable distance between Peter the Great and Stalin. Communism is itself an ideological imperialism, based on the conviction that it alone holds the map of human progress, it alone can trace the path. It is the twentieth century's projection of the eighteenth century's "Age of Reason," which is why it has strongly attracted many of the new nations that have emerged from their chrysalis of imperial control. Communism has no time for confusion. It never deals in doubt. It anchors all phenomena. All society has a blueprint; all history a plan. The world of nature itself can be planed and fashioned to meet the needs of mankind. Although space has yielded in part to this doctrine, and domestic agriculture hardly at all, its main principle—that scientific organization in every field, including the political, can lead men to unimagined prosperity—makes a powerful appeal. It can seem like a draught of refreshment to a people that has just arrived into an incoherent universe. Is there, then, a System, which has only to be followed? How reassuring to believe so!

But, if the methods of Communism are modern, its style is not. The great religions also base themselves on the principle of conviction. It has been their very dogmatism that has won them their victories, for where in the world today is there an imperialism more successful and deep-rooted than that of Islam, which since its ejection from Spain nearly five centuries ago has lost scarcely a yard of ground? Yet there does not arise, from the territories of the religious, the cry of "colonialism!"—the complaint that they are forced to conform to rules made by men long gone. The Koran, the Talmud, the Bible, the Vedas, the Papacy—all have their own empires. The peoples who gladly obey their rule do not consider themselves subject, in the sense of being subjected, to them. For not every form of imperialism undergoes the test of being seen and judged from below. Colonialism therefore, as a concept, comes into being only when the status of subordination is recognized as *unwelcome*.

More experience of this is available than those who pass

WINGATE COLLEGE LIBRARY
WINGATE, N. C.

through it are often ready to admit. Colonialism, although never so categorized, has long been rife in areas more familiar to us than Africa and the East. From the latter areas the demographers and ethnographers draw their examples of the plural society—a society, that is, wherein different races co-exist, as in Malaysia or Natal. (The point will later be developed that they do so only when they are made to.) In such societies it is color, physiognomy, language, and custom that emphasize the distinctions. But there are other badges of distinctiveness. Age and sex are two. Everyone lives in a plural society. In anyone's world there are two races—men and women. These are subdivided. There are the old and the young. There are the active and the passive, the agents and the patients. Amid these pluralities we have all to establish a way of living. We are judged by our skill at it, and we judge ourselves accordingly. We set store on the ability "to adjust," for we are made uneasy by those who cannot, or will not, so adjust: by adults who dislike children, by the young who make no allowance for the old, or by those who are not attracted by the opposite sex.

This social colonialism is indeed so widespread as to have avoided any such definition altogether. But it is there. A new word, it describes an old condition, an old captivity: for we all live our lives according to patterns we did not invent and might not, if we had power to decide it, repeat. Those who do not conform vary in type and impact from one age to another, but in any generation the saint, the artist, and the drunkard are all in their distinctive ways dissenters from the world as they find it, from the world as it has been bequeathed to them. This world has not touched them. It has not colonized their personalities. They do not belong anywhere in their place or time, and do not appear to have a way of life that anyone can adjust to or even understand. They suffer accordingly. For minds are more often, more easily, and more acceptably colonized than places—hence the insistence of psychiatry, a technique for mapping the historical geography of a personality, on the significance of what happens in childhood, for childhood is the period above all others in a man's life when the maximum amount of mental and moral colonization takes place. Mao Tse-tung's comment on humiliation applies beyond the borders of the purely political world: we have all had our "colonial period," whose bondage, light or heavy, we never forget.

And, if the history of personal motive is always so obscure, who can ever assess the full impact of great public movements upon the minds and souls of men?

What else, to those who did not know them, did not want them, did not believe in them, did not profit from them, were the processes of Hellenization, Romanization, and Christianity but examples of overriding and overbearing imperialism? (The story of Saul on the road to Damascus is, whatever else it is, also an account of the destruction of a personality.) History is usually content to record the successful imperialisms, and that history is written either by imperialists themselves or by those who admire and approve their achievement; as, for example, the writers who expatiate on "a great heritage," but who do not stop to consider those who were not mentioned in the will. What view of Athens and the splendors of Hellenic civilization has come down to us? Not that seen by a woman, by a Spartan, or by a slave. Annotated and commented upon by generations of scholars whose pupils have been drawn from the governing class, it is the photograph taken by a similar elite; by men who, whenever they debated the principles and practices of government, were convinced that this style of analysis must always remain the intellectual monopoly of their own kind. It is they who make the judgments in whose light the world thereafter moves forward. They determine the path that those to come will take; they landscape the vistas that those to come will admire. That the Assyrian "came down like a wolf on the fold" is a comment *post hoc,* made in the security that no outraged *démarche,* or even a posse of secret police, can ever descend upon the commentator from the palace in Babylon.

For "the verdict of history" is a verdict appealed to by those who believe it must go in their favor, since they suppose that those future judges who issue it will be circumstanced as themselves. The world as we know it today is the product of a series of imperialisms. It lies in the shadow of other men's victories and defeats, won and lost yesterday. We use a spiritual and an intellectual currency we did not ourselves mint. And this is what Rousseau so exclaims against, in his celebrated outburst that man is born free and is everywhere in chains. It is not a political system, it is life, he is railing at. Man is not born free. He is born into a family and into a society, into a time and into a place; and if he finds none of these propitious, he is bound to call them chains.

No one wishes for liberty who has not first recognized his state of bondage. Cultural colonialism is seldom so recognized. In western society chains have been fashioned for everyone to wear. Every woman acknowledges the imperial authority of the dress-houses of Paris and Rome. Dimensions are there decreed for them, as they are in Detroit for automobiles. Domestic "taste" can be bought at the interior decorator's. The world of the theatre is ruled from three capitals. From this little resentment results, since most of us prefer to live in what the novelist Anthony Powell has called an "acceptance world." Only when this acceptance is withheld, is recognized as entailing a loss of self-respect, does a "movement" against it develop, similar to the anti-colonialist resentment in modern nationalism. Are the articulate young delinquent? Do they fail in their duty to a standard of social conduct they did not invent? Or are they merely assertive? Are they trying to construct a new order for the society which they will in time come to control and operate? The controversy is just, since no one can tell the wrecker from the builder; and the young themselves are no judges of this either.

A clearer case of nonacceptance can be seen in feminism. The cry of "Rights for Women!" has now disappeared into the history books, but *there* was a classic anti-colonialist movement, the twentieth century's first and perhaps still its most significant. The empire of men over both women and their property was as old as the record of men themselves: it is indeed arguable that the very success of Islam is attributable to its earliest warriors' practice of confiscating the women of conquered countries and by its promotion of polygamy. Yet the movement to emancipate women has not, in the West, made much economic progress; and in the non-western world it has made no progress to speak of in any sphere. In consequence, half the human race still lives beneath the imperialism of the other half.

The "class-struggle" as depicted by the Marxists has an obvious affinity with anti-colonialism. The masses, to be formidable, had only to stand motionless: the workers of the world had only to

unite. What and whom they were to unite against needed no explanation. The imperialism of the feudal ages had gone, but it
had been replaced by the imperialism of the *bourgeoisie*. Marx
did not arrive at the conclusion that the next stage in this continuing revolution would be the establishment of the imperialism
of the proletariat. He supposed that when the proletariat was
sovereign, because there would be no need to exercise power, no
one would want to exercise it. Yet, as he often emphasized, the
mercantile class itself had been revolutionary in its day. It had
struggled to obtain its place between prince and priest, doing so
laboriously in a society wherein rates of simple interest were
regularly denounced as usury. For a long time it was not in the
Christian, but in the Islamic world, that the merchant had any
status, any prestige; and an even greater odium was attached
to the merchant who had not even the status of a Christian, but
belonged to the despised race and religion of the Jew.

For the concept of status argues an authority somewhere, allo-
cating it, recognizing it, and establishing clubs and institutions
wherein all those adjudged worthy to hold it can gather together.
Status can be won, but always and only on someone else's terms.
One graduates into a world one has not made. Or, alternatively,
one does not graduate at all: hence, the long series of stereotypes
about women, children, "youth," "the lower classes," natives,
Negroes, Jews, "Papists," "white trash," "box-wallahs," "untouch-
ables," and whomsoever else the controllers of a particular society
at a particular time have decreed are not to be granted a place of
influence within that society. This habit of mind is not peculiar to
white men. The Negro in British Guiana and in Trinidad has always had a contempt, heartily reciprocated, for the "East Indian"
there, and his is possibly the only English-speaking community
where the term "coolie" is still freely used. Syrian traders in
tropical Africa have long earned more money than respect. The
Chinese of Canton look down upon their own kin in Singapore.
The upstart is a universally recognized unpleasantness. The world
over, we can enhance our own status only by diminishing someone
else's.

And we do.

How vast, then, is the area covered by Professor Langer's "what-
not." How many are the upsets that imperialism, whether classical

or unclassical, whether spelled fiercely out in history books or never once mentioned there, can cause. Always to work in a world of other people's arrangements, to make a way of life out of a set of other people's assumptions, is a wearing business. In the best-regulated families blank misunderstandings occur between parents and children—who are, normally, people who *want* to live in harmony with one another. Modern Africa and many parts of Asia use English and French as their *linguae francae:* but it is simpler to learn a foreign vocabulary than to absorb the ideas that support it. Responsibility, loyalty, and authority have more to them than their literal definitions in a dictionary. They are part of a social code. They express a social creed. They represent a cast of values. Behind the abstract terms lies something concrete; and if, under an alien sun, the concrete is not there because it was never put there, attitudes will be sooner struck than principles grasped. The *évolué,* moving out of one society into another, is native in neither. There can never have been many with the aplomb of Prince Haidar Fazil of Egypt, "who divided his devotion between the mystical order of the Bektashi in a cave under the Mokattam hills, and an *étude approfondi* of the works of 'mon maître révéré, Gustave Flaubert'."[13] (And who knows what it cost him?) The politics professed by the average *évolué* are as tense as himself. The element of bewilderment is always there. The ex-colonial society in the West Indies breathes an atmosphere permeated by public principle that was born to serve the needs and express the aspirations of other, and freer, communities. This kind of intellectual colonialism is often as deeply resented as the most direct forms of exploitation.

What these have been is clear to anyone who can read a map. Imperialism, coming as cargo in a ship, marked its routes with its language. Spanish sea power divided the world with Portuguese sea power under the imperialist benevolence of the Catholic Church. Sea power got for Holland rich emporia the world over. Sea power made Great Britain the neighbor of every country that had a coastline. It made possible the colonization of North America, southern Africa, and Australasia. It allowed the Atlantic slave trade to flourish for a century and a half. It riveted the

[13] Ronald Storrs, *Orientations* (London, 1937), p. 87.

Indian subcontinent to an economic system half the world away.
It studded the map with alien and arbitrary names, most of them
from a dead language— for how many in the West know the name
the "Syrians" give to Damascus, or what the "Indonesians" call
"Indonesia"?[14] Imperialism carved out an area it called the Middle
East, indicating the area's relationship to places beyond itself.
It invented another known as the Far East. It put both into the
strategic control of Europe. The signposts of the world are imperialism's landmarks, the guides that men must follow, whether
they will or not.

In this compulsion lies the cause of the hatred that imperialism
has drawn down upon itself. The present, the only time of opportunity that we have, is conditioned by what happened in the past,
which nobody can alter; although some, like the political bosses
in George Orwell's novel *Nineteen Eighty-Four* (1949), opt out of
this predicament by concocting a new and far more popular version of the past.

We judge our times as out of joint *now* because our forebears
did not take some obvious action *then*. This charge imposes the
assumptions of one generation upon all others and makes hind-
sight the criterion of conduct: should William the Conqueror be
upbraided for not introducing the industrial revolution into England? Because we interpret the past emotionally, we do not judge
the present rationally. A student of imperialism in particular must
traverse some difficult country, confused by ill-drawn and con-
flicting maps, and he may himself be carrying a mental baggage
that impedes his own progress. He is, as Schumpeter pointed out,
with all of us among the atavists, for he too has his own preconceptions of the world and its ways. And he will certainly find
himself among just such ideologues as Napoleon objected to,
people whose habit and satisfaction it is to criticize the existing
order of things. It is a habit that leads them, inevitably, to as
trenchant an objection to the order of things in the past. As Leslie
Stephen pointed out, the English economists before the appear-
ance of *The Wealth of Nations* claimed only to be adepts in the
mysteries of commercial accounts. After it, in reflected glory,

---

[14] The name "Indonesia" appears to have been coined by the German an-
thropologist Adrian Bastian, about 1888.

they began to regard themselves as investigators of a new science, *capable of determining the conditions and the limits of human progress.*[15]

Thus, both "economic history" and "political science" began their academic careers less as disciplines than as attitudes. They still bear the marks of their origin. Although their pioneer Adam Smith never quitted his conservatism, both gravitated towards society's left wing, and there they bred sociology: an academic discipline whose right-wing practitioners have never made a crowd.

For, once the present is seen not as a context but as a phase, which, as is the nature of phases, must pass, it becomes possible of discussion. Discussion leads to criticism, since men are bound, who have imaginations at all, to be discontented with the present, which is so plainly not what it "should" be. And somebody is certainly responsible for this state of affairs. But who? Who is it that has prevented, that now prevents, the true present from holding power? Who is it that supports this usurper? Who blocks that future, which ought to be the here and now? Under this barrage, those whose interest it is to keep things as they are take to the defensive, and often enough with poor grace. From this radical perspective, imperialism in particular deserves the lash. Those who support the cause of empire are seen as merely perpetuating their own power. They impede the free movement of the human community. They turn the key on liberty. Imperialism, to a trained observer, stands out as the most readily recognizable expression of the will of the dominant economic order.

This trained observer (who may not have observed the nature of the bias in his training) will still insist that imperialism is not a target to be fired at, but a phenomenon to be studied. And this must be done scientifically, all illusion pared away. Science (unlike philosophy, of which it was once part)[16] is often seen as a constant, as a body of knowledge "out there," like heaven itself— unaffected by the imperfections in the human intelligence through

[15] Writer's italics. Leslie Stephen, *A History of English Thought in the Eighteenth Century* (London, 1876), II, p. 284.
[16] In the curriculum of the Scottish universities "physics" still appears as "natural philosophy."

which all its manifestations, like those of everything else that is "known" or appears to be "manifest," must pass. Yet there may be less detachment in the study than its students claim. Clinical diagnosis becomes moral judgment. Enthusiasm for truth leads to a love for hypothesis. A desire to explain converts into a zeal to expose. The attachment of the suffix "ism" to the adjective "imperial" serves notice that a series of events, whose significance has been heretofore clouded by emotion and prejudice, is to be subjected to a process of calmly rational classification. But—to docket, to label, to categorize: how better to expose? To display the business in all its nakedness will shock everybody, and at the same time deactivate the entire concept of empire. With its mysteries removed, so also will be its menace.

Or so it is hoped.

Yet not every process of *ismus* identifies with blame. "Materialism" has a critical content, but "industrialism" is still merely descriptive, an innocuous word—innocuous because no one on either wing of society complains of it. Russians, Chinese, and Africans all identify it as the key that unlocks the door to success and power in the modern world. Imperialism in contrast is seen as a dead end. Time has bypassed it: it is yesterday's means of assertion. What was empire but just another stamping ground for the hard-souled *bourgeoisie,* whose natural predacity was not even trammeled, in those wide but not open spaces, by the hypocritical morality that at least prevented them from doing exactly as they pleased at home? The profound hypocrisy and inherent barbarism of the *bourgeoisie,* Marx observed, "goes naked in colonies." This *voyeur's* image continues to entrance: as Richard Koebner noted in his influential article "The Concept of Economic Imperialism,"

The reader cannot but think of special economic interests whenever the word Imperialism is brought out.[17]

This reader, so envisaged, has been trained by two generations of thinkers firmly encamped on the Left—or, alternatively, by that liberal American tradition which sees the power of virtue but no

[17] Richard Koebner, "The Concept of Economic Imperialism," *Economic History Review,* II, ii, no. 1 (1949), pp. 1–29.

virtue in power. Imperialism, then, describes that kind of alien control which, since it has been so glaringly exposed, is assumed, in losing all its attraction, to have failed.

Every generation makes its own assumptions on success. None can assume they will last. When writing his *Imperialism, the Highest Stage of Capitalism* in 1916, Lenin did not claim, as so many of his disciples have done, that an exposure of the economic motivation of empire builders would by force of logic alone demolish the empires they had built. He stops to remark that there are "non-economic aspects of the question" which he is not going to touch, "however much they deserve to be dealt with"; and he refers to without illustrating "the numerous 'old' motives of colonial policy." He criticizes Karl Kautsky's identification of the *political* part of imperialism as a striving for annexations: "It is correct, but very incomplete, for politically imperialism is, in general, a striving towards violence and reaction."[18] This curious generalization he does not work out, perhaps because its working-out might have complicated his stand against Kautsky: for Lenin's insistence that imperialism is a phase in the economic process, that the balloon of capitalism will soon burst from overinflation and that the time of the social revolution of the proletariat is at hand, directly rebuts Kautsky's declaration that imperialism is a *policy* and therefore, like all policies made and carried out by ordinary men, exposed to good or to bad luck, capable of good or bad handling, of meeting either success or failure. Thus, although concentrating on the economic part of imperialism, Lenin on his own showing did not suppose that, product and stage of capitalism though it was, imperialism had nothing in it but a single-minded drive for monopoly and profit. It would have been odd if he had thought so, since he openly acknowledged his debt to English mentors, with J. A. Hobson's work on *Imperialism* (1902) in pride of place.

It has long been a European axiom, promoted the most assiduously by the type of German scholar Lenin most disliked, that it was the British who invented the doctrine of imperialism. Devoted to this, they had gone out to do remarkable things in the

---

[18] V. I. Lenin, *Imperialism, The Highest Stage of Capitalism* (Foreign Languages Publishing House, Moscow, n.d.), pp. 19, 146, 201.

world. They had arranged for themselves a destiny which they could not now escape. The world position they gained, with all its magnitude and success, has fascinated every observer: even the most recent analysis, by Koebner and Schmidt (1964), concentrates almost exclusively on British precept and practice.[19] As for the British, who are most serious when joking, they have been willing to rest their case on an academic aphorism about absence of mind.[20] They have denied that they were at any time capable of laying down anything so fraught with logic as a doctrine. They have remained unconvinced by the categorists of behavior and have insisted that the suitable adjective to derive from empire is not imperial but empirical. Yet the English Liberal James Bryce, writing in 1871 not of the British but of the *Holy Roman Empire,* had this to say of imperialism—which at once deals in category and brings into focus those issues which Lenin later chose to avoid:

The sacrifice of the individual to the mass, the concentration of all legislative and judicial powers in the person of the sovereign, the centralisation of the administrative system, the maintenance of order by a large military force, the substitution of the influence of public opinion for the control of representative assemblies—are commonly taken, whether rightly or wrongly, to characterize that theory.[21]

This characterization is one that Bryce's contemporaries were applying to the practices of the Second Empire of Napoleon III, who had committed himself to a still older doctrine of benevolent despotism, and whose every move obfuscated his motives in a cloud of suspicion. Bryce's colleague Charles Dilke dismisses, in his *Greater Britain* (1868), "a mere imperialism, where one man rules and the rest are slaves."[22]

Writing thirty years later, Hobson took this standard assessment into his account. Imperialism manipulated the public mind.

[19] Richard Koebner and H. D. Schmidt, *Imperialism* (Cambridge, 1964).
[20] J. A. Seeley, *The Expansion of England* (London, 1883), p. 10: "We seem, as it were, to have conquered and peopled half the world in a fit of absence of mind."
[21] James Bryce, *A History of the Holy Roman Empire,* Third Edition, revised (London, 1871), p. 375.
[22] Charles W. Dilke, *Greater Britain* (London, 1868), II, p. 367.

Imperialism threw dust in the eyes of the masses. But this it did so expertly that social revolution became less, not more, likely. To Hobson imperialism was not the last, worst stage of capitalism before its collapse. It was, alas, an effective prop for the whole unscrupulous system. He wrote his book as an *exposé*, in the hope that an outraged democracy, the scales at last fallen from its eyes, would knock the prop away. But this it never did. Lenin came, commented, and went—and Hobson did not change his mind or his purpose. Indeed he deepened the emphasis, in the introduction he wrote for a new edition of his *Imperialism* in 1938. Those who promoted imperial ideas were still throwing up clouds of dust, were still seeking

to avert internal democratic struggles for economic egalitarianism by providing outlets for surplus goods and surplus population, together with emotional appeals to the combatant predacity which animates a spirited foreign policy.

And (no matter that to discover either a combatant predacity or a spirited foreign policy in the England of the 1930's was a task to tax the ablest) what manner of men were these who so occupied themselves? Why, they were the faceless "economic men" of the textbooks, come alive. They were men who in 1899 had been identified in Hobson's mind with capitalist Jews, busily exploiting and even inventing patriotic sentiments of predacity on the South African goldfields. They were men who had now made themselves less obvious but had become even more sinister; for was not the South of England

full of men of local influence in politics and society whose character has been formed in our despotic Empire, and whose incomes are chiefly derived from the maintenance and furtherance of this despotic rule?[23]

In this reading, imperialism cannot be a doctrine, since doctrines by definition declare themselves aloud. It is not honest enough. It is only a smokescreen, put out by *rentiers* playing squires, to mask anti-democratic intentions. It did this effectively at home, and even more so overseas. Just how effectively can be

[23] J. A. Hobson, *Imperialism,* Third Edition (London, 1938), p. 58.

calculated from the acidulousness of the tone of nationalist historians, who resent having constantly to treat of a cast of characters whose principal role is the nonheroic one of dupe. R. C. Majumdar, in his *British Paramountcy and Indian Renaissance* (1963), speaks of "the mask of benevolence of British imperialism," and, in a reference to the welfare of the masses, calls this the *raison d'être* of British rule in India, "according to its supporters."[24] A confidence-trick was played, and so successfully, it appears, as to anger even those who were not taken in by it.

Edmund Burke liked to insist that men give their allegiance less to law than to custom. Ideas and institutions, doctrines and dogmas that survive a series of campaigns against them become respectable through the very fact of their endurance. Durability is a sign of success: and names once derisive, such as Quaker, convert to titles of honor. After Waterloo the world was compelled to accustom itself to the fact of British power, since no one had the means of challenging it. In international as in domestic affairs the privileges of power were acknowledged to include action and influence; and therefore the question of justifying their use did not arise. The point of Lord Palmerston's celebrated "gunboat diplomacy" was not that it was a diplomacy of force, for all diplomacy depends ultimately on this: but that so little force, a symbol of it only, needed to be used. It was, possibly, a fortunate thing for the world at large that it was the English themselves, bred to a liberal tradition that valued contract and distrusted power, who raised more complaint about this than did any foreigner. In the nineteenth century there were always a number of influential men who feared that the fact of Empire might wrench English liberties from their context, and who saw imperialism as a conspiracy against the British Constitution (which, as some even argued, it might really be prudent to write down). British statesmen, mindful of this climate of opinion, were as determined to stay clear of "entangling alliances" as though George Washington and Thomas Jefferson had never transferred their allegiance: for alliances with European powers were inevitably alliances that en-

---

[24] R. C. Majumdar, *British Paramountcy and Indian Renaissance*, Part 1, in Bharatiya Vidya Vharan's "History and Culture of the Indian People," vol. ix (Bombay, 1963), pp. xxii, xxvii.

tangled with military despotism—which could also easily be construed as a conspiracy against the British Constitution. The British took this point of view abroad with them into the world and, even when (especially when) establishing a firm authority, were hobbled by their conscience. Given this lead, others fastened on the advantages it could get them. Criticism of any arbitrary use of British power could, and did, catch the British themselves off balance.

The governance of India in particular provided a standing contradiction to the principles the British held dear: government by consent, no standing army. As Indians learned their liberalism from Mill, Macaulay, and Mazzini they came to know how to reach Achilles' heel. They drew their sharpest weapons from a moral armory. The essence of imperialism, says one who is himself the product of an alien, "imperialist" education,

is to be found in a moral relationship—that of power and powerlessness—and any material consequences which would spring from it are not enough to change it.[25]

This was ever Mohandas Gandhi's own theme—when he would urge his countrymen that they must learn to say no, that it was not an alien bondage but one they had fastened on themselves that kept them subordinate:

as soon as we have discarded the awe of the British, and ceased to consider ourselves as cheap as dirt, we shall be free.[26]

Gandhi's reference to awe throws light on the nature of the prestige, the *mana,* a successful authority can wield and is a useful reminder that power of this kind has always existed. A nation that has it, whatever the state of its collective conscience, uses it—and it was not a faith in liberalism alone that caused England ultimately to retire from India, amid scenes of massacre. Power had gone; and with it died the will that animates all faiths.

Since power exists historians must deal in it, and it is better dealt with pragmatically. The older Empires have indeed been

25 Albert Hourani, "The Decline of the West in the Middle East," *International Affairs,* xxix (January 1953), p. 31.
26 Mohandas K. Gandhi, *Young India 1919–1922* (Madras, 1922), p. 648.

so treated. The histories are not yet written that condemn Alexander the Great and the Roman Emperor Augustus on the single ground that they promoted territorial expansion and held particular views concerning the proper governance of subject peoples. Even those who charge them with political immorality excuse them because they did not know any better. (The Victorians, however, did not let them escape the judgment of a higher Power, since they confined all pagans to hell: to Thomas Hodgkin, writing in 1880, Rome's Empire "fell" because God willed that it should do so.[27]) The prestige of the great soldier and the great emperor has remained: the adjective has not been taken from them. The Hellenic and the Roman Empires are still presented as something much more than two vast areas of imperialist exploitation. One reason for this immunity is certainly that no record has come down to us that displays the other side of these medals: no Gaul, for example, has left behind his *Commentaries* on Julius Caesar, or his reaction to the division of his country into three parts. But in our own age this great success on the one side, that greater silence on the other, have had no parallels. The ancient world was not shaken by social revolution. Our own world has experienced little else—hence the series of reassessments and reappraisals, which compel historians to rewrite their predecessors' works every generation.

"Imperialism" is itself a comment, made by the controlled about their controllers, and made in the assurance of impunity. Power seen from below has been adjudged as a usurpation. The devotees of liberty, unlike those of equality, have taken authority for their foe; and under freedom's banner everyone, however unfree, has marked his stand. No dictator arises who can afford to betray his genuine disregard for the welfare and security of his own people. No war is fought that is not just, since no one confesses to aggression. Karl Marx resented the power of the *bourgeoisie*, because he thought them unworthy to hold it; and he found it tolerable to contemplate at all only by imagining it as a phase in a grand, other-directed process wherein power itself would finally dissolve. But only a *bourgeois* era, whose masters concentrated closely on the trading part of life but were content to leave its

[27] Thomas Hodgkin, *Italy and Her Invaders* (London, 1880), II, p. 546.

other areas in a darkness into which everyone was free to take his personal beacon, could have produced both Marx and his critique. Only a society careless of what political theorists thought or felt or did would have left him the freedom of the British Museum wherein to produce his apocalyptic diagnosis.

In contrast stands the commonplace that peasants in the Middle Ages did not realize, since it was to no one's interest to point it out to them, that they lived their lives in the grip of a feudal system, or even that their Ages stood in the Middle of anything. "Feudalism" is *ex post facto*, a word coined in the early seventeenth century, when English lawyers were ransacking the statutes and reinterpreting Magna Carta to justify their opposition to what they considered arbitrary government. And so it is with "imperialism"; it comes after the fact. The older world knew nothing of it. It certainly knew of empire, but not of any intellectual comment concerning it. It would indeed have been a strangely disoriented Assyrian king who thought up the idea of "His Majesty's Loyal Opposition"; and from his day to these dissent in the "Middle East" has recorded itself through the single doctrine of assassination.

Born in the East, empire never lost its train of exotic splendor, for rulers in the West saw to it that it did not. The Roman Emperor Diocletian (A.D. 276) borrowed his trappings from the recently risen Sassanid dynasty in Persia; and it became accepted, or at any rate was never publicly objected to, that an emperor, heaven-born, was also heaven sent. In later ages, when lesser kings had lesser pretensions, monarchy was still a divine institution wherein a ruler lay under the protection of God. Time has not totally erased the mysteries that men attached to authority. Assyrian kings eleven hundred years before Christ called themselves Kings of the Universe: the present ruler of Persia bears the same name. Pope Alexander VI (Borgia) allowed the King of Portugal to call himself Lord of the Navigation, Conquest and Commerce of Ethiopia, Arabia, Persia, and India; Columbus was styled Admiral of the Ocean Sea; Tokugawa Japan drew its Mikado from heaven; King George III of England bore the title of the King of France; and Napoleon on occasion felt a stronger urge to rule in Cairo than in Paris. If imperialism, seen in the guise of a trapping of empire, has come under such heavy fire, it is perhaps because there is a certain human pleasure, experienced by all but the mighty, in bringing arrogance down to scale.

But something is due to great achievement, and honor is owed, not bought. Men are very willing to look upwards rather than sideways, and to grant their respect to those whose vision they sense to be broader than their own. In every age the recurrent *irrationales* of empire—the appeal to prestige, *la gloire*, motherland, Fatherland, destiny—relate to this need for assurance and reassurance. We wish to be part of something that is greater than ourselves. More than any other institution, empire depends not simply on success, but on the type of success that is so spectacular as to convince its beneficiaries that they are indeed a chosen people, clearly favored by the gods, since honored by such brilliance in their leaders. Rome's history still magnetizes our respect, because of the men and deeds it records. In Julius Caesar's Rome the patricians felt it vital to the safety of the Republic that the mob should be kept busy, for mobs were supposed to feel rather than think. A patrician revolution lost Rome its republican status, without however altering this conviction in the minds of its governors. The Empire, like the Republic, must be made popular; and Emperors, like the Consuls before them, respected. These things would surely be achieved under an administration that increased both the external power of Rome and the economic privileges and well being of its citizens. It was an accurate forecast; and these things were done. The emotive significance of "empire" was thus born on the Roman forum; and Richard Koebner begins his book on *Empire* by citing a case when Scipio deflected the people from their intention of bringing him to book by reminding them that he was a hero with African laurels, and by appealing to their sense of the dignity inherent in the *imperium populi Romani.*[28]

When the Roman people, citizens of the Republic, found themselves become the subjects of a Roman Empire under the rule of an imperial Caesar Augustus, this was still declared by such propagandists as Horace, Livy, and Virgil to be quite compatible with the aims and ideals of the Roman Republic. The image of *imperium Romanum* was designed to combine national pride with

[28] R. Koebner, *Empire* (Cambridge, 1961), p. 1.

dutiful service. Out of this grew a powerful *mystique:* and it was always the intention of its instigators that it should. Augustus liked to see himself as the second founder of the Republic, called himself *princeps,* and took as his main task the association of power with service, in order to justify both the ascendancy of Rome in the Mediterranean and that of the Caesars in the Eternal City itself. Other voices sang the same song. The plain purpose of Virgil's *Aeneid* was to supply an ethical sanction for the Roman Empire, by equating its achievement with the vaguer but inescapably romantic heroics of Hellenes larger than life, while at the same time charting a future course wherein the majesty of Rome would always spare the subjected and bring down the proud, *parcere subietis et debellare superbos.*[29] Rome's power must in essence and substance entirely differ from that of Carthaginian mercantilism, Hellenist dynasticism, and Asiatic theocracy. The secret of power was order. And order, to be secure, must be *just.*

Thus was the spirit of *Romanitas,* animating a political system controlled by the *pax Romana,* invoked and perpetuated. If it was a siren song, it was one that caught and held the mind as closely as the heart. The power of the Roman Empire at its zenith in the second century A.D., when its territories stretched contiguously from Syria to Scotland, bears witness to the magnetism of this doctrine of imperialism. No empire has since existed that has not sought to draw sustenance from the same spring, and to build its security upon what France's romantic poet Alfred de Vigny celebrates as the *Servitudes et Grandeurs militaires* (1835). *Romanitas* has outlived Rome. Although Roman roads and towns have been put to the imperial uses of others, they have retained a particular aura, one that summons up the memory of the role they once played in an organization so long gone. Rome's northern provinces—Britain, Gaul, Germany, Danubia—never had the resources to support themselves, so that their towns functioned better as garrisons than as markets; but even so, "each new town meant a new body of support for the imperial idea."[30]

---

[29] See C. N. Cochrane, *Christianity and Classical Culture* (Oxford, 1940), pp. 29, 72.
[30] Tenney Frank, *Roman Imperialism* (New York, 1914), p. 329.

This idea, that law and civilization were things possible to men, if they could but learn to discipline themselves to keep them, was never entirely buried beneath the weight of subsequent political history. A view of Rome's physical remains still calls out a response different from that evoked by the pyramid of a pharaoh. The success Rome achieved has been declared, by the series of educated generations that was given an exclusively "classical" education, to represent the highest secular achievement possible to mankind. A melancholic grandeur attaches to the concept of "decline and fall." A tragic significance marks the name of the "dark ages" which follow hard upon. No historian, diligently explaining these misnomers, will ever supply in their place anything of quite their kind. Everything that concerns empire has in it an element of drama: its heroes may be good men or bad, but they must be cast on the great scale, Virgil's own, and play their parts on a stage Aeneas might tread. Napoleon I knew this: Napoleon III did not. The prestige on which all successful empires have been able to call, to reinforce their physical control, rests in part on the need of others to share in such reflected glory, and on their willingness to become "subjects" so that they may do so.

Accordingly, just as it assists understanding to call the Middle Ages by that name and to identify the habits and context of those then alive as feudal (provided we remember we are using a form of mental shorthand), so the pretensions and powers of emperors and empires, together with the doctrines they used to reinforce their rule, are genuinely clarified if we use the concept of imperialism to describe the context in which empires do their particular work.

A number of scholars have dealt with the ancient Empires in just this way, while at the same time trying to avoid the barrage from the committed Left. Tenney Frank, in his *Roman Imperialism*, published in 1914, says that

Imperialism, as we now use the word, is generally assumed to be the national expression of the individual's "will to live,"

but he does not think this was true of Rome. Popular sovereignty in the Republic in the early third century B.C. brought on, to be sure, "a mild form of imperialism," but Julius Caesar was Rome's first "candid imperialist." Frank argues that in the time of

Augustus a Roman control of Egypt had become a political necessity, and that the reforms of the civil service which occupied his reign were necessarily bound up with his establishment of an efficient system of imperial control in the provinces.[31] Certainly, if necessity is a doctrine it has had its many adherents, as also has the notion of a large imperial system as constituting a useful bureau for full employment.

Joseph Schumpeter agrees with this interpretation of necessity, but for him Republican Rome was the more aggressively imperialist of the two polities. The Republic was overpopulated with displaced persons and landless soldiers. Its political machinery was controlled by landlords. The alternative to war, another means of full employment, was agrarian reform—and this no one put in hand. Imperial Rome, in contrast, lived its life on the defensive. This argument has not convinced C. Delisle Burns, for whom the Roman Empire is the last of the great predatory empires based on slavery: and it would not have impressed James Bryce, for whom Rome was above all the empire of system. No power, he wrote, was ever based on foundations so sure and deep as those that Rome laid down during three centuries of conquest and four of undisturbed dominion.[32] It could hardly have done this had it been compelled to spend its days on the defensive.

Pierre Jouguet, in his *Macedonian Imperialism and the Hellenization of the East* (1928), also thinks that imperialism is best defined as "a will to power and betterment,"[33] and with this in mind finds an analogy between the rise of Macedonia and that of Prussia. He agrees that true imperialism is of eastern origin, but he is convinced that the idea of empire was foreign to Hellenism, since neither Athens nor Sparta tried to incorporate states other than Greek into their Empires. But Isocrates (436–338 B.C.) may surely be classified as an imperialist writer, since he believed that it is civilization, not race, that truly makes "the Greek" (another idea that was to cast a long, long shadow, particularly over the history of *la France d'outre-mer*). His contemporary Thucydides also holds this opinion, although on his general posi-

[31] *Ibid.*, p. 330.
[32] Schumpeter, *op. cit.*, p. 52; Bryce, *op. cit.*, p. 367.
[33] Pierre Jouguet, *Macedonian Imperialism and the Hellenization of the East* (London, 1928), p. 3.

tion there is scholarly doubt. "Some have made him an apostle of imperialism and others its opponent," says Jacqueline de Romilly in her *Thucydides and Athenian Imperialism* (1963). (And it is also fair to say, since it shows how intellectual preoccupations vary, that some in discussing Thucydides have not considered the matter at all.) She believes nevertheless that the will to dominance and power "springs from the character of the Athenians, as water from a fountain," and that Thucydides is certainly "the son of Athenian sea-power"[34] and therefore, if we believe in the influence of a blue-water school staffed by men whose eyes are constantly narrowed on the horizon, an imperialist by association.

Moreover, the Greeks in their exuberance ran risks that others coming after were to weigh with greater care. The notion of *hubris* is one of our most notable legacies from the Greek experience. For everybody knows that success can go to one's head, that a reach may be longer than a grasp, that pride goes before a fall, and that good intentions line the road to hell. Dressed in a little brief authority, we no doubt make the angels weep. Shakespeare's point underlines another Greek miscalculation: for the Greek idealization of human nature did not prove a sure guide for imperial or even for the more humdrum forms of security—since when human nature reigns it lets predatory passions loose and in so doing brings about its own disaster. Passion has an imperialism of its own. The failure of Athens, says F.W. Walbank in his *Decline of the Roman Empire in the West* (1946), epitomized the failure of the city-state. And what was that, but a gathering of a self-centered elite, determined on luxury and resolved to mold everything and everyone to suit its own convenience? Built on a foundation of slave labor, or on the exploitation of similar groups, including the peasantry, the city-state certainly built up a brilliant minority civilization, but

. . . precisely because it was a minority culture [it] tended to be aggressive and predatory, its claim to autonomy sliding over insensibly, at every opportunity, into a claim to dominate others.[35]

[34] Jacqueline de Romilly, trans. P. Thody, *Thucydides and Athenian Imperialism* (Blackwell, Oxford, 1963), pp. 312, 367.
[35] F. W. Walbank, *The Decline of the Roman Empire in the West* (New York, 1946), p. 67.

Even an elite, then, can reach beyond its grasp. Yet still this does not alter the fact, in Mlle. de Romilly's view, that there is such a thing as a law of political necessity, a law of force, as the Greeks themselves well knew. And so long as it remains prudent, keeps itself within reasonable bounds, imperialism merely follows the way of the world. It expresses the desire of the strong to assert themselves, for without such acts of assertion who will think them strong?

Here, then, is a series of assumptions about the ancient world made by twentieth-century writers. (Who is to judge, one might wonder, the reasonableness of the bounds?) It shows that imperialism can be related to character, to will, to self-fulfillment, and to a doctrine of manifest destiny. It also asserts that civilization contains an innate authority which gives it the right to proselytize itself. These good scholars take care to mark out the premises from which they start: the title *Roman Imperialism* cannot have been arrived at, in 1914, without long consideration. But, if publicists less bound to standards of professional accuracy see history through the same, if in their case darker-tinted, spectacles, who can blame them? It is a fact that the Syrians under the Roman Empire, and the Italians under the Austrian Empire, have nothing in common save their condition of subordination; but this condition is reckoned as enough, this has been taken as sufficient warrant to classify the activities of these two very disparate systems of authority under the heading of imperialism, leaves on the selfsame tree, and that a rotten tree, ripe only for the axe. Imperialism serves as a useful, positive, and immediately comprehensible generalization. It argues that someone had power, and misused it.

And herein lies a half-stated, indeed hardly half-realized assumption: that power, in the best of all possible worlds, ought not to be used at all.

That power is its own justification is a doctrine recognized as morally wicked, from whose grip men must struggle to free themselves. Great wars have been fought in this twentieth century to destroy the doctrine; but although the victories ultimately gained have slaughtered its immediate exponent, they have not managed to drive it from the context of human thought and action. Imperialism would never have been so vilified had power itself not been so feared. Power may indeed tend to corrupt, but it is the kind of corruption sooner seen in others than in oneself. It has become the totem of a goddess who must *not* be placated, so seductive is she. No one, and certainly not Lenin's heirs and disciples, now whole-heartedly believes that a diagnosis of imperialism as a desperate measure of economic exploitation at the end of its capitalistic tether does much to resolve the problem that the very existence of political power sets before every generation.

The recurring issue about power is, simply—Who shall wield it? Some generations spend and expend themselves fighting to get an answer to this to which they, or at least their children, can subscribe: others live in an age of security and acceptance. There is a second question—To what end shall it be directed? But this is also a secondary question, for it cannot be answered out of its turn. This is a point that many commentators have chosen to miss, preferring "systems" of their own making to those whose challenge confronts them. As an example, a doctrine of constitutional right, bearing with it the right to appeal to specific terms of reference, will not profit or even avail an individual whose society has changed its terms of reference, whose environment is now controlled by those who look on constitutions as an old-fashioned style of window dressing, and who anyway place no importance on individuals or on their egocentric rights.

This modern predicament has many past parallels. There is a history that Ireland did not have: it is one that many Irishmen have recorded in their hearts, and some have died to establish. But since Ireland did not have it, it is not, in fact, *in* her history, and cannot be put there now. Imperialism is fixed into the historical record of every nation that has an ascertainable past at all. It has its basis among very many peoples, and it has generally depended upon the capacity of the few whether the many would at a particular time be members of the imperial, or of the subject, race. It is within this inescapable context that the bitterness against imperialism and colonialism, which is so often a bitterness against race and life itself, has been bred. It may indeed be an intolerable thought that

The people who have endured a wrong must be incapable of rectifying it,[36]

[36] David Urquhart, *The Progress of Russia in the West, North, and South* (London, 1853), p. 16.

but some men feel compelled to harbor it. They indict their ancestors accordingly. They do not do so with grace, for the austere assessments Gandhi was always making were never popular—"Our mental training has been one of feeling helpless."[37] Nations that do not wear the accolade of a successful popular revolution will continue to envy those who were not *given* their freedom, but won it.

No discussion of power stays rational too long—and perhaps, anyway, it ought not to. The entire German academic discipline of *Historismus* was based on the idea that knowledge is power, that history is something that can be guarded against in future that its lessons can be learned, that it *has* lessons to be learned, and that there is a formula for human behavior. This belief is likely to last as long as human beings themselves. It in part accounts for the magnetism of the concept of imperialism, since within the context of empire human behavior most clearly exposes itself. The essence of empire is control. To control, whether of others or of oneself, everyone must bring a philosophy. This philosophy may be difficult to define—as the officials of the Bengal education department must have felt in September 1920, when they issued a circular urging that teachers should be asked to co-operate

in bringing about a right understanding of the meaning of the [British] Empire and in dispelling the idea that the Empire is based on force and militarism.[38]

Yet behind this protest at calumny certainly lay that "unformulated philosophy of life and politics" that Professor Eric Stokes has so brilliantly analyzed. "At its heart," he writes,

was the belief that political power tended constantly to deposit itself in the hands of a natural aristocracy, that power so deposited was morally valid, that it was not to be tamely surrendered before the claims of abstract democratic ideals, but was to be asserted and exercised with justice and mercy.[39]

Here is a doctrine of far greater significance than the calculated

[37] Gandhi, *Young India,* p. 677.
[38] *Ibid.,* p. 808.
[39] Eric Stokes, *The Political Ideas of English Imperialism* (Oxford, 1960), p. 10.

risks of *rentiers*, one that in its day had the rare effect of making an equal appeal to Englishmen and Frenchmen in their respective imperial outposts. Power had privileges, certainly, but it also had responsibilities. These included the dissemination and the guardianship of civilized values, whose nature was such that they not only did not need but were actually injured by constant parsing and analysis. This "natural aristocracy" earned its social place by performing a genuine social service. This it could not abdicate, whatever pressures came from the articulate either on the Left or from somewhere below, whether from domestic radicals or from Indian Congressmen, without a very serious dereliction of duty. And, if this kind of power was to be asserted and exercised, there were good guides how best it should be done. John Stuart Mill had already diagnosed, in his *Representative Government* (1861), that the greater part of all political power consisted in will; while Rudyard Kipling, writing in the heyday of self-confident imperialism, laid the stress on the end product of will—which was work.

An examination of power and the assumptions that have been made about it, both by its supporters and by its enemies, will help keep a student of human affairs from wandering in Utopia, in some bright garden of images of his own landscaping. It will not, however, keep him from scaling its walls if he finds its gates shut. Wishful thinking has never been the monopoly of the dialecticians and the committed. Most of us are committed not to systems but to ourselves. For every genuine social reformer there are probably a hundred daydreamers. These are people who put their faith in urges and impulses. They easily discover trends and phases, they readily find their hopes mirrored in great concepts. These are the Romantics, the enhancers of life, who did not die with the passing of a particular school of literary fashion. Because they are so well worth leading, they are very often misled by those who can speak their own language. The imaginative among them will look for, and be certain to find, in the strivings of poets and artists a will to power unappeased. They may not have read Nietzsche on this subject but they know what he said, and they can see in Byron dying at Missolonghi an immensely satisfying symbol of Romance, Imperialism, and Death, a trinity of fulfillment.

They are the men of feeling, and they are owed a great deal, for without them the concept of social justice would never have been born. To the true nineteenth-century Romantic, to Château-briand and his cloud-capped school, Napoleon I was the Great Individual, the captain of his soul. Because he was this he was readily forgiven his philistine outlook on all things spiritual; and the Bonapartism that was bred in St. Helena (that "eagle's cage," what else?) was to nurture a brand of romantic fascism all its own. And even if these notions, and others of the kind, on the whole infected those whose practical abilities were few, and are anyway too high-flying ever to be digestible as a daily diet, at least they take their place on the side of the truth. The basis of history is idealistic, as Elie Halévy said. It is idealism that promotes revolution and wages wars.

This is no new idea. It had impressed Tertullian in Rome, who pointed out in his *Apologia* (A.D. 198) that the attempt by the "natural aristocracy" of that day to suppress Christianity by force and to dismiss its arguments unheard implied in itself a lurking suspicion that the doctrine might, after all, be true. If the persecuted have a strength, it is not one that is material. This argues that ideas have more power than the men who hold them. Such ideas may build and grow as they pass from one generation to another: and this act of transmission, of colonization of the future, itself creates custom and the habit of allegiance to it. The *avant-garde* holds a height, whose strategic importance it was the first to realize, until the main body comes up to occupy it. The success of any such idea dispenses with the need to formulate a philosophy to explain it: it is failure, not success, that men question. The very concept of good government, for example, begs a host of questions about morality, purpose, and method, which no one is inclined to put so long as the government is effective. Thomas Hobbes, whom this whole matter fascinated and whose disenchantments still trouble the liberal conscience, observed in his *Leviathan* (1651) that

Kings, whose power is greatest, turn their endeavours to the assuring it *at home* by Laws, or *abroad* by Wars.

The kings he spoke of saw this activity as something both right and necessary and as approved by God. In that assumption lies the entire philosophy of what now goes by the name of the *ancien régime*.

But that *régime* faltered amid the shallows and fatuities of court ceremonial, and the powers of rationalism arose to combat it. The aristocrats, men as rational as any and sometimes, because of their superior education, more rational than most (as Tocqueville himself stands to bear witness), themselves lost faith in the necessity of their own function. In an enthusiasm for the new doctrine of popular right, they were aristocrats who in the National Assembly in Paris on 4 August 1789 stood up to vote their own privileges out of existence. Thereafter aristocracy everywhere became an embattled order. The "Vienna settlement" of 1815 was more like an encampment, from whose walls the Right looked down to gauge the strength of the Left. Its authority restored the Bourbons to Paris, but not for long, for it could not bring back the world in which Bourbons, whether French or other, could be at home. Kings of France had once ruled by divine right: but now their actions had to be authorized by Charter, and a prince of Orleans, propelled to the throne by the revolution of 1830, chose to describe himself as "king of the French."

This identification with the idea of a *nation en masse* had been Napoleon's own practice, who always liked to see himself as the embodiment of the principles of 1789; and his nephew, when in 1852 he climbed to imperial status, also called himself "Emperor of the French"—thus incurring the contempt of the Tsar, whose allegiance was to God and Russia, not to Russians. Yet, as an institution, aristocracy survived the nineteenth century—and indeed stockaded itself in some style, since in Germany, where the majority of European nobles were now congregated, Bismarck had deprived nationalism of its previous association with liberalism and had given it both a rigid military control and a new fervor of imperial patriotism. Even "militarism" itself contained an idealism of a kind: for it sought to formulate a new philosophy for aristocratic authority. Yet, again, the process of *ismus* shows that the Left wing was determined to publicize just what it was the Right wing was about. The powerless, by now politically conscious, were also extremely vocal.

Accordingly, in the last quarter of the nineteenth century were bred many new concepts, ideas, and definitions, which were all

designed to rebut or reverse the codes, habits, and preconceptions
of the traditional ruling class. Life was judged no longer from on
high, but from below. This was done in what were declared to be
impersonal terms, as much in sorrow as in anger. The presence
of the poor, long sanctioned by the religious, becomes the problem
of poverty, which is not to be sanctioned at all. The business of
exchange and investment becomes known, and disliked, as
capitalism. Radical attacks on property, and on those who own it,
stand forth as part of the new doctrines of "socialism." "Materialism" condemns those who make profits. "Social justice" emerges,
at first less as an ideal to be pursued than as a writ to be served:
for this form of justice is to be meted out, it appears, by the poor
to the rich, who, since they are less numerous than the poor, have
fewer rights. Art depicts not the world that men recognize but
the world as the artist sees it somewhere at the back of his mind.
Throughout literature the cry resounds for personal fulfillment—
a fulfillment which, if Ibsen is taken as a guide, quite properly
entails the destruction of the extant social order, with all its
utilitarian bonds and conventions. It is a world of the critic, of
higher thought, even of "new women": it witnesses an invasion by
the unaccommodated, who cannot find room until they have displaced those now in possession, and have made Heartbreak House
flourish in place of Horseback Hall. It is a world that has no use
for a "natural aristocracy," which it sees merely as a body of men,
out of touch with the genuine issues of their own time, usurping
a power to which they have no longer any moral claim.

It is against this background that the campaign against imperialism, together with that against all other forms of political and
social power, was fought.

For aristocracy and empire were naturally linked. This link had
long been taken for granted (which is what we usually mean when
we call a thing natural). The mode of thought that established
the one upheld the other. Successful predators, once they had
stopped freebooting and had secured themselves as monarchs of
all they surveyed, had remained in command of a social structure
that used authority and allegiance as its pillars. If and when they
moved abroad from this secure base, they took both their powers
and their lieges with them: the Normans, for example, carried an
identical code of function and service into Cyprus and into Sicily,

into the "Latin Kingdom" of Jerusalem, into Wales and into Ireland. They adapted it to the circumstances of each area but never altered it out of recognition.

If, as has been noted, "feudalism" is still an intangible term, land and property are not intangible and never have been. Property is fact, not fiction; and a system of governance that uses it for a foundation must necessarily be solidly constructed. Time never erased the feudal concept of *nulle terre sans seigneur*. Spanish and Portuguese *conquistadores* wrote and entailed their own title deeds wherever they went. In Quebec, whose original French colonizers were in the main from Normandy, the *seigneur* became the master of secular society. This was true also of St. Christophe, Guadeloupe, and Martinique in the Caribbean. In the Spanish island of Jamaica, taken by a raffish offshoot of Cromwell's army in 1655, property was allocated and laid out regiment by regiment, with the lion's share to the officers, as both payment .and reward for their success. Empire, seized by force, was merely an extension of property (as was prize money in the detailed regulations that governed the disposal of captures at sea); and the social codes that governed "the manor of East Greenwich" in England were transplanted by landed proprietors to many areas in North America throughout the seventeenth century, in the confident expectation that they would perpetuate themselves there.

Colonies, or "plantations," were from the outset possessions in the fullest sense. They belonged to someone. Who their sovereign was might be at any one time a matter for hot dispute between the kings themselves, but that there was such a thing as sovereignty, either to hold or to usurp, was never in question. This in part explains the common *de haut en bas* attitude adopted by the statesmen in the imperial metropolis toward the world of the frontiersman, the settler, and the planter. In this perspective they were social subordinates. They constituted a lesser rank in society. They were expected to realize it and to act as such. And many colonists who did indeed realize it but were not prepared to act as such, could never entirely shake free from a sense of their own temerity in breaking the bonds that their world accepted as natural.

Property, as most men who had any were disposed to agree, had

its own rights and privileges. The English constitution could afford
to remain unwritten because these rights and privileges were
tacitly accepted as valid by all ranks of society; and an Empire
whose rulers were able to appeal to this deep sense of propriety
among their own subjects, while at the same time entailing their
social supremacy upon their own posterity, was one that could
afford to live a confident life. Macaulay's schoolboy is supposed
to have defined an island as a piece of land entirely surrounded
by the British Navy. The definition has its wry truth. In the spring
of 1887, while on a world tour, the English historian James
Anthony Froude came upon a Spencer-Churchill administering
the West Indian island of Dominica, and exclaimed that this was
"a post which an English gentleman ought not to be condemned to
occupy."[40] His point of course was that this particular estate was
too poor to merit the management of so distinguished an estate-
agent; yet this forgotten outpost, however far behind God's back,
was nevertheless as much a piece of property as was India under
the Crown, and for that reason alone as much deserving of good
husbandry as any estate in England.

That Dominica was commercially useless, was socially a puzzle,
and unlikely ever to be worth its keep were matters beside the
point: besides, there were a great number of British colonies of
which precisely these same things, and even more gloomily, could
be said. For although the imperial possessions were for the most
part originally appropriated for commercial purposes, in the hope
that they would bring in some harvest of a marketable kind, that
fact and its subsequent disappointment did not alter the context
of their governance. Commerce whether on land or sea had never
been able to defend itself successfully from its own resources.
Men of commerce were therefore compelled, and were anyway
willing, to appeal to the social and military hierarchy whose
function it was to protect all the property of the realm.

This paternalist system of government, based on the aristocratic
tradition and established from the outset in all colonial territories,
long lived free from radical criticism. There were always Irishmen
who objected to the presence of the English Ascendancy in their

---

[40] J. A. Froude, *The English in the West Indies; or, The Bow of Ulysses*
(London, 1888), p. 172.

island, but since they were able to make only sporadic and unsuccessful efforts to circumvent it, they never established in English minds any sense of their right to dissent. Elsewhere (and even in Ireland) the habit both of ascendancy and of deference to it became ever more deeply ingrained. Time and thought moved more slowly in Europe's imperial annexes than in Europe itself. The small European cadres overseas were closely knit. In a small society there is no room for originality, and if one wished to be accepted by H[is] E[xcellency] at Gov[ernment] House (as what woman did not?) one did not air unacceptable views. Expatriates had their own local authority and precedence to maintain: they had therefore no interest in promoting any brand of thought that might be construed as disloyalty, for radicalism, as everyone knew, had a contagion of its own. What travelers came among them were usually of their own nationality, whose comments on an exotic scene, if sometimes barbed, were generally good-natured: Victor Jacquemont, raising Parisian eyebrows in 1832 at English manners in India, is an exceptional case.[41]

Colonials thus tended to assume that "home" would never change, that the world they would retire to when their time came would be the same world, grown that much older, which they had left in their youth. In the meantime, the isolation they lived in, in fact the major weakness of all colonial societies, became in many cases looked on as a trophy to be preserved. It became a form of insulation. The Europeans who fused together in South Africa to make up the Boer stock missed both the agricultural and the industrial revolutions which literally changed the face of Europe, and took pride in having done so; for they had thus avoided all taint of cosmopolitanism, which would have injured or at least compromised their hard-won sense of community and purpose. Similarly tea planters in Ceylon, rubber planters in Malaya and the Dutch East Indies, tobacco growers in Rhodesia and cattle farmers in Kenya were to let time pass them without marking how late it was growing.

Yet a colony's ignorance of European horizons was well matched

[41] Victor Jacquemont, *État politique et social de l'Inde du Sud en 1832*, ed. A. Martineau (Paris, 1934). There is a selective English edition by C. Allison Phillips, *Letters from India 1829–32* (London, 1936).

by Europe's ignorance of its own. The intellectuals who led the campaign against the accepted views and establishments at home were deprived of any reflecting images from the world of their own kinsmen overseas, and only on rare and distinctly unofficial occasions was this situation changed. Douwes Dekker's novel *Max Havelaar* (1860), with its shocking revelations of how life was lived on the Dutch plantations in Java, sold widely in Europe more because it brought firsthand news from that other world than because of the quality of the news itself.

Thus the campaign against imperialism had to get under way on a battleground for the most part shrouded in fog. Popular ignorance of the actual conditions of empire as well as of the policies that controlled it was a commonplace in every country that owned one. For long in English speech "the colonies" was a phrase less descriptive of actual places in the world under the British flag than a category of oblivion, devised by the ruling class, to which the younger or in whatever other way the more unsatisfactory members of their own order could be thankfully consigned. The slavery issue was the only "colonial question" guaranteed to arouse a genuine and general public interest. In the 1820's the humanitarians were writing pamphlet after pamphlet depicting West Indian plantation conditions, and selling them all; but the 1840's can show no such literature and no such interest, and what was happening in the West Indies after the great emancipation of 1833 was known only to a very few officials who never had, and did not want, the public ear.

Similarly, Algeria was a field of military maneuver (or *champ d'honneur*) for the French Army for forty years (1830–70) without the majority of the French people ever becoming aware of its existence. Muhammad Ali of Egypt, who might well have made himself Sultan at Constantinople and set about renovating the disastrous Ottoman Empire, was never allowed to emerge from the veils of diplomacy in which French, Russian, and British statesmen always encased him as soon as his actions seemed likely to disturb a *status quo* in the Levant which was distinctly to their own interest. Empire, like diplomacy itself, was a minority interest, but since it was the major preoccupation of this minority, and since this minority was also the one that ordered the social and political conventions at home, it survived and thrived without benefit of democratic scrutiny, and felt no loss in doing so.

Scholars have recently pointed out[42] that this mid-century era was no less imperialist than the subsequent age, as a great many annexations and expansions were made during it. This is true, but not significant. Imperialism indeed went on for a very long time before it was classified as a phenomenon detrimental to the welfare of the people. It was the amount of popular notice that was taken of it that makes the 1870's a watershed in the story of imperial affairs, not the amount of imperial property that was amassed. Empire was an irrelevance to the majority in the earlier period: in the later it became relevant, and thus fell into the arena of public discussion. Power now seemed, to the waiting democracy, no longer something so far beyond its grasp as not to be worth its attention. Hard calculations were made about it. Its assumptions were questioned, its stereotypes broken up. Phrases that had lived a quiet life, such as "the interests of England," "the interests of France," "the balance of power"—which were all of aristocratic origin, coined to describe habits and ideas with which the masses were not familiar—had now to undergo a close scrutiny. And so did empire itself. Empire was a form of property which fell pleasingly into an instantly identifiable category. For what else was the property of empire, but loot on a large scale?

And what was imperialism, but the policy that acquired it?

The empire builders, as spokesmen for the empires they had built, had therefore to come into the arena to discuss the principles they had long taken for granted and sometimes forgotten to formulate. They had to counter the doctrine that declared they were totally fraudulent with doctrines that declared they were not. This battle must now engage our attention, for it is not yet

[42] See in particular R. Robinson and J. Gallagher, in their "The Imperialism of Free Trade," *Economic History Review*, (second series, VI, no. 1 (1953), pp. 1–15; *Africa and the Victorians* (London, 1961); and Chapter 23 in the *New Cambridge Modern History*, vol. xi (Cambridge, 1962), "The Partition of Africa": "The groundwork of European imperialism had been truly laid long before the cartographical exercises at the end of the century . . . . Only after Africa lay divided and allotted did European opinion embrace the mythology of empire," pp. 593–594.

over, and the din from the combat zone shows no signs of diminishing. What did these men think they were doing? What did they believe in? What did they want? On what foundations have empires in the modern world been laid? And if things have since gone so wrong, was this because imperialism was a house built on sand, or does the fault (if there is anyone conveniently to be blamed) lie elsewhere? Rome was not built in a day; but her achievements are so easily and commonly demolished in two minutes that an investigation of the principles on both sides of this business cannot be out of place.

It is time, then, to look in turn at the doctrines which attached themselves to empire: to power, to profit, and to the whole concept of a superior civilization, and the mission thereof.

TWO

The Doctrine of Power

Every doctrine of imperialism devised by men is a consequence of their second thoughts.

But empires are not built by men troubled by second thoughts. Hence the mutual irritation, mixed with bewilderment, that is generated between the man who does and the other man who watches what he does and dockets his doings. Thought without action seems as absurd to the one as action without thought to the other. The latter feels that institutions *ought* to relate to some philosophy, to specific terms of reference, against which their conduct can be checked. But empire, when considered as an institution, furnishes material for jurists to verify, but seldom for anyone else. It lies within an area of impulse, and impulse possesses neither a good map nor a reliable signpost.

The structure of an imperial bureaucracy, its methods of recruitment and employment, the powers of the imperial officials and the codes they work by—all these can be traced and pronounced on. The "course of empire" is not so simply plotted. Imperial ideas are less ideas than instincts, the sum of a series of factors which cannot be precisely calculated. An imperial policy can be attributed, say, to Disraeli or to Kaiser William II; but neither were monarchs of all they surveyed (William's Chancellor Bethmann-Hollweg later protested that his master's personality "was profoundly penetrated by the ideal of peace")[1] and what is allocated to them under the heading of policy might signify more under the heading of hope. The poet may deal with hopes and dupes, fears

---

[1] Theobald von Bethmann-Hollweg, *Reflections on the World War* (London, 1920), p. 20.

and liars—but not the categorist. Reduced to conjecture, he will sometimes take a revenge, and expand the element of the irrational. He presents the empire builder as a cardboard figure, a comedian unawares, who confuses activity with action and police work with progress—and is at last caught by surprise by events whose significance he did not have the wit to see.

For this judgment such a critic can marshal evidence from the colonial record. He pauses at a time of his own choosing to ask what, exactly, is going on here? Not many of us can give a completely satisfactory account of ourselves when suddenly halted in the midst of our routine: the great religions all know this. But the imperialist has not been granted this grace. Nor has he often felt he needed it. Expanding frontiers and administering new provinces is hard work. It is also regular and continuous work, totally absorbing the time of those concerned, who are therefore not inclined to any deep reflection on the ultimate consequences of what they are doing.

In time, if that is given them, officials and public servants come to take the whole thing for granted—their own image of their official status, their own image of the public, their own concepts of service, of the imperial institute, of its policies, and of the entire doctrine of power supporting it all. They develop a habit of authority whose strength reflects the depth of deference paid to it. They know that power is a responsibility: they are certain they handle it responsibly. Sir Alfred Lyall, who recorded the India he had served, had this in mind when he remarked that most of his countrymen would never own to a "doctrine of imperialism" at all. For, far from closely examining the tale he told, of *The Rise of the British Dominion in India* (1893), so that they might learn its lessons and better plan its future, they looked on the whole business "as an almost incomprehensible stroke of national good fortune."[2] Luck was part of the equipment of the successful; let others trouble whether or not it was deserved.

It is against this backcloth of massive mental passivity that the striking gestures of the determined and purposeful few, the true *entrepreneurs* of empire, are played. These men possess a dynamo

---

[2] Sir Alfred Lyall, *The Rise of the British Dominion in India* (London, 1893), p. 1.

of a kind not found in institutions, supplied with an energy that is not statistically calculable. One such can speak for them all. "When I began this business of annexation," Cecil Rhodes told an admiring Cape Town audience in July 1899,

They would ask me to stop at Kimberley [Griqualand West], then they asked me to stop at Khama's country [Bechuanaland]. I remember Lord Salisbury's chief secretary imploring me to stop at the Zambesi.[3]

Everyone could share his amusement—for how typical were these reactions of pettifogging bureaucrats to the openhanded drive of the man on the spot! Was not the expansion of the Empire above and beyond the Zambesi, or as far as the Mediterranean itself if Rhodes could get there, only a matter of commonsense business enterprise? Like all such enterprises, did not its health depend far more on its own innate vitality than on any stimulation (or lack of it) from without?

The vitality that sets itself to the work of conservation and protection differs from that which maps a sphere of influence and takes the frontier far: but its source is the same. That source is confidence, of the kind that whets itself on the sense of superiority and sees in victory a trophy as much of moral courage as of military skill. From this point of view, power is the product of will.

It therefore follows that powerlessness is bred from poverty of spirit.

Imperialists (a name here given to those who expanded and consolidated the area of their own and their country's power) inevitably took this stand. Men of high spirit, firm believers in destiny ("a doctrine which is not to be tolerated as a plea among Christians, however valid it may be in Mohammedan casuistry"[4]), they did not stop to weigh nice propositions in ethical behavior and usually despised those who did, seeing in that conduct only a means of escape from the predicaments of positive action. As an English administrator in Burma once rasped, "Let us avoid the pernicious cant that our mission in Burma is the political educa-

[3] Vindex, ed., *Cecil Rhodes: His Political Life and Speeches, 1881–1900* (London, 1900), p. 642.
[4] F. W. Chesson, ed., *The Political Writings of Richard Cobden*, Fourth Edition (London, 1903), II, p. 456.

tion of the masses."[5] Schoolmastering was beside the point of the imperial exercise, which was, to bring law and order to parts of barbary and maintain them there. All life was a challenge, all survival a gamble. All history was a succession of chances, chances taken or missed. If the Romans had not built an Empire, then the Carthaginians would have. If the Russians had not done so, then the Swedes or the Poles. Every generation, grappling with the especial circumstances it has inherited, produces its own contestants for the stakes of power. Opportunity has few doors, and most of these are already manned. This must be so—and what does it serve, or whom, to debate whether or not it should be so? The world will not wait for the hesitant, and will never belong to the halfhearted.

To meet opportunity's challenge, every available aid must be mobilized and sent into the battle line. Two such are character and geography. The emergence of geography as a separate curricular subject in European schools and universities was a direct consequence of the world-probing, fact-finding imperial ideas of the 1890's, while the breeding of character and the training for leadership more than intellectual brilliance was always the *raison d'être* of England's private "public school" system. On any scene where these two auspices were favorable, the sun was not supposed to set. But, in contrast, an unkind trick of terrain could defeat prodigies of valor: see how the fate of all the islands of Europe was one of seizure. At one time or another Crete, Rhodes, Cyprus, Corfu, Malta, Sicily, Sardinia, Corsica, the Balearics, Britain, and Ireland were all taken by predators, and all the Atlantic archipelagoes colonized. In none of them did the original race survive intact. Their best destiny was to help form the plural society over which the rulers presided. It was a kind geography that led the people of the young United States of America to believe that their nation's manifest destiny lay in the building of an empire by westward migration: it was an unkind geography which made it inevitable that no one in Latin America ever came to believe any such thing.

[5] Sir Herbert White (a former Lieutenant-Governor of Burma), *A Civil Servant in Burma* (London, 1913), p. 153.

This conviction, that character and geography can be riveted into a framework for success, is one that turns naturally to mysticism, to the belief that since things have turned out so, they were planned so, by a Providence which may indeed be inscrutable but whose purposes may still be gauged by men of superior instinct, who will make even the clouds and shadows of the future a part of their patterns of power. This reading of the human situation, as fatalist as Karl Marx's own, makes a profounder appeal to the romantic spirit. The French historian Hippolyte Taine responds to this when he lyricizes the opportunities that can be seized wherever there are men with the wit and fire to seize them. There is Race. There is Milieu. Above all there is Moment. Perhaps no one man can accurately and absolutely diagnose the hour of their fusion; but men of stature are the helmsmen of the age, and they will surely sense its spirit, that *Zeitgeist* which favors them and will carry them, have they only the faith, to spectacular success.

But imperialists were men of affairs, who did not often dream these dreams. They preferred to weigh one interest with another. They calculated likelihoods and invested in reasonable certainties, in much the same frame of mind as the ancient mariners who, while plotting their ships' course by the stars, did not speculate in their logs how the stars got there in the first place. Germany's Bülow strikes the note of hard commonsense when commenting on the treaties with Tonga and Samoa recently arranged by his country. These treaties (June 1879) represented, positively,

No colonial or monopolistic policy, but merely the principle that where I have planted my foot, there shall no one else be permitted to place his.[6]

This note is heard again when England's High Commissioner in South Africa, Alfred Milner, reports to the Colonial Secretary in London, Joseph Chamberlain. While watching the machinations of the Boers against the current British doctrine of paramountcy,

. . . I have had to show my teeth a little and intimate that while I am, of course, neutral in colonial politics, I could not accept resolutions

[6] Mary E. Townsend, *The Rise and Fall of Germany's Colonial Empire* (New York, 1930), p. 56.

which exceeded the legitimate bounds of party controversy or verged on sedition.[7]

It emerges clearly from the official explanation given to the House of Commons in February 1900 concerning Britain's actions in Uganda. The object for which protectorates in the Lakes country of Central Africa were first established was not merely that they should become media of civilization, and certainly not because anyone wanted to acquire territory for its own sake,

—But the considerable liabilities attaching to them were undertaken in pursuance of a definite policy of securing territory which had to do with the headwaters of the Nile, which are absolutely necessary for the [British] control of Egypt and the Sudan.[8]

This plea, of absolute necessity, was reckoned self-explanatory. The imperialists saw it as their plain duty to define the boundaries of the arena of every political action.

Nor could they see anything to quarrel with in the aphorism that the ideas of an epoch are those of its dominant class. Why not? What other ideas could have any hope of success? They were ashamed neither of their dominance nor of their opinions. To them the only wickedness lay in inaction, in an acceptance of privilege, without any corresponding discharge of duty: to be told that they had too selfish an idea of their duty, was an impertinence, a gibe at ability from those who had yet to prove their own. They intended to entail both the privilege and the duty on a posterity of their own breeding, since only if they did this could they be sure that all their work and thought would not be wasted. As Louis Faidherbe, France's architect of Empire in Western Africa, declared, "Our intentions are pure and noble, our cause is just; the future cannot fail us."[9] His true point was, that it could not be allowed to do so. This conviction, that the future like the present must stay in authority's grip, governed all of its policies. Its context included every aspect of the national life. But it was not a context that made room for the principle of democracy, and this

[7] Alfred Milner to Joseph Chamberlain, 29 August 1897: C. Headlam, ed., *The Milner Papers* (London, 1931), I, p. 90.

[8] 22 February 1900: *Hansard's Parliamentary Debates,* fourth series, vol. 79, p. 880.

[9] Quoted in Mary Kingsley, *West African Studies* (London, 1899), p. 280.

made it inevitable that an attack on one enclave of power, from wherever mounted and for whatever reason, symbolized an attack on authority itself.

Nineteenth-century statesmen listened to all rumblings from below with this in mind. England's Prime Minister Sir Robert Peel saw that a principal danger in the protracted struggle to repeal the Corn Laws was that other interests would be damaged: already "the system of promotion in the Army, the Game Laws, and the Church, were getting attacked."[10] The social authority of the English gentry could not be divorced from their political supremacy without risk. *Quo warranto* proceedings brought against one branch of the established order might easily establish a precedent that future radicals would be happy to exploit. In this particular case, Peel thought it better to repeal the Laws so that the sense of general agitation which was stirring in the unseen depths would lose its focal point and evaporate. Thus would society be saved.

Society, as a concept, argues the existence of bounds, regulations, and codes of behavior, on which someone, for society's own good, has to keep an eye. This is equally true of empire. Both need to be controlled, and their controllers need to be certain of acceptance. That the price of liberty is eternal vigilance is a dictum that must always be referred to a context. Who is free? Who is to be watched? The ideas of the governing class, which could never admit that guardians like other men bore watching, insisted on being, and on remaining, all-pervasive. There was no real distinction between domestic and external affairs: the attitudes prevalent in one prevailed in the other. The whig quarterly *The Edinburgh Review* illustrated this condition neatly when it declared in 1899 that any system of compulsory insurance against old age, controlled by the government, was "generally felt to be repugnant to the genius of English liberty."[11] For this equates one assumption with another. "The genius of English liberty," as a piece of aristocratic shorthand, had been in vogue since the Revolution of 1688–89. Abroad, however, the exclusive and self-regarding nature of this "genius" had long irritated appraisers of the English scene. The Marxists

[10] A. C. Benson and Viscount Esher, eds., *The Letters of Queen Victoria,* first series (London, 1908), II, p. 50.
[11] *The Edinburgh Review,* vol. 190 (October 1899), p. 339.

still describe the "Glorious Revolution" as "the name given by English *bourgeois* historians to the *coup d'état* of 1688 which deposed the English king James II supported by the reactionary feudalists and brought to power William of Orange, who was associated with big landowners and the upper strata of the commercial *bourgeoisie*."[12] Similarly, "the freedom of the seas," which in England calls up stirring images of a host of redoubtable tars, has always been judged very differently by Americans and by Frenchmen, who have found in it as large a symbol of overbearing British imperialism as "gunboat diplomacy" itself. Peel's contemporary, the French historian Jules Michelet, dismissed all these assumptions as spurious. What was English liberty, he demanded, but the fruit of aristocratic pride and selfishness? Hence, the emphasis put on traditional liberties, on individual freedom, and on local self-government, instead of on (what all true Frenchmen sought) social, universal liberty.[13]

Perfide Albion is, of course, the Frenchman's shorthand for this disseminated mendacity. Albert Sorel, in his influential *L'Europe et la Révolution française*, underlined Michelet's point. In England the possession of common rights before the law had made Englishmen indifferent to the great diversities in their own social condition. This indifference had produced a callous society, impervious to the doctrine (not even understanding the principle) of social justice. Feeling themselves free, its members did not choose to appear equal; and had been utterly bewildered when the democratic principle had asserted itself among their own expatriate colonists in America. As a consequence, no men were less likely to promote a high idealism in their international relationships. England was governed by self-styled aristocrats, whose pedigrees were more commercial than feudal; and although they kept aloof from their mercantile contemporaries, it was a mercantile *ethos* that governed their national policies. England, in sum, was "une île marchande," controlled by men who, in the true spirit of the countinghouse, subordinated everything to self-interest.[14]

---

[12] Editorial footnote, in *Marx and Engels on Colonialism* (Foreign Languages Publishing House, Moscow, n.d.), p. 354.

[13] Quoted in J. L. Talmon, *Political Messianism: The Romantic Phase* (London, 1960), p. 247.

[14] Albert Sorel, *L'Europe et la Révolution française* (Paris, 1885), I, p. 353 ff.

They were imperialists to a man. Frenchmen who realized that French history and imperialism were scarcely strangers to one another insisted nevertheless that a distinction had here to be made. For, clearly, the universal *assimilation* promoted by France

> is not that of which England and Rome have dreamt in their egotistic and materialistic policies. It is the assimilation of intellects, the conquest of wills.[15]

To set out to conquer anyone's will is surely to betray a remarkable degree of egotism; but the French continued to reserve their thunderbolts for Napoleon's "nation of shopkeepers," many of whom never developed any imperial ideas at all.

Certainly the English avoided a logical, intellectual approach to empire. But they were not too stupid to notice that this attitude was itself an irritant. To recognize the extent of their own pragmatism was to compound the already severe state of annoyance elsewhere. Cecil Rhodes said he well understood the French anger at the objections currently being put forward by England to France's monopoly of the commerce of Madagascar. He put words into France's mouth: " 'It is all very well for you English to talk about equality of trade, but that equality means that we shall not be in it at all. We find that you English are always admirably logical on any point that is in your favour.' "[16] But Rhodes in making this point on the French behalf was merely underlining another, purely English, and highly infuriating attitude: that one could understand a foreigner's standpoint without, of course, intending in the slightest to take it into serious account.

The all-encompassing nature of the control which a confident ruling group can exercise over a deferential society has provoked comment from others beside those irked by patriotism. Karl Marx insisted that all social power was economic at root. Others have illustrated the consequences of this, without adhering to his cataclysmic resolution of the problem it sets. The American sociologist Thorstein Veblen, in his *Theory of the Leisure Class* (1899), anticipated Joseph Schumpeter's views on the atavistic nature of imperialist conduct. In a leisure class, which is simply that part of

---

[15] Jules Michelet, *Introduction à l'Histoire universelle* (Paris, 1831), p. xii.
[16] Vindex, *Cecil Rhodes,* p. 651.

the ruling group which can afford to do nothing, and under the leisure-class scheme of life, which is the resultant of political and economic power long established, "traits and types . . . reminiscent of the predatory culture" survive, often buoyantly. Witness for example the leisure class' general enthusiasm for war, which sometimes comes as a relief from a surfeit of too much leisure, whether at Heartbreak House or Horseback Hall. The pacifist Richard Cobden had noted that the honors, the fame, and the emoluments of war did not belong to the middle class: was not the battleplain the harvest-field of the aristocrat, watered with the blood of the people?[17] An upbringing in the middle class, however, did not protect its sons from catching an aristocratic tone, for a generation later Joseph Chamberlain was declaring that he did not care in the least about New Guinea nor was he afraid of German colonization, "but I don't like to be checked by Bismarck or by anyone else."[18] This toughness of attitude certainly exemplifies Veblen's point: what, anyway, was government itself but a predatory occupation? And, if this was true of a domestic government, how much more true was it of imperial government, which, not content with pervasion by influence, actually invaded by force of arms all spheres of life within the area of its control! "In Asia," explained a Russian military hero, "the duration of peace is in direct proportion to the slaughter you inflict upon the enemy."[19] Nor did one have to be the servant of a despotic system to believe this. It was also the long-held opinion of generations of free white men on the western American frontier, best expressed in the axiom coined there that there was no good Injun but a dead Injun.

For the doctrine of self-preservation, even though it may be the most consistently propagated by a governing class, is no monopoly of that class, nor is a predatory culture an invention peculiar to the privileged, or a state of being which only they work to maintain. The French Revolution showed to the world that democracy

---

[17] Cobden, *Political Writings*, I, p. 34.
[18] Chamberlain to Charles W. Dilke, December 1884: J. Strauss, *Joseph Chamberlain and Imperialism* (Washington, 1942), p. 26.
[19] General Skobeleff, who routed and massacred the Tekke Turkomans at Geok Tepe in January 1881: quoted in Charles Marvin, *The Russian Advance upon India* (London, 1882), pp. 98–99.

could prove itself a most terrible and warlike power, and it had thrown that shadow far: universal conscript military service, with its twin brother universal suffrage, had mastered all continental Europe—"with what promises of massacre and bankruptcy," cried Taine, "for the twentieth century!"[20] No socialist creed invoking the brotherhood of man would fundamentally alter the nature of this case. France's socialist leader Jean Jaurès knew this, knew it sadly. He pointed out that since the French Revolution, in France and Spain, in Germany and Italy, democracy had become inseparable from nationalism; for if the proletariat had really been indifferent to their respective fatherlands, would not Europe have already been given up to the Cossacks?[21] He was proved right when in 1914 the German Social Democratic Party, the most organized and influential socialist movement in Europe, threw in its lot with the military imperialism of the Hohenzollerns. Americans, too, had ignored Tocqueville's pessimism on this matter. They had hoped that a sovereign democracy would show itself purged of old-world sin and delusion, that it would never be guilty of predatory action, never traffic in imperialism. But, as the twentieth century turned, they had to confess their error. At this particular stage in the development of the United States, one commentator noted gloomily in 1900, territorial expansion was as certain as the advent of spring after winter.[22]

Particularly in a "frontier situation" did the doctrine of self-preservation ally itself to that of power. This was a commonplace in all the European empires, whose "men on the spot" confronted a hinterland that they did not, or not yet, command. The frontiersman, living in a perpetual state of emergency, was governed by atavisms of his own. These had little in common with those of the metropolis from which he had come, where his homekeeping kin had privileges of time and ease that allowed them to develop

[20] Hippolyte Taine, *Les Origines de la France contemporaine* (Paris, 1891), p. 14.
[21] Jean Jaurès, *L'Armée nouvelle* (Paris, 1910), pp. 542, 544.
[22] For a survey of viewpoints, see "American Imperialism in 1898," ed. Theodore P. Greene, in *Problems in American Civilization* (Boston, D. C. Heath & Co., 1955); F. H. Giddings, *Democracy and Empire* (New York, 1900), p. 270.

peace of mind. The frontiersman saw the utility of force as a solution for a local problem. The metropolitan saw only its brutality. The man on the spot relied on force more because he felt he had to than because he wanted to, although too long a reliance on it would often make him want to. He was under social and physical pressure. Since he was not free to afford magnanimity in the conduct of his affairs, he never prized this as a quality worth having. Private advantage he understood; public justice was often beyond him.

This was an attitude beyond the comprehension of the safe. The British metropolis became more "liberal" in its outlook than did any other center of empire, or any dependency, because it needed no standing army to guard its home frontiers. The nation had no enemies except those that its rulers went out and made, beyond the island's shores. As a result, the British people did not feel that foreign politics was any of their business and trusted their governors not to involve them needlessly, or ruinously, with other powers. But as a further result, British subjects, both at home and abroad, were subject not only to the king but to the mental and moral assumptions of those who managed the king's business—a race of men who slept easily in their beds, who expected tomorrow's sun to rise upon a selfsame scene, and who were therefore very slow to fathom the attitudes of those whose position did not allow them to take as much, or indeed much of anything, for granted.

This detachment bred a distrust of other, more emotional judgments. The third Earl Grey, England's Colonial Secretary from 1846 to 1852, saw no value in the seventy year old precedent of the American Revolution. He insisted that representative government better fitted the colonial situation than responsible government, for colonies were places at the far rim of civilization, places where men had no tradition beyond that of rugged individualism, a doctrine not well fitted to deal with complex issues. In 1846 he reminded the governor of the newly organized colony in New Zealand that "the otherwise inestimable advantages of colonial self-government" were attended with at least one serious danger. This was, that the powers conferred by the franchise on the representatives of the people might be perverted into an instrument for the oppression of the less civilized and the less powerful races of men inhabiting the same colony.[23] In this particular case of New Zealand, which had at that time a population of only 3000 white men, 3000 British troops, and nearly 105,000 Maori, the opinion was well justified. It was one whose implications were to trouble other generations of statesmen, not in Great Britain alone.

Grey felt that it was practicable to give a colony representative institutions and then stop—"something like the English constitution under Elizabeth and the Stuarts."[24] But colonists felt they deserved better. Edmund Burke's principle, minted when he opposed Charles Fox's India Bill in the House of Commons (December 1783), that all power exercised over a native race ought ultimately to be used for the benefit of that race, was too exotic a concept to serve the settler overseas. It was hard for such a man to feel convinced that his own power, over whatever race was his neighbor, was at all secure, as he stood amid the smoking ruins, say, of his farmstead on Cape Colony's eastern frontier. Instead he could very easily envisage a future wherein the power of the native race would be exercised over *him*, and exercised without regard for *his* ultimate welfare. Only his own efforts, brutal and without benefit of clergy though they might be, could stop this future taking shape. Not all the thunderbolts of denunciation hurled at him by "Aborigines Committees" at Westminster, or by the humanitarian sects which had their London headquarters at Exeter Hall, or by any subsequent Liberal or Fabian, ever deflected him from his position. No argument drawn from the field of Indian governance could impress him: for in India at least power was secure in the hands of the British minority. In such circumstances, but in such alone, was there room and time for intellectual conjecture on the rights of native races and for the practice of genuinely benevolent and paternal despotism.

Three degrees of latitude nearer the Pole, Pascal tells us, reverse all jurisdiction: "A meridian decides what is truth." European expatriates living three or more degrees nearer the equator

[23] Earl Grey to Sir George Grey, 23 December 1846: H. M. Stationery Office, *Parliamentary Papers*, 1847, xxxviii, Cmd. 763, p. 64 ff.
[24] G. E. Marindin, ed., *The Letters of Lord Blachford* (London, 1896), p. 297.

have long testified to his insight. White men who live beside, but not among, a colored proletariat will insist that they cannot afford to deal in ethics that do not relate to that predicament. That they choose to stay in it is beside the point. They resent the social analyses that issue from a commentator's armchair, because they see in them only a menace to their own security; to preserve which is, and must always be, their first duty.[25] To such men liberalism is an irrelevance at best: at worst it is a subversive activity.

Colonial frontiersmen who could not share Burke's ideas nonetheless found that they had to live in a world his ideas had shaped, the official world of Westminster and Whitehall. As the nineteenth century developed, this world of high policy grew ever more sophisticated and even more impatient with the obscurantism of primitives, whether white colonials or black savages, who did not because they could not keep pace with its own kind of progress.

The improvements in world communications served only to emphasize this time lag in ideas, attitudes, and practices between the metropolis and the colonial outpost. Its consequences have set forth a major theme in imperial history. They contribute alike to the American Revolution, to the Indian Mutiny of 1857, and to the Boer War of 1899. American colonists were defending the currency of principles minted in the seventeenth century (which they had seen no reason to change) in the teeth of a British oligarchy that had forgotten their original point. Hindus without hope in a future that would not be of their own making were casting wildly back to a medieval state of life wherein they had enjoyed at least some status. The Boers of South Africa, too, were stockading themselves against the blight and mendacity of the incoming twentieth century, which would assuredly wreck their concept of a gathered community. In these three cases the rulers of empire assumed the right to mold opinion. They saw themselves as progressive, their subjects as reactionary. For their subjects were to be governed by more than mere legality. They must also walk a line, adhere to a way of life, laid down for them by their governors. They were patients, not agents. This, was assumed in the colonial status from the outset.

To Burke, for example, the whole point of the first "Regulating

[25] These points are developed in Chapter IV.

Act" passed by Lord North's ministry in 1773 was "to form a strong and solid security for the natives against the wrongs and oppressions of British subjects resident in the province of Bengal."[26] Anyone who objected to that was plainly wicked. Similarly, in 1833, a British government decreed the emancipation of slaves throughout the Empire: the most arbitrary interference with private property on the national record since the days of Cromwell's Protectorate. This particular social revolution was imposed on colonists who, if they had been self-governing, would never have legislated on the matter at all. This is clearly borne out by the subsequent conduct of the ex-British colonists in the South of the American mainland; thirty years later they suffered an even harder imposition and had this same doctrine of the rights of men enforced against them, at sword point, by those of their own countrymen who were not committed to a slave economy.

Liberalism, in the hands of the confident, had thus a very cutting edge, and had not much to do with that doctrine of *laissez-faire* with which political scientists most often connected it. The compulsory veto placed on slavery by men acting under a primarily religious impulse is perhaps the most significant illustration of the entire doctrine of benevolent despotism, which had by no means died with the rationalists who so admired it in the eighteenth century. The West Indian planters, a body of men that had always displayed a vociferous loyalty to the British Crown and had often helped to finance its wars, were ordered to give up their legally acquired property. And, having no alternative sponsor, nor any chance of successful resistance, they did as they were told. When its turn came, the "Cotton Kingdom" of the American South did resist, but unsuccessfully: and its world, too, was forcibly reconstructed.

Imperial authority, therefore, in the opinion of those who held it, was there to be used. Indeed it was a dereliction of duty not to use it—an argument of which much more was to be heard. By admitting a twenty million pound compensation for the slaveholders in the West Indies, in Mauritius, and in Cape Colony, the rulers of the British Empire tacitly admitted they were dealing hardly with their own subjects. It was a matter of priorities, a matter of

[26] Eric Stokes, *The English Utilitarians and India* (Oxford, 1959), p. 2.

necessity. And here the two views of power, the view from the metropolis and the view from the frontier, tend to converge. When faced with emergency either moral or secular (slavery within the British world, or savages in the kitchen garden), both the statesman and the frontiersman saw virtue and utility in the policy of force. Both, when put to it, expressed the ultimate confidence of their race and situation. Both obeyed the doctrine of necessity and did what they had to do.

It was thus their condition, not their attitude, that so greatly differed. It is one thing to proclaim and proscribe a moral evil. It is another to kill someone in order oneself to stay alive. The one has a respectability the other lacks. British liberalism was both the product and the expression of British power. It ruled the fifty-five years that span Waterloo and Sedan. In these years, on this plateau of security, attitudes grew that had not flourished in the past and were not to flourish in the future.

In international relations the eighteenth century is more like the twentieth than the nineteenth is like either. The eighteenth century saw the working-out of a struggle for power on a global scale. While this was under way doctrinaires did not appear to comment on it. Adam Smith's *Wealth of Nations* would not have been written (or, if written, welcomed) twenty years earlier, when no one yet knew whether the master of both India and North America would be an Englishman or a Frenchman; nor would the English colonists in America have mounted a rebellion with a liberal bias in an era wherein the fate of the French in Quebec (1763) might well have been their own. Statesmen of that time, like those of this, were accustomed to a world in disorder. The statesmen of the intervening century were not. They believed in progress. They believed that they had made progress and that they would make more. They thought disorder a phase, an obstacle that intelligence could, and certainly would, remove. To get rid of it, indeed, was the highest mission to which a civilized man could set himself. "We find by practical experience," wrote one civilized man deeply committed to the task, "that the affairs of the world will not work while there is disorder about."[27] The implication here is that of course the affairs of the world could be made to work, so long as

[27] Francis Younghusband, *India and Tibet* (London, 1910), p. 436.

all the civilized nations combined to establish a harmony. And of course they would do so: was not this the great world-impulse that underlay all things?

No one then supposed that this world-impulse could suffer a change, that any nation would choose to embark on a "revolution of destruction," or that men in power might prefer to commit themselves to disorder and disharmony.

To seek to "balance" power was both a moral and a practicable aim. Power was a *datum*. Utopias that sought to dispense with it would always attract men of good will and high hopes: but the fact of the matter was that societies were fashioned by ordinary men, who *needed* bounds and limits within which, and only within which, they could thrive. The insistence of Englishmen that their first task anywhere they went was to establish "law and order" had always more to it than a misplaced devotion to police routine. It had a moral basis. Security of life and person within the bounds of an organized imperial control was at once a symbol of a disciplined civilization and a hope expressed for greater things to come. It established a safe base, on which these things could grow. David Livingstone, Christian missionary though he was, set his priorities for Central Africa as "commerce and civilisation," in that order. Commerce could thrive only amid conditions of peace; and only peace could foster those other conditions wherein the civilized values and virtues, the Christian religion among them, could take genuine root. Cecil Rhodes, not cast on Livingstone's scale yet with much of his range, affirmed his judgment. A child of the mid-century (1852), he was always under a driving compulsion to finish his work. It was as if he understood that not only he but his very ideas were never going to enjoy a satisfied old age. "I knew," he said in 1894,

that Africa was the last uncivilised portion of the Empire of the world, and that it must be civilised; and that those who lived at the healthy base, with the energy that they possess, would be the right and proper individuals to undertake the civilisation of the back country.[28]

It is a magnetic phrase, "the Empire of the world." It has laid a spell on every nation wanting to assert its own sphere of in-

[28] 6 January 1894: Vindex, *Cecil Rhodes,* pp. 339–340.

fluence in the record of mankind. For "the back country" was always there, pressing against every civilization, and challenging all its principles.

The claim of the Russians, for example, that theirs was the task and the honor to bring enlightenment both into eastern Europe and Asia under God's especial favor was well known to the great powers, but had never been given their serious attention. They made it an axiom that all Russian justification was innately spurious, since all Russian motives were genuinely sinister. The fate of the Poles in 1863 confirmed this. Russia was a rogue power, a comet power, the only one free enough of the European state-system to be able to envisage its overthrow without damage to itself. A mixture of incomprehension and suspicion had bred in both the French and the English a Russophobia that their diplomacy never seriously tried to dissolve.

But the Russians made one attempt to clarify their view of life. In October 1864 the city of Tchemkend in Central Asia was stormed by General Tchernaiev's forces. In November the Russian Chancellor, Prince Gorchakov, issued a "circular" to Russia's consular officers abroad, briefing them on the situation, so that they might parry local protest.[29] This circular, printed in full by the St. Petersburg official press, was hailed derisively in diplomatic circles as Gorchakov's *ballon*—and when Russian forces in Turkestan continued their forward move, taking Tashkent the following summer and thus inaugurating a series of frontier campaigns that were not to be completed until the absorption of Merv in February 1884, the onlooking diplomats were able to congratulate themselves on their percipience, that Russian guile and Russian style had not changed and never would. In fact Gorchakov's circular was issued in good faith, for he really did expect, as its peroration announced, that its message would receive "a just and candid appreciation." When the content of optimistic bombast, natural to the prince's temperament, is discounted, the language used remains significant.

For it pleads the doctrines of necessity, power, and civilization. No one could deny that the Muslim khanates in Central Asia

---

[29] Gorchakov's "circular," dated 9/21 November 1864, is printed in W. K. Fraser-Tytler, *Afghanistan,* Second Edition (Oxford, 1953), p. 319 ff.

were haunts of slave-raiding, slave-trading barbarians, ruled by tyrants. The position of Russia in Asia was that of all civilized states which came into contact with half-savage, nomad populations. It was anyway a peculiarity of Asiatics to respect nothing but visible and palpable force. No diplomatic *démarches* concerning their mistreatment of Russian nationals would ever have the slightest effect on such people. No civilized country could afford to allow such a situation to continue in territories which directly abutted on its own. It was necessary to put a stop to it, to clear out the Alsatia and to establish a settled regime there. Had not a similar necessity been admitted by others in just such a position? The North Americans, the French in Algeria, the Dutch in their colonies, and the English in India, all

. . . All have been irresistibly forced, less by ambition than by imperious necessity, into this onward march, where the greatest difficulty is to know where to stop.

Everyone knew that the best agent for promoting progress and civilization was the establishment of commercial relations. But for the development of such relations everywhere order was necessary. Stability was necessary. In fact (as Livingstone would have agreed in Africa's context) a complete transformation of the habits of the people was necessary. The peoples of Asia would not transform themselves, could not do it even if they wanted to. Someone must do it for them. And this was no self-centered task. The Imperial Russian cabinet in assuming it took as its guide, certainly, the interests of Russia. But it believed that at the same time it was "promoting the interests of humanity and civilization." The Prince-Chancellor remained confident that the governments of Europe, staffed by men of good will, could not but look at the business in this light.

More, much more, was to be heard of these sentiments. It is especially ironic that Gorchakov's parting shot should have been the first expression of an imperialist doctrine that British officials were to publicize and popularize fifty years later: the doctrine of the "dual mandate," or double trust. This declared that the paternalism of a colonizing power benefited not only a particular subject race, but also served the interests of the world at large, by extending the area of civilization.

Despite their cool reception, the Russians had effectively given Europe notice of their good intentions. In doing so they put themselves at an advantage which other powers, busy about their imperial business, would have done well to copy and were to live to envy. The British in particular found themselves unable to protest effectively against Russian imperialism. St. Petersburg was ever afterward able to counter with a straight face the series of "Notes" from London in regard to further advances into Central Asia.

The British suspected that one day the Russian armies would discover exactly where to stop, that their terminus would be India's northwestern border, that it would be British India itself and not some degraded *caravanserai* which would give Russia her long-sought "civilized neighbor" in Asia. Khanates in Turkestan and emirates in Afghanistan had hitherto provided the British with a buffer zone between their own imperial limits and those of Russia; but the Russians now seemed to have begun a policy that would in time do away with this zone altogether. A straight consequence of this was that any independent policy mounted by England in Europe, and particularly towards Turkey and the Balkans, would be paralyzed. If the two great powers in Asia ever came directly to confront one another, their soldiers patrolling a common frontier, England at that moment would become as much a landlocked, "continental" state as any of her rivals. So the British continued to ask what was going on and were repeatedly met with the excuse that some unforeseen, indeed unforeseeable, situation had arisen in Turkestan or Transcaspia which had made the *status quo*, so much desired by the Russians themselves, impossible to maintain.

So clear a statement of the duties of civilization, so confident an assertion of the superiority which clothed the civilized, made it easier for Russia than for anyone else to appeal to the guidance of a manifest destiny. Whether it covered Pan-Slav activity in the Balkans or direct expansionism into the Far East, this was evoked without any of the defensive self-consciousness with which the same doctrine was invoked by Americans, who, when their destiny was achieved and their continent colonized from sea to shining sea, kept a sense of unease about all the dead Injuns who were the inevitable victims of the business of imposing one culture upon another. No ill-fated United States' government treaty with

any Red Indian tribe speaks such a language of rectitude as that
found in the terms of the treaty (also ill-fated) between Russia
and the Muslim state of Bokhara, signed by the Amir at the dic-
tation of the Russian governor-general in Turkestan on 28 September 1873. The seventeenth article intones that

> In deference to the Emperor of all the Russias, and for the greater
> glory of His Imperial Majesty, His Eminence the Amir . . . has resolved
> that henceforth and forever the shameful trade in men, which is so
> contrary to the laws of humanity, shall be abolished within the limits
> of Bokhara.[30]

If conquest needs the intoxication of a doctrine,[31] the Russians
certainly seem to have known how potent to make the brew.

But few outside Tsarist Russia developed so sublime a self-
assurance. The striking of romantic attitudes fell into disfavor, as
Germany's William II, an Ajax born too late, found out more than
once. Mankind, Montesquieu tells us, "although reprobates in de-
tail, are always moralists in the gross." Gross moralism dogged the
public action of the imperialists, and none of them could find an
intellectual appeal strong enough to demolish their difficulties.
Newspaper editors in Paris and London would from time to time
pontificate that the French, or the British, were chosen people,
entrusted with a particular mission. The French were inclined to
believe it; but English irony was always too deep-seated. One historian did remark that the Indian Empire had been reared for his
countrymen as for a chosen people, but few of them agreed.[32] A
colleague was later to say, with greater accuracy, that the structure of governance in India had been as much the work of Indians
themselves as of the invaders. Writing of the establishment of the
East India Company's power in the second half of the eighteenth
century, Lyall commented that "the military classes of the Indian
population very soon began to transfer their services to the standard of leaders who always paid and usually won."[33]

---

[30] D. C. Boulger, *England and Russia in Central Asia* (London, 1879), II,
appendix.
[31] H. R. Trevor-Roper, *Historical Essays* (London, 1957), p. 169.
[32] J. W. Kaye, *A History of the Administration of the East India Company*
(London, 1853), p. 64.
[33] Lyall, *British Dominion in India*, p. 109.

Since no one nation could ever convince any other that its own style in imperialism was essential if civilization was to survive, they had all to fall back on to the more concrete, but even more debateable, ground of "rights." This lies in egotists' country. "We hold these truths to be self-evident," avers the American Declaration of Independence, at once clearly, and quite accurately, implying that there are others who do not hold anything of the sort. The Declaration of the Rights of Man was, because it was the most popular, also the most detested doctrine of the French Revolution, and Englishmen and Scots were transported to the antipodes for having Tom Paine's *Rights of Man* (1791) in their possession. All statements about rights are assertions of opinion, with a defiance stamped on them. They declare that the condition of things is not what it should be. Something must be done to change it; if that something is not done, a great wrong goes unredressed. Conscience will not allow him who sees this to stay silent. He must speak. Rights, therefore, are the things that I, the self, the enlightened critic of the established fact, want.

What Tom Paine, American colonists, and French attorneys wanted was something so simple that a complex society could not grant it without shattering itself. "All men are created equal," which was their doctrine, is one that also argues (since it is not demonstrably true) that all men ought to *remain* equal; and that there is something wrong with the social system, and even indeed with the cosmic scheme, that allows inequality to exist. The doctrine of rights thus grows in controverted soil and thrives in an atmosphere of charge and countercharge, passion and prejudice. The man who is at home on that ground, who breathes that air, has left the world of things as they are for the world of things as they ought to be: the world which he, the man of destiny and the hour, will make them. He has entered the world of romance.

Romance has ever had an imperialism of its own. Of all empires, it has the most loyal subjects. Yet these subjects have never formed a fraternity. They are the alumni of too many schools of thought. The claims of right put forward by romantic imperialists are not welcomed by critics of the social order who wear another style of romance. If the nineteenth century owns a Romantic movement at all, then certainly both Victor Hugo (1802–85) and Louis Napoleon Bonaparte (1808–73) are its products: and how bitter was their mutual enmity, is notorious. Among romantics the charge of betrayal is endemic: and a Bonaparte had a great deal to betray.

The general suspicion that greeted the Emperor Napoleon III on his self-elevation in 1852 quickly attached itself to the policies he promoted on France's behalf. The word "l'impérialisme" was coined to describe them: like "colonialism" in our own time, it was a debased coinage from the start. Since the "man of December" was a Bonaparte, it went without saying that he was also an egotist, an adventurer, *capable de tout.* And what anyway was a Bonaparte but a hero whose feet were clay, someone who had not fulfilled the dreams others had dreamed about him? Since the uncle's capacities, admittedly heroic, had clearly been denied to the nephew, the latter's claim to any right to rule was dubious. Louis Napoleon made no secret of the serious superstructure he wanted to build upon his uncle's flimsy intuitions of good governance; but he never diagnosed that the weakness of those foundations would forever threaten his plans and his Second Empire with them.

The first Napoleon, although declaring a loyalty to Roman fashion, had in fact been more inclined to hunch oriental trappings around his imperial shoulders. He had made of the Church a brood of spiritual police. He had despotically ruled through his army and his bureaucracy, taking care that even local functionaries were independent of the people they governed. His Empire had replaced the *ancien régime*'s notorious Bastille with eight more of the same, less notorious but equally effective. He granted all his imperial honors to *gendarmes* of one kind or another: his *Légion d'honneur* was, and fundamentally still is, a military decoration, so that "the highest reward to which an administrator, a scientist, a scholar, a poet can aspire is the decoration which comes almost automatically to nearly every captain or major at the end of twenty years' garrison duty."[34] Since he wanted only to rule, he saw no use for political convictions.

The third Napoleon had, if anything, somewhat too many of these. Caesar was buried, yes: but *he* came to restore him. The

[34] Albert Guérard, *Reflections on the Napoleonic Legend* (London, 1924), p. 89.

Caesar he invoked had never lived, but Napoleon III was resolved to make him live, to mold a Caesar of Democracy, at once the ruler and the tribune of the people (a role that Napoleon I had shuddered away from, even in his last extremity of 1815's hundred days). The nephew's *Idées Napoléoniennes,* published in London in 1838, sees empire as a sphere of rule for an hereditary executive. Its head should be confirmed by the vote of the people, by their universal suffrage, in a *plébiscite.* In a proclamation issued on 14 January 1852, while he was yet only the Prince-President of the Second French Republic, he embellished these notions. The actions of the chief executive, since he was responsible to the sovereign people, must be spontaneous and without check. Hence, he must have ministers who would act as his honored and powerful auxiliaries. But each of them must be responsible to him alone. What a chief executive had no need of was a "responsible" council, which would form "a daily obstacle" to the projects he put forward. As experience showed, any such council would express only the shifting politics of the chambers, which bowed to every wind and prevented "the steady application of a regular system."

It was just this claim to systematization that caused alarm. What dynamo operated this system? Egotism: converted into a widespread activity through a bureaucratic channel, or, to use the new term, imperialism. The Emperor, himself spurious, would conduct spurious policies. His annexation of Nice and Savoy (1860), taken in reward for the exercise of French idealism on behalf of the unification movement in Italy, confirmed this general view, which was echoed by the thunder of Victor Hugo against *Napoléon le petit.* Imperialism was thus stamped from the outset with the imprint of something not accurately definable but at any rate meretricious and self-deceiving. It would always pretend to nobility while busily furthering its self-interest. This was the central accusation against the Second Empire: not that it was an Empire but that it sailed under false colors, with which the *tricouleur* had little to do. Whatever the plans of Caesar, Empire could not be equated with democracy. The democrats of Europe had gone down to defeat in 1848–49: their previous grievance was now a genuine wrong, to nurse and remember. The critical barrage thus grew more intense. Imperialism met with a contempt that empire had never had to cope with. Empires, as wielders of power, had of course incurred honest hatred throughout the ages; but they had not pretended to be something they were not.

Power, efficacious and successful, should not need to wear a mask. Self-interest which did not lay claim to high morality was preferable to a self-interest that did.

Diplomats, for example, stayed free from the mistrust that dogged the imperialist, whose very breadth of idea made him of necessity a demagogue, drumming up support. The diplomat worked in a polite *incognito*, but everyone knew what he was doing. His stock in trade was his country's self-interest, and the better he promoted this the more he was worth. It had become the diplomat's habit to personify whole states with the policies that he and his kind, a French-speaking fraternity, were working on. "It is the opinion of France," "England will not permit," "Germany views with displeasure" are all commonplaces of diplomatic language. This trick of speech has been borrowed by professional historians, who write a shorthand about "France in the Levant," and so forth. The language is natural to those whose business it is to think in terms of power: it is a genuinely imperialist habit of speech, unclouded by the justifications that beset the louder-styled imperialists who insist that the *mystique* of imperialism somehow transcends mere self-interest. For in the eye of heaven it might be as *just* for China to have a base in the Isle of Man as for Great Britain to have one in Hong Kong; but no diplomat, troubled enough by the matters that actually confront him, can ever feel he needs his attention drawn to a philosophical consideration of that kind.

Examples of this language clearly display the assumptions that support it. In *The Diplomacy of Imperialism* Professor Langer notes how Lord Rosebery, England's Liberal Prime Minister, was in 1894 "disposed to allow Russia to occupy Armenian provinces of Turkey in return for the recognition of Britain's special position in Egypt, and perhaps with some compensation for France in Syria."[35] Rosebery's successor was a tory,

[35] William L. Langer, *The Diplomacy of Imperialism,* Second Edition (New York, 1950), p. 197.

but this did not signify. When in January 1898 Lord Salisbury explains to his envoy at St. Petersburg his own view of some pressing issues, the tone is the same. The two Empires of China and Turkey, says he, are so weak that in all important matters they are constantly guided by the advice of foreign powers. In giving this advice Russia and England are constantly opposed, neutralizing each other's efforts much more often than the real antagonism of their interests would justify. He hopes that this "evil" can be removed; and perhaps it may be, if the Russians would only believe that "we aim at no partition of territory, but only a partition of preponderance."[36] No doubt crosses his mind that there can be any question as to a right of preponderance. Nor is this attitude peculiar to the late 1890's (generally accepted as the zenith of imperialist sentiment). Thirty years earlier Lord John Russell had struck exactly the same note. Her Majesty's government, he tells *his* envoy at St. Petersburg, do not want to enter into a struggle with Russia for influence in Central Asia

. . . but what we aim at is that Russia shall not take advantage of her relations with Persia and her means of pressure on the states of Central Asia to encroach upon countries which it concerns us should remain in the possession of native rulers, and be undisturbed by foreign intrigue.[37]

Here is one British assumption about power which was forever to infuriate Russians, Frenchmen, Germans, and Americans alike: that what England did in a particular situation beyond her own shores was bound to be just and proper. What everyone else was up to was foreign intrigue.

Imperialist statesmen expected, as these examples show, to have rivals in the field. There would be frontier problems. Spheres of influence would clash. An agenda with these items might sometimes perplex but would never startle them. They reckoned that possession was nine points of the law and could look back to a tradition of international conduct that supported this. In the

[36] Lord Salisbury to Sir Nicholas O'Conor (St. Petersburg), 25 January 1898: G. P. Gooch and H. W. V. Temperley, eds., *British Documents on the Origins of the War* (London, 1927), I, no. 9, p. 8.
[37] Lord John Russell to Sir John Crampton (St. Petersburg), 31 March 1860: Public Record Office, London, Foreign Office Papers 65/867, no. 66.

sixteenth century Spain, the dominant imperial power, had provided the envious with an obvious target. When Charles V inherited both the Spanish and the Habsburg properties in 1519,
he found attached to every portion of his dominions a long-
standing feud with its neighbors. All these feuds were at once
transferred to Spain; and Spain pursued them all. Among her
enemies were Frenchmen, Moors, Turks, Lutherans, and English,
corsarios luteranos on a Spanish Main. But none of them brought
the charge that Charles was a usurper, with no right to his great
imperial position. They merely asserted their own self-interest
against him; and, as Spanish power was the context of action,
this could only be done by singeing the king of Spain's beard.
Aggression was a part of everyone's program, justified by the
doctrine of necessity. "No one calls it imperialism," Schumpeter
says, "when a State, no matter how brutally and vigorously, pursues concrete interests of its own."[38]

But by the late nineteenth century the moral idea of rights
had attached itself to simple envy. It made ambition fiercer.
Empires of emulation, protesting their right to a place in the sun,
were emerging. They accused those who already owned freehold
under the sun of an immoral degree of greed, exercised when
everyone else had been too busy, or too weak, to intervene. Once
they had taken an inventory it was plain to Frenchmen and to
Germans in what ways Great Britain had made opportunity work
for her since Waterloo. The British Empire now stood forth as a
phenomenon. It had to be classified, and, when classified, explained. This was the proper, scientific approach. To ignore
such a material challenge would have been to confess that events
were governed by chance (or else that God favored the English,
an intolerable notion) and that science was an irrelevance. It was
heresy to believe either. The British Empire was the product of a
historical process. What process, exactly? If intelligence was applied, the answer would be found. The analytic approach would
provide a key to history: it remained only to find, in this particular case of Empire, the lock that it fitted. And then, of course,
to mold one's own key, to construct one's own lock, and go
through the opened door to the goal of world success.

[38] Schumpeter, *"The Sociology of Imperialisms,"* p. 5.

If the British Empire was a growth, the German Empire was an artifact. It has instantly verifiable dates for its inception (10 May 1871 in Europe, 24 April 1884 overseas), and it arrived on the world's stage armed with the necessary doctrine on *Imperialismus,* justification in advance. *A priori* theory was to the German taste. Things did not merely exist. They existed because they fulfilled a need. Therefore it had to be proved that empire, and especially a German Empire, did just this. What need? The need for self-expression, for one. "Every virile people has established colonial power," Treitschke told his students at Berlin, insisting also that the victorious Prussians ought to have compelled the French to disgorge their properties in Cochin China, together with Tahiti, the Marquesas islands, and Réunion in the Indian Ocean.[39] (This doctrine of virility reached its middle age in the 1930's, when it became Mussolini's refrain that "Fascism sees in the imperialistic spirit a manifestation of its vitality.")[40] But, when looked at from this angle, the British Empire repelled the Germans because it rejoiced in no "spirit of empire," laid claim to no *raison d'être,* contenting itself instead with an old-fashioned, unscientific, nonintellectual concept of *raison d'état.* It puzzled the elder von Moltke, for example, that the British should have been among the most warlike, but also among the least military, of peoples. This seemed, indeed, a wounding comment on some inefficacy in the German system.

Of all the English statesmen who took empire seriously and proclaimed its cause, justifying it by an appeal to the economic necessities of his country, Joseph Chamberlain was at once the best known and the clearest-headed. But Chamberlain's disregard for economic truth in his claims made obvious the inadequacy of a strictly doctrinaire approach, for Chamberlain was a fine example of the hard-headed businessman in politics; a man who ought, if the stereotypes were of any service, to have been thinking of nothing but finance capital (another German invention)[41] and to have spent most of his time adding up trade returns. But Chamberlain, whose imperialism came not from his head but

---

[39] Quoted in Townsend, *Germany's Colonial Empire,* p. 56.
[40] *The Times,* London, 25 May 1937.
[41] Rudolf Hilferding, *Das Finanzkapital* (Vienna, 1906).

from his heart, very often contradicted both himself and his own evidence. Opposing politicians pointed this out, but without any genuine sense of shock. It was precisely this irrationality in the British "imperial idea" that upset both Hobson and Lenin, who, as true to their own natures as Chamberlain was to his, were forever looking for reason, for logical pattern.

Even those friendly to England often expressed concern about this lack of applied thought. Admiral Mahan (sourly described by a fellow American[42] as the distinguished formulator of *Machtpolitik*) was one of these. "They are true prophets," he remarked in his first book on sea power, which became an Anglo-Saxon imperial handbook,

. . . though they seem to be having small honour in their own country, who warn her [England] that the continuance of her prosperity at home depends primarily upon maintaining her power abroad.[43]

The British were carrying pragmatism, which after all was not one of the fine arts, to the point where it would mislead rather than promote an intelligent international policy. If, then, the Germans paid more attention to theory than it was sometimes worth, the British were too apt to assume that no theory was worth anything.

Neither changed their outlook. The experience of war between 1914 and 1918 confirmed the Germans in their notions of *Machtpolitik*, while at the same time it made even more remote any British effort to establish a philosophical basis for policy. The Germans, because they had not won, attributed this misfortune to some error in their practice. They saw none in their theory. It was still their right to be powerful; their mistake had clearly lain in not being quite powerful enough. The British stayed as free of preconceived ideas as ever. They evolved no thought how to shape the future they wanted. What they wanted was what no empire has ever known—a quiet life, a life free from care, jealousy, and all "foreign intrigue." Peace and prosperity were still the major British interests, and British politicians continued to suppose that everyone else thought them valuable too. The upshot was that

[42] Charles A. Beard.
[43] Alfred T. Mahan, *The Influence of Sea Power upon History*, Fifth Edition (London, 1890), p. 38.

the misapprehensions of Neville Chamberlain about National Socialist Germany were thoroughly matched by Adolf Hitler's misconceptions about England. For the German *Führer,* no less than the British Prime Minister, thought it quite possible "to do business" together. He never did come to understand why his several offers of "a free hand" for the British Empire elsewhere than in Europe (since Europe was clearly Germany's own imperial responsibility) were not accepted. What else could the English possibly want? From the traditional English standpoint, what other policy could have been more acceptable to English statesmen, who were always declaring that all they wanted to do with power was balance it?

For many Germans never saw any reason to change that view of the British Empire which was first brought to it in the 1870's. They had hoped by diligent study to uncover the motivations of British policy, to assess their driving force. Study uncovered nothing of the kind. The British Empire was only an emporium, operated along countinghouse, marketplace lines. German imperialists took the Manchester School of economists as their guide to English political motive, in much the same style (and for much the same reasons) as Russian communists still consider Charles Dickens as a reliable reporter of the contemporary English scene. The English, needing peace in order to prosper, would subordinate everything to getting it. For them to pretend to higher thoughts while they went about this business was an hypocrisy of just that kind that Europeans had long diagnosed as native to English soil. "The assimilation of the interests of humanity with those of the British Empire, which is peculiar to English thinkers, is, of course," said Bethmann-Hollweg, "unacceptable to Germans."[44]

What was acceptable to Germans proved equally unacceptable elsewhere. A French observer defined the German doctrine of imperialism as one

directed towards the domination (*Imperium*) of the Germanic elements of the world over the non-Germanic.[45]

[44] Bethmann-Hollweg, *Reflections,* p. 167.
[45] Jacques de Dampierre, *German Imperialism and International Law* (New York, 1917), p. 22.

It was based on clear principles. The interest of the community was superior to, and must therefore override, the interest of the individual. The supreme community, whose authority was unimpeachable, was the State. German gifts of discipline, German powers of organization made Germany the inevitable pioneer in the task of fashioning the collective human community. When fashioned, this community could enjoy no better destiny than to remain under the authority of the German culture. *Deutschland über Alles* was not a shallow slogan, a piece of drum-beating: it was a consecrated formula, at once the product and the symbol of the philosophy that governed the teaching of history, and indeed of everything else, within the German State.

The historian Wilhelm Giesebrecht declared that science, the century's most shining tool, ought not to be cosmopolitan: "It ought to be national, that is to say, German."[46] His own history of the Holy Roman Empire (1856) he dedicated to Frederick William IV of Prussia, then the rising star of the German nationalists. It invoked the splendid *Kaiserzeit*, the time of the Emperors, whose Roman Empire had lighted the path to future imperial success and had imperishably proved the worthiness of the Germans for their world-historic vocation (*Berufung*). James Bryce in his own study of the Holy Roman Empire later noted the effects of this intoxicating version of history on the contemporary German Empire. The Empire proclaimed in Versailles' hall of mirrors reflected the baroque splendors of Vienna. The inheritance of the Roman Empire had once made the Germans the ruling race of Europe, "and the brilliance of that glorious dawn could never fade entirely from their name."[47]

Since history proved so useful a tool in the hands of the scientific investigator who knew what he was looking for, it was to be expected that the new biology and the evolutionary theories of Darwin should have been set to the same work. Only the strong and the fit were awarded the prizes of life, and who were stronger or fitter than the German people? The naturalist Ernst Haeckel popularized Darwin's ideas, fertilizing ground already sown by Joseph Gobineau's *Essay on the Inequality of the Human Races*

[46] *Ibid.*, p. 31.
[47] Bryce, *Holy Roman Empire*, p. 431.

(1853–55). Their belief in racial superiority did not incline the Germans to practice reciprocity in their dealings with other nations. No true reciprocity, in such a situation, was possible; and it would be hypocritical to pretend that it was. The idea of Pan-Germanism could never adapt itself to the presence of other races. The imperialism of the Hellenes, the Romans, the Arabs, the British, and the French was a force of assimilation, "but German imperialism was a force of elimination."[48] The Germans conquered, or planned to conquer, *territories* and *areas*, not nations. Germans needed above all, if their ideas were to grow and develop fully, space. If the space was not physically there, it had to be created. It had to be cleared. They spoke of *Lebensraum*, as if the provision of room for German elbows was the only function such cleared areas could have. They saw themselves as constantly faced with a Task. When not actively at work on this Task, they were betraying the cause for which they stood. From the facts of the time they deduced a challenge, and at once declared their response.

A German Empire, then, a true world state with a true world policy, would be nothing like the British Empire. Ah, it would be something far otherwise. It would be animated by a patriotism of a nobler stamp. It would be kindled by a zeal for the spreading of Germanic *Kultur*. It would give to the world more than the British, shopkeepers to a man, could ever dream of. It would not count pennies, or suffer a fall of honor. The new Imperial Germany, remembering the *Kaiserzeit*, informed by the *Zeitgeist*, pursuing a *Berufung*, aware of the responsibilities of *Weltpolitik*, blessed by sufficient *Lebensraum*, and populated by a race of men whose efficiency was a European watchword, would square joyfully to its Task. It would unlock the future. It would usher in that Golden Age for which all peoples, even those only dimly aware of science and all its wonders, were waiting and hoping. And it went without saying that those who opposed these ideas, or perpetuated conditions which obstructed their success, were enemies not only of Germany but of all mankind.

It also went without saying that if the Germans could improve upon the British Empire, so could the French.

[48] de Dampierre, *op. cit.*, p. 44.

Frenchmen would do this less solemnly and without such pro-
longed reference to political science; but they would do it, since
it was a thing that ought to be done. The building of an empire,
like the building of anything else, was in the main a matter of art
and style, an affair of *élan* and *esprit*, in all of which Frenchmen
excelled. It was also their axiom that in all these the English were
woefully deficient.

The young Francis Garnier, about to make his first visit to the
Far East in 1848, speaks more vehemently on this than did many
French empire builders, yet still in the language of most. Imbued
with the romance of the East, he cherished in consequence a romantic hatred of the English, who appeared to be impervious to
it. What, for example, had England done in India, beyond impov-
erishing that country both spiritually and physically? Was that
the part a civilized nation ought to play towards a vanquished
people? Had England fulfilled the duty which her very conquests
imposed upon her? No she had not: so, *évidemment*, England was
not a civilized nation at all. Garnier echoed here his contemporary Michelet: what anyway was England but "an infamous
melting-pot in which the lives of men were exploited for the
profit of the few?" She was assuredly a colossus, but a colossus
"with rotten feet."[49]

French patriots continued to share this opinion. Napoleon III's
mystical and incalculable brand of imperialism had departed
with him, but the new Third Republic was as eager as any French
government had been or was to be for a position of established
power, with the respect that the world accorded such. *L'Empire*
under the two Bonapartes had contained a great deal that was
fraudulent. In the Second Empire the Cochin China business, like
that in Mexico, was never thought through by anyone. In the new
age these *aventures exécrées* were tabu; but, surely, the old
concept of *la France d'outre-mer*, France extended in majesty
throughout the world, was still viable?

If this was only a postwar trauma, it went deep. In 1946 as in
1871 Frenchmen looked outwards in nostalgia for happier days.
In 1946 an anthology was published of the imperialist sentiments
pursued by *Les Constructeurs de la France d'outre mer*. Its edi-

[49] Hugh Clifford, *Further India* (London, 1904), pp. 132–135.

tors insisted how, under the German occupation between 1940 and 1945, "le sens de l'Empire français outre-mer était la seule liberté qui nous restât." But they also insisted that they were not burying their emotions in the past. The territories of the French Empire had still, in 1946, a great and fulfilling future before them, a future of fraternity with metropolitan France. Frenchmen had not lost that *génie colonisateur* which was so striking an illustration of the national spirit. It was true that some Frenchmen, regrettably many Frenchmen, might feel and indeed always had felt that the story of French enterprise overseas, of the development of great possessions by the guiding lights of French civilization, was an irrelevance, since France's true historic role was that of founder and arbiter of Europe's culture. To the anthologists, these were misguided men. Those who did not look to France overseas did not understand France herself. From Champlain's era to Lyautey's, from Richelieu's to Ferry's, true patriots had realized that France owed it to herself, to her own greatness of spirit, to establish an Empire—had realized indeed how great an abdication of responsibility it would be not to do so. They had known, as all should know, that the story of Empire was a symbol of "le roman de la France sur la vaste terre." A matter of the heart, a matter also of style: "Tel est l'Empire, et il a besoin d'une foi."[50]

Such high sentiment had not roused the sluggish in the earlier era. Yet in 1871 a French Empire was already in existence. It consisted of about a million square kilometers and five million people, mostly in Algeria. It cost the citizen-taxpayer some twenty-two million francs a year. These facts intoxicated few and irritated many. Memories of the Prussian invasion did not die; and men who concentrated their emotion on Alsace and Lorraine and kept their watch on the Rhine had no patriotism to spare for the security of the Maghrib or the Mekong. They had to have it proved to them that France gained anything from her establishments in such unknown parts.

By uphill and protracted effort, Jules Ferry did just this. It was he who forged a coherent, reasoned doctrine to animate a new

[50] R. Delavignette and Ch. A. Julien, *Les Constructeurs de la France d'outre mer* (Paris, 1946), pp. xii, 43, 47.

era of French imperialism. His best weapons were logic and a keen perception of the situation as it was; but he found it harder to make headway in an emotion-charged atmosphere than Frenchmen are supposed to do.

He did not arrive with a doctrine (this indeed would have pleased his critics better): he later evolved one out of his own imperial activities, after he had been ejected from office on 30 March 1885, with the cry of *le Tonkinois!* pursuing him. He was not wholly a rationalist: a fervent patriot, he too could thrill to the magic and power of a great challenge, one to which, surely, all true sons of France could respond? Was not the whole matter of empire "un immense steeple-chase [*sic*] sur la route de l'inconnu;"[51] fascinating for that very reason? But his guiding principles were clear. He wished to promote the maximum industrialization of France. The economic battle must be fought: the high German and American tariffs marked the enemy positions. These industrial giants would grow ever more powerful; and France, in order to compete with them, must find new markets for herself and as rigorously protect them. This entailed a planned program of colonial expansion. Only by this means would French industrialism prosper. Only by taking this route could French economic independence be reached. These things were in the national interest, to which all patriots must subscribe: and the national interest must override all other considerations, even those sacred "principles of 1789," which were, to Ferry, a species of "métaphysique politique." The modern world was a world of might, not metaphysics: a world of power, not principles; at any rate, not of principles fashioned to deal with a very different order of things, with an age that had gone. Economic strength was the new mainspring of power. It affected everything. It affected the way Frenchmen lived now, would live in the future. For social prosperity depended on how many markets France could monopolize: "la paix sociale est, dans l'âge industriel de l'humanité, une question des débouchés."[52]

---

[51] *Ibid.*, p. 302.
[52] "Social security, in mankind's industrial epoch, is a matter of markets"; *Ibid.*, p. 305. See also Henri Brunschwig, *Mythes et Réalités de l'Impérialisme colonial français 1871–1914* (Paris, 1960), pp. 79–102.

In sum, the colonial policy of the Third Republic was the off-spring of her industrial policy. If France did not promote an effective industrial policy she must step down from the ranks of those who counted, those who had something to say, indeed everything to say, about the shape and nature of the future.

Ferry made these ideas a commonplace; and his disciples related them firmly to the kind of international behavior France ought to adopt. His friend Paul Leroy-Beaulieu, whose *De la Colonisation chez les peuples modernes,* first published in 1874, had become a political textbook by the 1890's, insisted that France for example must become a great African power lest "in a century or two" she become a weak European power.[53]

So it was not Germany's Bismarck only whose map of Africa lay in Europe. France's imperial quest in Africa had already involved considerable trouble with the English and would involve even more—but what of that? France's view of England's establishment of world influence was similar to that held in medieval Christendom concerning the power of Islam: she could not understand how it could have happened in the first place or why it continued to succeed. The French needed colonies overseas to remind the English, who forgot what was not constantly brought to their attention, that France was a great power. It was no bad point to make: for English officialdom, which knew a great deal about local conditions and attitudes on the Zambesi and the Nile, knew far less about these same affairs on the Seine and on the Loire.

The French hoped that England would no longer be able to adhere to her selfish but profitable doctrine of balancing power in this new era wherein stakes of power were being set down in Africa and in Asia by a ring of imperial competitors. She would be drawn actively into the European arena, where she properly belonged. She would have to come down from her platform of splendid isolation. She must now learn to negotiate and to bargain —and to lose, like all other lesser mortals always classified by the English as "foreigners." England, with an extended Empire, in an age in which the other powers were extending or founding their

[53] Quoted in Stephen H. Roberts, *A History of French Colonial Policy 1870– 1925* (London, 1929), p. 19.

own empires, was no longer an island, impervious to winds of change. She was in fact as vulnerable as her nearest colonial frontier: the problems that had always beset her in regard to the Canadian border and to India's northwest were now to be attached to innumerable tracts of African bush. France's drive for economic strength would thus prove a major factor in the diminution not only of the wealth, but also of the strategic immunity, of her principal rival.

Thus France joined Great Britain in the business of making an empire of trade. The countinghouse mentality of the English was adaptable by men of ideals, since their idealism at once purified it of the native English dross. Where the English were content to run a commercial emporium, the French would establish their imperial conception of trade. In their own history were experiences that could guide them in this task. The circumstances facing France in the last quarter of the nineteenth century reflected those of the age of Louis XIV. What Ferry said echoed the principles that Colbert, Louis' *surintendant des bâtiments et manufactures* and later (1669) his minister of marine, had worked all his life to establish.

Colbert, like Ferry, had insisted that colonies were needed to increase French commerce, for only by this means could the royal treasury be kept filled and the royal wars financed. Colonies provided a market for French manufactures. They produced raw materials for France's sole benefit, while themselves remaining exclusive possessions; as much a part of the realm, and as precious, as any province of metropolitan France. (This exclusiveness was the core of high policy: economists later gave it the name of mercantilism, but it was not in the first place promoted by merchants.) The rivals in the field were not the English, but the Dutch, then the world's carriers who, according to Colbert's own estimate, owned 16,000 of the 20,000 ships that made up Europe's mercantile marine, and whose assets in their East India Company amounted to 800 million livres. For the burghers of Amsterdam the French monarchy had a profound contempt: but if Dutchmen could do all this, what might not innately superior Frenchmen do in their place? Royal favor was therefore awarded to Colbert and his schemes, and merchants for the first time were admitted into the royal suite. "Oversea commerce is the means to bring happiness to our subjects,"[54] states the preamble to the letters patent authorizing the incorporation of a French East India Company, to whose capital of ten million livres the king, queen, and courtiers all subscribed. A royal edict of August 1664 announced that trading *to India* was *not* derogatory to a man of noble birth.

The world's other half was also spanned. A French West India Company, with a capital of some four million livres, spoke the day's imperialist language. This Company's charter (May 1664) allowed it to exploit the mainland of South America from the Amazon to the Orinoco, together with "other islands, and the mainland of North America from the north of Canada to Virginia and Florida"—with a monopoly of the trade of that distinctly non-French area for forty years.[55] A great deal was thus sketched out that was never to be completed. Yet Colbert's work in establishing both a navy and a mercantile marine for his country laid the foundations for the great imperial successes of the next century and presented a legacy to all Frenchmen who in later times looked out to sea. One of Ferry's contemporaries, writing in 1886, awards to Colbert and his ideas the best accolade in anyone's gift. "Good or bad in theory," says he,

in conformity or not with the principles of economy, Colbert's policy had one merit which was more valuable than many: it was successful.[56]

And only the State could best organize success on the national scale. Free trade might suit the book of merchants in a sellers' market, and indeed many a merchant and many a planter in colonial America had seen with great regret the harrying of the Dutch supplier and all other so-called "interlopers" from his door. But it did not accord with the policy of competitive national States. Trade had to be nationalized. The tariff wall was not to be demolished, it was to be exported: and, when exported, buttressed.

European views on this did not change. The English doctrine of free trade, which did not lack an idealism that hoped to promote a universal condition of peace and stability, was never

[54] S. L. Mims, *Colbert's West-India Policy* (New Haven, 1912), p. 9.
[55] *Ibid.*, p. 69.
[56] *Ibid.*, p. 338.

adapted, or its adoption even seriously considered, by England's emulators in the business of empire. In their work of colonization the Germans shared the exploitation theories of Frenchmen, Dutchmen, and Belgians. They concentrated on the production of raw materials, by forced labor where necessary. They backed this policy by military force and used it without misgiving: thirty "punitive expeditions" (the adjective symbolizes the attitude) were set on foot into the German colony of Kamerun in West Africa within twelve years (1891–1903). They backed it, too, with their genuine belief in "scientific" method. This must be applied to agriculture, to money, and to markets. It must also be applied to men themselves, whether their own colonists or some native race within the colony.

This devotion to science was what lifted the matter of colonial rule on to a higher plane than any mere grubbing for profit could reach. The Germans were as indignant as Belgium's King Leopold II to be accused of brutality, and to be told that they cared everything for the produce but not at all for its producers. Their answer repeated the Russian assertion of 1864: native races had to be compelled to come into the modern world, since they would never of their own accord do so. The task of governing from a distance the inferior races of mankind, wrote the English sociologist Benjamin Kidd, would be one of great difficulty, one that would tax every resource of intellect and character. But it was one that must be faced and overcome,

if the civilised world is not to abandon all hope of continuing its economic conquest of the natural resources of the globe.[57]

The civilized world was not going to do anything of the kind. Profit and prosperity remained the pillars of national power.

To win for itself the respect and even the fear of rivals, this power had to formalize itself in ways not customary in the pre-nationalist era. Nations had long flown flags and banners; but only in the age of professed imperialism did these become sacred symbols, dishonor to which was dishonor to the nation itself. Other symbols joined it, each insistent on its own ceremonial. The German Navy, sprung from nothing (or from the imagination of

[57] Benjamin Kidd, *The Control of the Tropics* (London, 1898), pp. 284–85.

Admiral Tirpitz), became at once a tool of the imperialist trade and a notice served on the world that no engine of power owned by anyone anywhere was not also going to be owned by the great German Empire. As an English politician had written, "the necessity of maintaining the consideration due to ourselves"[58] was the first element of all political power and influence.

The French Army, whose most influential officers were aristocratic Catholic monarchists, anti-radical and anti-masonic (a group whom the civilian rulers of the Third Republic were naturally happy to see, and keep, fully employed on the far perimeter of the civilized world) was another such symbol of power. The Russian armies in Transcaspia and Turkestan, controlled by military governors-general who paid as little attention as they could contrive to the civil arm in St. Petersburg, were others; as, in another fashion, was the Russian concept of Pan-Slavism, a missionary miasma that obscured all Balkan politics and penetrated as a result into every chancellery in Europe. Americans learned to remember the *Maine* and were exhorted while doing so to take up the white man's burden.[59] Hubert Lyautey, the future master builder in French Morocco, reflected while still a cadet at St. Cyr in 1875 on the importance of *l'école de caractère* and on how great an empire might be built by the disciplined alumni of such a school. "Character" itself was to become a symbol of the superior civilization.[60]

Emulators fell heir to this confusing accumulation of symbols. The Italians were ready to adopt all of them without stopping to consider whether in fact their country owned anything which they accurately symbolized. Jules Ferry had made a reciprocal equation out of the relationship of a metropolis to its colonies: the expansion of colonies would cause an expansion of the home industries. But clearly *some* industrial power in the metropolis must first exist to make any process of expansion, whether colonial or domestic, possible at all. Nevertheless, one month before Ferry's enemies forced his resignation, the Italians occupied the port of

[58] Urquhart, *Progress of Russia*, p. 58.
[59] Rudyard Kipling's poem, "The White Man's Burden" (1899), was addressed to the government of the United States.
[60] 19 May 1875: quoted in Delavignette and Julien, *op. cit.*, p. 469. See also Chapter IV.

Massawa on the Red Sea and began a colonial policy whose purpose it was to make Italy, a country as notorious for its poverty
as Spain, rich and resourceful. This was, after all, as a Fascist
apologist explained in 1930, a legitimate aspiration, a matter of
right.[61] Expansion was neither good nor evil: it was only inevitable. The Italians, according to an earlier propagandist, set out
on their imperial way determined to avoid the pitfalls that had
entrapped those that had gone before them: Spanish formalism,
Dutch egotism, French concentration, and the "too diverse" conditions of English colonization.[62] They did not, however, have
much luck.

The list of this series of symbols and attitudes makes it plain
that nationalism was everywhere rampant. Imperialism was indeed only an extension of its field of operation, for nationalism
only becomes a living thing, capable of being grasped by a majority, when it goes out into the world to measure itself against
some other form of itself. The idea that some kind of international trusteeship could be applied to the governance of the tropics had been sketched out at a colonial congress held in Berlin in
1884: but when Belgium's Leopold II had taken hold of the area
(the Congo basin) for which this experiment had been marked
out, the notion lapsed until towards the close of the war of 1914–
18, when the Americans reproduced it in the form of "mandates"
for ex-enemy colonies.

Colonies were national property, estates that must be developed
by improving landlords using the most up-to-date methods. It
was not aspiration only, nor even extent of territory, which would
fertilize that place in the sun. What was needed was a simple
competence. In England this was the constant theme of a small
group of militant, enthusiastic Imperialists—men who claimed
both the name and a capital letter for it. British imperialism was
the counterpart of the various nationalist movements in Europe;
but it was not so much the extension of a fervent patriotism as
an exotic breeding ground for it, and for that very reason it was
thought of by many influential Englishmen as something entirely
unnecessary. England did not become more English by extending

---

[61] Luigi Villari, *The Expansion of Italy* (London, 1930), p. 7.
[62] Quoted in A. Keller, *Colonization* (New York, 1908), p. 520.

her possessions overseas: was there not indeed a risk that she might become less so? For in England patriotism had never (because it never needed to in a uniquely favorable geographic position) taken on the racial aspect adopted by embattled European nations, jealous always of the inviolability of their respective territories and of the habits and attitudes their frontiers enclosed.

But Chamberlain and his school drew attention to the vulnerability of an England that did *not* own a world position. Their speeches and writings presaged that half the population would starve if England was ever reduced to "Little England," if ever the British Empire narrowed down to mere United Kingdom dimensions. Imperialism was therefore not only a form of survival. It was *the* sole policy for survival. Not to adopt it was flying in the face of facts, of commonsense, and of the future. Because this was so, Chamberlain advocated abandoning the free trade system. This too had become a form of "métaphysique politique." It had been an admirably serviceable policy in the days when Britain was the unchallenged workshop of the world. It had indeed been the natural imperialist policy of the mid-Victorian manufacturers, although Cobden and Bright would have shuddered had they ever heard it called by that name. But now around the workshop was a scattering of new buildings, put up by rival firms. Their machinery was bright and their prospectuses ambitious. Chamberlain therefore called for a return to a planned system of protection and imperial preference. "Protection" was more than the name of a particular economic policy: it meant what it said. "England without an Empire!" he exclaimed in 1906; "England in that case would not be the England we love!"[63] Love, like everything else, exacted a price; but who would resent paying it?

What Adam Smith had emphasized in his *Wealth of Nations* (although a book primarily aimed at mercantilist targets) was still true: defense was more important than opulence. Mercantilism since Smith's time had been in an intellectual pillory; but, when taken out of its stocks and dispassionately examined, it proved to have acted as a useful defensive policy in a day of hot competition. Just such a day had returned. It was time for the English to leave that comfortable plateau, where they had raised

[63] Speech at Bingley, Yorkshire; *The Times*, London, 10 July 1906.

and so greatly admired the flowers of free trade. Opulence needed defense, and defense could rest only on power. The German Empire, which from the outside appeared to be a more unified organization than it really was, was often cited as the example to follow. The power of the State had to be used to regulate its own future, to safeguard the destiny of its own sons. On this point English imperialists, voting Conservative to a man, found themselves in an odd harmony with social planners on their Left, who were trying to engineer a shotgun marriage of socialism with the Labour movement. Both believed that every sphere of public life had its place within the arena of political responsibility. Both detested the vacuities of the "incompetents," men who had no notion of the size of the job it was their duty to tackle.

Paternalism, like liberalism itself a product of power, thus kept its place as a principal creed on both Right and Left in England. The social reformers adhered strongly to a doctrine of power, since only by means of one could they refashion the world to their hearts' desire. Physic had to be administered to people who did not know what was good for them: here was the "Crown Colony" *ethos* of government, which was, even while the first National Health Insurance Act was passing through the House of Commons (1911), successfully creating the country to be known as Nigeria. The imperialist saw it as part of his mission to disseminate law, order, justice, education, peace, and prosperity. He could not logically burke the same tasks, different only in degree, in his own country. "Protection," his new enthusiasm, threw its shadow far beyond the arena of commerce. But, while he saw this, he did not see any need to change the social structure. The very concept of social welfare summoned up, as liberty itself had always done, the image of its necessary guardians. Which guardians were necessary, was of course the issue on which Right and Left parted company.

As the socialist Robert Blatchford insisted in his *Britain for the British* (1908), Britain did not belong to the British. It belonged to a few of them only, men whose doctrine of power demanded that they should employ their fellow countrymen as workers or servants. This vast majority was kept "below the salt," like the contemporary population of India—a land also ruled by a handful of British tories, first cousins to those upper middle-class persons who now maintained the *Raj* in Britain itself. The Empire was a closed circle of power and therefore an irrelevance to the destiny of the British people. It deflected the attention of their rulers from the matters that should properly have engaged it. The educated classes continued to send their sons to govern the imperial possessions; but the paternalist rule of distant natives drew little attention at home. No one was of less significance in public life than the retired colonial official, as the great proconsuls Milner, Cromer, and Curzon all found out. "If we personify the Empire," said a writer on *Conservatism* (1911), "our imaginations recoil like Frankenstein from the monster we have made, the monster of a heterogeneous personality."[64] H. G. Wells' comment was more incisive. Nineteen people out of twenty, the middle class and most of the lower class, knew no more of the Empire than they did of the Argentine Republic or of the Italian Renaissance[65]—in other words, nothing at all. The English workers were not yet so strongly impregnated with the doctrine of the brotherhood of man as to care about the absence of Factory Acts in British-controlled Egypt; the twelve-hour day put in by women and children in the cotton-ginning mills there; the one pound a month pay-packet which the Calcutta jute-mill worker took home; or the kind of home he took it to.

But the imperialist tried to awaken his countrymen to a sense of their duty by insisting on the gravity of their predicament. "Little England," her gaze riveted on her own navel, was, he sincerely hoped, a phantom of a future that would never come to pass. Indeed he saw it as his own clear duty to ensure that it did not come to pass. Imperialism was not a burden or an irrelevance. Nothing could be more relevant. It was a *sine qua non*. The exercise of power in international affairs ought to be regarded

as a normal and peaceful function of the national life, to be steadily provided for—not as a spasmodic war-call, to be insured against grudgingly.[66]

[64] Lord Hugh Cecil, *Conservatism* (London, 1911), p. 64.
[65] H. G. Wells, *Mr. Britling Sees It Through* (London, 1916), p. 79.
[66] On this theme see the collection of essays and speeches by Lord Milner: *The Nation and the Empire* (London, 1913).

Milner, pioneering for British paramountcy in South Africa, would as eagerly have affixed the same authoritarian system on Britain too if he had been given his head. The respected soldier Lord Roberts urged that true efficiency could only be obtained by imposing military conscription, which he was the first to euphemize as National Service. He argued also, in front of chambers of commerce as well as to applauding cavalrymen, that to abandon the Empire would also be to abandon the country's mercantile wealth. For years Cecil Rhodes had been saying the same thing. Great Britain's world position depended on her trade, and if her people did not take over and open up those areas of the world that were at present in the grip of barbarism, they would be shut out from the world's trade, since other nations would do the job for them. He had once said this to Gladstone, who had answered that he would have quite agreed if he had really believed Rhodes was right; since if hostile tariffs were raised against Britain in every new country taken by another power, "it was a poor look-out."[67] But he, Gladstone, believed in the success of the free trade principle, and in liberalism, and in a future where the imperial sway of all these would never be disturbed.

Rhodes realized that these principles were as hallowed in England as were those of 1789 to the conservative French, who were prepared to recognize only those revolutionary conditions that were safely interred in the past. He agreed with Ferry's diagnosis, how to preserve social peace. The current social nostrums in England were so much humbug. And the working-man was finding them out to be so, was coming to realize that he "must keep the world and the trade of the world if he is to live."[68] The Empire was the future. Without it England had no ascertainable future at all—and how would this profit the working-man?

Poor look-out or Golden Age to come, this fascinated preoccupation with the future was common to every imperialist outlook, from whatever nationalist standpoint. That the progress of industrialism and the contraction of great areas of the world within its grasp was a revolutionary business, likely to loose forces of a kind that no one could accurately gauge, was something plain

[67] Vindex, *Cecil Rhodes,* p. 650.
[68] *Ibid.,* p. 698.

to see. That it was a business likely to be as dangerous as it was exciting was also clear. Imperialists, although optimists by nature and temper, never lost sight of the element of risk. To plan, to scheme, to gamble, to apply intelligence and foresight to circumstance—these were essentials, matters of straight commonsense, if disaster was to be avoided. Prediction might not be accurate, but no generation, no national entity, could afford to be caught entirely by surprise. One had only to look around. The nineteenth century had caught by surprise those static nations that had expected, if indeed they had expected anything, that the conditions of the eighteenth century and for that matter of ages past were going to continue forever. Hence, as the twentieth century came in, the writing was on the wall for the Chinese Empire, for the Ottoman Empire, for the tribalisms of Africa, and even, at long, long last, for the stubborn and impermeable Tsardom itself. But such should not be the fate of the virile, of the confident, if the virile and the confident seized the opportunity that was always there for those with the will to find it.

The imperialists enjoyed the world they lived in. They were at home in it. They agreed with (because they had drawn up) the terms of reference that governed it: strategic, commercial, diplomatic, social. They wished to extend it by building annexes overseas whose peoples should be trained to acquiesce in these same terms. They were convincd that, by so broadcasting the soil on which they themselves thrived, over so wide an area, they could not but broaden the sphere over which civilization ruled. They had a function to fulfill. They had the determination to fulfill it. If this was to be called a doctrine of imperialism, then let it be so. They would take the name of imperialist in pride. It was better to do that than to fold the hands and shake the head, to absent themselves from the conduct of the world's affairs, to have a voice but not raise it for fear they would be criticized for selfishness, for insensitivity, for ruthlessness, or whatever. Inaction and silence would be construed not as magnanimity but as weakness. And so it would be, in truth. It would assuredly precipitate the process of letting the weak go to the wall, of ensuring that only the fittest survived the battle for existence. They themselves would be the weak, they themselves would die at that wall —if they bowed to radical opinion and allowed all that they had done, and caused to grow, to wither and perish for lack of simple care.

But simultaneously all over the industrial world radicals, socialists, social reformers, communists, and anarchists were speaking a language as robust. Their own type of imperialism was designed not to govern the world as it was but the world as they were resolved to make it. They had drawn up new terms of reference and were ready to serve them on mankind. They worked not to extend the existing system but to get rid of it.

The props of that system had been put there by the capitalists. They must first be knocked down and the ground cleared. On how to do this there were many opinions. The majority of European socialists believed in the pursuit of happiness as fervently as American liberals had ever done, and did not suppose that much happiness would be found by plunging society into bloody revolution. Moderate social democrats normally spoke of happiness attained as a state of social justice and did not scare themselves with yellow or other colored perils, phenomena that came from beyond the industrial world. They saw a foe closer to home, coming not from strange continents but from the continent on which they themselves lived. They saw the major menace coming from below, from those untraveled kingdoms, the unvisited parts of town, where dwelt a mass of men who must be supposed to have made in silence a tally of their own wrongs. These were men who did not know and were not moved by the hopes and fears of the comfortable, since they had no comfort. They were men who could not look forward to dying in their own beds in their own houses, since they owned neither bed nor house. They were men who were native to the areas that "society" (a concept invented by the educated) had not colonized—men among whom some humanitarians had established what were known as "settlements," a term borrowed from the vocabulary of the pioneer Christian missionary, who had used it to describe his clearing amid some Kaffir *kraal*. If such men were driven, as much by *bourgeois* complacency as by outright oppression, into the hands of the anarchists, the true revolutionaries, then the outlook was poor indeed.

Jean Jaurès had expressed this in a famous cadence. The *bourgeois* masters of the Third Republic, who called themselves Radicals, had in their self-centered attack upon the Catholic Church, in their laicization of education, "interrupted the old lullaby that had long cradled human poverty." They had awakened the disinherited, who would demand their rights with more urgency in this world if they had lost hope of a future world in which the balance would be redressed.

This stirring was everywhere noted as a portent. Even in America some felt that an eighteenth-century political charter did not necessarily interpret all twentieth-century social problems: the Socialist Party of America, a counterpart of England's Social Democratic Federation, polled close to a million votes in the presidential election of 1912. By 1914, while Britain's Independent Labour Party could muster only some thirty thousand members, the Social Democratic Party of Germany stood strong at more than a million. Thus, even if the workers of the world had not united as Karl Marx had urged them to do, at least they had become collectively conscious and resolved in one form or another to take political action. The times were poised for their success. The dawn seemed near. But *der Tag* found for itself a different connotation. No wonder then that every section of the British socialist and Labour movement demonstrated in Trafalgar Square on 2 August 1914 to oppose the idea of any British participation in the dynastic, militarist, imperialist struggle that was getting under way in Europe. For it was clear that war on the European scale, which would involve and waste every nation's industrial and spiritual potential, would be a blank denial of mankind's best hopes.

Every liberal mind felt this shock. In October 1912 the imperialist Lord Roberts had declared his conviction that the German Social Democrat, that representative figure of all the socialist movements, would make war on his French, Russian, or English "comrades" if his superiors ordered him to do so. The event proved him quite right: and his accuracy especially saddened those liberals who had long thought that all military judgments were outmoded to the point of absurdity.

Yet the events of July–August 1914 also proved to liberals that they had been right to see in imperialism the menace to every hope and plan for the future. They had been right to disbelieve its apologists, the men who were constantly brandishing plans and programs and insisting that only the unremitting application of imperialism to the problems of world policy would make England a greener and pleasanter land. The war of 1914–18 was to convert Hobson's *Imperialism,* itself an angry reaction from the South African war, from a contemporary critique to a textbook in political science for new generations. Imperialism was now to be seen not only as an irrelevance, but as a wicked misuse of the national resources. For the imperialists had committed the supreme irrelevance. They had gone to war for trifling reasons, careless of their duty to their peoples, unaware, it seemed, that they had any duty at all. They had gone careering off on their chargers down a blind alley, taking civilization with them. They had chosen a path of glory that, as it turned out, was not even to lead to the grave; since it was the "unknown soldier," a faceless and indeed bodiless conscript whose grave was never to be found, who emerged as the democratic hero of the war. Imperialism was and would ever be fraudulent. It did nothing for anyone that anyone would ever want.

For the imperialists, even supposing them to be capable of realizing their dream of industrial "progress" all over the world, even if every Hindu hereafter were to pass his life-span dressed in Manchester's textiles, would only too plainly never put their profit where it would do the most good, where the social pressure was at its most dangerous. Richard Cobden's anatomy of the condition of the English people, made in 1840, was still true of their condition, and it would also remain true of the people of any nation which was whirled by imperialists towards some private goal of their own making. There was no country, Cobden had said,

... where so much is required to be done before the mass of the people become what it is pretended they are, what they ought to be, and what I trust they yet will be, as in England . . . It is to this spirit of interference with other countries, the wars to which it has led, and the subsequent diversion of men's minds from home grievances, that we must attribute the unsatisfactory state of the mass of our own people.[69]

In this diagnosis, the doctrine of power—backed by calls to honor, buttressed by and dependent upon success, its declared

[69] Cobden, *Political Writings,* II, p. 375.

purpose the better security and prosperity of all the people—was only a doctrine of profit; and "imperialism" itself, shorn of the spiritual clouds that masked it from the common sight, only the name that best described it.

To this diagnosis we can now turn.

THREE

The Doctrine of Profit

If it is true that a doctrine consists in a body of principles, can a doctrine of profit be said to exist? Is not profit its own principle? And is that principle the kind that doctrinaires normally have in mind?

Such questions have always seemed beside the point to those who are going for gain, which makes its own point. We do not preach all we practice; and how consistent is this particular practice the record plainly shows. Desire for profit is a common guide to action, even though other motives are declared for it. Any study of imperialism must pay close attention to it; indeed, many such studies pay close attention to little else. This is not surprising, since both the imperialists themselves and their socialist critics saw imperialism and capitalism as indissolubly linked together. From where they all stood the prospect was the same. It was their prognosis that was different.

The imperialists insisted that their doctrine of profit was a necessary part of their task of spreading the ideals of a humanitarian civilization. Money brought power, and only the powerful could act with success. How could they perpetuate their imperial ideals if empire itself was not securely based on good business foundations? How would the world prosper and its peoples multiply while they pursued a common happiness, raising their standard of living every generation, if care was not taken of sound investment and "securities," the very name of which brought solace and the conviction that the future was bound, under the imperialists' paternal guidance, to be only a greater and sunnier projection of the present? "I have before me a document," wrote Sir Charles Dilke in January 1888, with his eyebrow only slightly raised,

. . . referring to an Indian railway, the interest of which is guaranteed by Government, in which shareholders are asked as to their wishes with regard to the nature of their stock after 1 January 1959.[1]

Imperialism, to its propagandists, made excellent economic sense, indeed the only economic sense. In England Joseph Chamberlain and Cecil Rhodes, the Royal Geographical Society and the foreign missions, all firmly believed that the most valuable thing that money, properly invested, could buy was a lien on the future. What anyway was profit, but another name for the just reward that was due to those who exercised valor and virtue and energy?

Their critics' deepest fear was that this map of destiny was indeed a true one. Because of it they invoked a moral lightning against empire and all the works of imperialism. Alas for the hope and dream of the sons of men, if they were to be turned over to the hard-faced and the crass-souled, to the merchants in "philanthropy plus five per cent," to that complacent *bourgeoisie* whose members flattered themselves that God could fashion no finer heirs to His creation than their own kind. What possible virtue could exist in a doctrine of profit whose sole purpose was to perpetuate the imperial rule of those who were its profiteers?

This attack on imperialism was only a part of the socialists' campaign against the foundations of society. Imperialism was not itself the primary target. For imperialism was only a tinsel palace reared on capitalism's rock, which one day would be shattered by the application of the correct amount of social dynamite. Socialists were not in the least interested in bringing Africa or China or wherever within the fold of European civilization, since they were convinced that there was a great deal, indeed everything, to be done in Europe itself before its own natives could lay claim to a civilization at all. Converted to Marx's philosophy that all political and social power was economic at base, they waged this campaign with such diligence and skill that the "economic interpretation" of imperialism is still, to the majority of those who interest themselves in its doings,

[1] Sir Charles Dilke, "Modern Armies," *Fortnightly Review,* January 1888.

the only one worth discussion. Recent works, such as Messrs.
Robinson and Gallagher's *Africa and the Victorians* (1961),
discuss just what *type* of economic interpretation best illuminates
the imperial scene; they do not question the interpretation itself.

This image is not likely to change, since it reflects an inner
conviction so all-encompassing. The profit motive can never
expect to enjoy the esteem of, say, a doctrine of strategic
advantage. Self-preservation, which that doctrine embodies, is
reckoned one of the rights of man; but men are ready to admit,
when not themselves busy in the market place, that what Adam
Smith called "the human propensity to truck, to barter, and to
exchange one thing for another" is a propensity very possible
of abuse. Rudyard Kipling has exposed the underside of this
natural instinct:

> Who shall doubt the secret hid
> Under Cheops' pyramid
> Was that the contractor did
> Cheops out of several millions?[2]

Cheops' contractor, it seems, took a gainful advantage of his opportunities: and it is he who, according to those who interpret
imperialism as an entirely economic phenomenon, supplies the
model for imperial action.

The interpretation, then, chooses, explains, and finally har-
monizes the series of events that tell the story of national
expansion. It finds their motive force in the lust for profit alone.
That the industrialized nations broke beyond their own bounds
to search for this wherever they could get it is the core of this
theory. It throws a shadow into every other. Behind every profession of a civilizing mission, it claims, must lurk in fact only
the desire of industrial capitalists, men whose real interest in
human welfare must ever be slight, to multiply the number of
consumers who are at their disposal within the ring of their
system of monopoly. These industrialists use what the German
socialist Rudolf Hilferding was the first to describe as finance
capital—capital set free for manipulation by the expansion both

[2] Rudyard Kipling, "A General Summary," *Departmental Ditties* (Lahore,
India, 1886).

of industry and credit, in such abundance, or surplus, as to make it possible for its manipulators to change from their former habits of short-term marketing to a new practice of long-term investment. Their ideology is that of power; and they call with confidence upon the State to give the full support of its political power to the foreign business interests of its own nationals. Their doctrine is in fact predicated on the conviction that the State will recognize that it is by means of these manipulations in money that its own authority, territorial as well as fiscal, will become ever more widespread.

In their practices the financiers can count on the support of small investors, whose knowledge of power and policy is non-existent but whose appetite for profit is just as considerable as their own. The small men, like the large, are looking to get from the use of surplus capital abroad higher rates of interest on their money than can be got at home: the difference may in some cases amount to as much as that between two or three per cent in Europe and twelve or more per cent in areas that cannot withstand the lure of a European loan and a dip in the European pool of capital. To find such areas one had only to look at a map of places well beyond this center of gravity. The states of Latin America accordingly display throughout the nineteenth century a remarkably recurrent history of foreign loans, high interest rates, and local default. The Ottoman Empire borrowed over one billion dollars from European exchanges between 1854 and 1875, before it collapsed beneath the weight of its own fiscal inflation.

Since the masters of capital were then English and French, their two nations are considered as pioneers in the field of economic imperialism, armed with the techniques gained over the centuries from their experience in commercial imperialism. As the *Journal de Débats* remarked in 1862, "At London and Paris there is sufficient credit for all the governments of the universe."[3] Both in "the City" and in "the Bourse" the eyes of the capitalists were turned with particular interest upon the Levant. During the Crimean War (1853–56) the governments

[3] 24 March 1862: D. C. Blaisdell, *European Financial Control in the Ottoman Empire* (New York, 1929), p. 22.

of both England and France had assisted the Ottoman government with loans amounting to eight million pounds. But this type
of State action had been made possible only by the emergency
of the war itself. Enterprizing capitalists could not normally call
with confidence on anything beyond their own judgment, which
was usually referred to by others, in no very good humor, as
speculation. The *laissez-faire* principle was strong, particularly in
English government circles. Even though England was the
country in which industrialism had progressed farther than in
any other, and was thus the first to experience a supposedly
"saturated" capital market, her politicians were neither economists
nor financiers and would at that time have taken offence at being
called imperialists of any kind. Private enterprise, conducted at
its own risk, was permissible, but even that had its limits, as
Baron Julius de Reuter found out when he could get no support
in London for a grandiose scheme which would have obtained
for him a stranglehold on the economic life of Persia (1872).

At the beginning of this period *The Times* well expresses this
attitude of amicable detachment:

The great wealth of England and the desire for more profitable invest-
ments than are offered within the limits of a country of redundant
capital, have caused and will cause the East to be explored by the
enterprising and speculating,

and a little later awaits with equanimity the outcome of just such
enterprise:

The Turks have a fine territory and no money, energy, or skill: we
have all three, and they pour into Turkey as naturally as water finds
its level.[4]

And as it nears its close, England's Foreign Secretary Lord
Derby makes much the same point. Commenting in 1875 on the
attitude of the Conservative government not to interfere with
the movements of capital, he declared that this principle was
sound: for, if it were understood in England that persons lending
money to foreign states would be given the official support of their
own government, the obvious effect of that would be to enable

[4] 20 February 1857: *Ibid.,* p. 58.

the poorest states, or those with least credit, to get money on
much better terms than they otherwise would.

Foreign capital had therefore to do the best it could on its
own terms. It could not complain of hardship. The terms it
obtained for itself under the "capitulations" (indulgences granted
by the Ottoman government allowing foreign nationals the protection of their own laws and courts and not that of their country
of residence) put the bulk of the import and export trade of
the eastern Mediterranean into its own hands, for one of these
capitulations placed a limitation on the customs duties that could
be levied on foreign goods, thus giving the foreigner an advantage
he could speedily exploit.

But when Turkey defaulted in its interest payments in 1875
and European governments came to the support of their bondholders, the modern age of economic imperialism, a public not
a private affair, may be said to begin. The preservation of the
Ottoman Empire was a major British and French interest. To
allow it to collapse through sheer financial and fiscal ineptitude
would be to give a hostage to fortune, and in all probability to
Russia, of a kind that might never be redeemed.

Here Britain and France could genuinely declare that they had
the "Concert of Europe" behind them. This concert now took on
an especial form. To Cairo as well as to Constantinople went
foreign inspectors, treasury-bred, who uncovered every last in-
competence. As a result an Anglo-French "Dual Control" was
established in Egypt in 1879, whose "Commission of the Public
Debt" oversaw all matters of revenue and expenditure, and
whose English and French representatives were appointed not
by their governments but by the bondholders. This pattern was
followed at Constantinople, where henceforth the Sultan, like
his Khedive in Egypt, had to live in the light of other people's
superior knowledge. In 1882 an organization called the Administration of the Ottoman Public Debt was set up. It had a Council
of six, representatives of holders of Turkish securities worth one
hundred million pounds, drawn from Great Britain, Holland,
France, Germany, Italy, and Austria-Hungary. These representatives were still, officially, private persons; but no one reckoned
them anything of the kind, least of all themselves. The unofficial
approval by European governments of the appointments of

members to this Council; the official viewpoint and training of the appointees; the Council's responsibilities to the Deutsche Bank and to the Ottoman Bank, themselves administered by foreigners; the system of interlocking directorates employed by those banks and their associated enterprises in dealing with the Ottoman Debt—all these, in the opinion of the Council's historian, made it "an instrumentality of European imperialism." It functioned "as the colleague of modern European capitalistic society intent on the economic exploitation of the Ottoman Empire."[5] It steered all public enterprise in the way it thought it should go, paying particular attention to railways. By 1914 fifty-eight per cent of Ottoman Empire government bonds were held by French citizens, and the Deutsche Bank and the Ottoman Bank (largely French) were still the most important driving forces in the European economic penetration into Turkey.

This example is perhaps the one that best illustrates the theory that a cohesive, single-minded *bourgeoisie*, motivated only by profit and careless of all other human values, possessed of the power to summon up all the resources of the State, set to work to expand the area of capitalism beyond anything it had previously known. The magnitude of this aim appeared so highly dangerous to those who detested capitalism and all its agents and agencies as to call down upon it, in the indignant works of Kautsky, Hilferding, Lenin, and a host of others, malediction upon sins it did not commit and aims it did not promote.

In time this *bourgeoisie* became vilified as the hard-faced men who not only did well out of the twentieth century's First World War, but actually brought it about. They are the true imperialists, to whom the world owes all its present woes. They are the men who forced a pattern upon the world, not only on its map but on its thinking, which another century of political "emancipation" will hardly suffice to dissolve. It was they who, for example, partitioned Africa and made it a European annex (although this particular piece of rapacity leaves unexplained the profound disinterest in the whole project expressed by very many chambers of commerce, presumably the spiritual homes, at every local level, of this policy-forming *bourgeoisie*). It was they who manip-

[5] *Ibid.*, pp. 233–234.

ulated the economies of the weak to reinforce those of the strong. This they still do, still chanting of welfare and civilization. Economic imperialism is, simply, "the establishment of exploitation of dominion for continuing material advantage." The process needs, as wine does, time and security in order to mature. This it has had. The exploitation that these imperialists promote

consists in the employment of labour at wages lower than would obtain in a free bargaining situation; or in the appropriation of goods at prices lower than would obtain in a free market.[6]

Imperialism is accordingly a denial of liberty, promulgated most often by those who profess liberty, and by those whose standard of civilization is entirely determined by the extent of their own comfort.

The Dutch Empire in the East has often been singled out to play the role of Cheops' contractor. Under the culture system promoted by the Dutch East India Company from the seventeenth century onwards, the Javanese were required to devote a part of their lands to certain cash crops and to deliver these to the government at fixed prices. The Dutch imperial officials got a portion of the proceeds. This system pressed not only on commerce but on the entire social structure: for when the Company made its demands for "contingents" and forced deliveries, these were not supplied through agreements made with the peasants themselves (nor organized by western contractors as was the practice in the late nineteenth century) but sprang from the obligation of the natives to supply goods and services to their own chiefs. The chiefs, pressed by their Dutch masters, pressed harder on those whose welfare should have been their concern, since they extorted more than they intended to transmit. The cornerstone of the Dutch system was the limited production of tropical raw materials for sale in the home market at high prices; and it is because the system was brought to such a high pitch of efficiency that the economic interpreters of imperialism use it as a textbook case.

There are many such cases in the textbook, well deserving their

[6] David S. Landes, "Some Thoughts on the Nature of Economic Imperialism," *Journal of Economic History* (December 1961), pp. 496, 499.

place. And behind their presentation, whether done with figures or with feeling, lies the conviction that profit, like power, is itself a sin. Men who hold either in their hands will inevitably, such is their nature, use it to other men's woe.

Within the bounds of empire itself, many critics who took no credit to themselves for economic analysis arose to take this same moral stance. Victorian England was itself the posterity of an imperialist era well supplied with men whom Cheops' contractor would have hailed as brothers.

Gladstone once summed up a widely held opinion when he declared that the foundations of England's Empire in India "could ill bear examination":[7] for although before its political dissolution in 1859 the English East India Company had managed to live down its past of peculation—a generation of hay-making in the sunshine of ceded Bengal (1765–91)—the realization that grand imperial ideas had their seamy side, that human beings in positions of supreme power were unable to live always, or even often, on a plane of high and selfless endeavor, provided a legacy of frailty to challenge the conscience of those mid-Victorians who were determined to interweave morality with politics. In 1858, when India was about to become a direct political responsibility of (although not a direct financial charge upon) the English government, the Radical John Bright remarked that he had never known and did not know now a man capable of governing India.[8] All such imperial tasks, whatever clouds of glory they trailed, were bound to be too great in scope for ordinary men; and in any one generation, how many extraordinary men could a nation be expected to produce? The correct conduct of the business of empire, where the will of an alien ruling class was law, where that law had to be upheld by a standing army, and where no one in authority had any wish to obtain nor any means of obtaining the consent of the governed, would always demand more of virtue than a normal man had in him to grant.

But many people who were directly concerned with the daily work of imperial administration did not often mount this high

[7] W. E. Gladstone, *Political Speeches in Scotland 1879–80* (Edinburgh, 1880), I, p. 39.
[8] Speech at Birmingham, 24 June 1858.

platform. They were too preoccupied; and doubts as to their own capacities do not often afflict the competent. The medical missionary Mary Kingsley, who had sharp eyes and sharper opinions, and whose knowledge of western Africa exceeded that of the many officials who peppered it with dispatches from London, believed firmly that one sort of exploitation deserved another. The founding and maintaining of a colony, she pointed out in her autobiographical *Travels in West Africa* (1897), annually drained some thousands of the most energetic and enterprising of its nationals from the service of a mother country. This game was clearly not worth the candle if no profit of any kind was going to accrue to anybody. Energy and ability should not be poured into sand. No nation could afford so to waste its substance. Such effort expected, and could legitimately claim, reward. The opportunity to win such a reward was there for all to see and, for the ablest, to take. West Africa was obviously destined to remain "for hundreds of years" a region admirably fitted to supply the European manufacturer with his raw material. It would take his products in exchange, thus "giving him a good margin of profit." Was this anything to flinch from? Here indeed was a common interest and purpose for administrator and merchant alike, one with no need to shirk the limelight. To Mary Kingsley the traders of the Slave and Ivory and Grain Coasts and of the Bight of Benin, frontiersmen who had labored under a ruffian reputation for nearly seventy years, were not exploiters cynically battening on the benighted. They were "heroes of commerce" and ought to be recognized as such.[9]

The tone is combative, for the lady intended to provoke. In England the frontier dividing the man of rank from the man of trade was still clearly drawn, and still respected on both sides of it. The tradesman was reckoned a useful member of the community but he was expected, as was everyone else in an aristocratic society, to keep his place. He was not supposed to be of the stuff that heroes were made. Not bred to higher notions of duty and service, he was not asked to acquire them. He was asked only to do the best he could according to what lights he had, however dim. Dr. Samuel Johnson once remarked that

[9] Kingsley, *West African Studies*, p. 691.

The business of trade could not be conducted by those who conduct
it if it presented any difficulties,

an aphorism that illuminates an entire social scene as well as a
personal prejudice. A century later Matthew Arnold in his *Culture
and Anarchy* (1869) attached to the manufacturing middle
class the name of Philistine, which was neither easily forgotten
nor got rid of.

English commentators on public affairs, themselves men of
the middle class who derived their incomes from sources they
did not divulge (since it was vulgar to talk about money), accustomed their educated readers to this high line with commerce
and its practitioners. When they spoke and wrote of England, its
place in and its duty to the world, they seemed to suppose that
the country needed no economic foundation at all. This attitude's obvious function as a façade gave to the foreign observer
still more ammunition for his general charge of English perfidy.
Thomas Babington Macaulay, for example, was able to save an
estimated sum of some twenty-five thousand pounds after only
three and a half years in the East India Company's service (1834–
38); and thus his celebrated *History of England,* the product of
his leisure (1848–55), owes at least a backward nod of recognition
to the fact of empire. Lord Ashley, the Evangelical who instigated
the humanitarian factory legislation of the early 1840's, withdrew
his motion to suppress the trade in opium from Bengal to China
after listening to a debate punctuated by the assertions of knowl-
edgeable Members who insisted that the government of India,
busy about its beneficent tasks, literally could not afford to
relinquish a revenue that annually brought in over one million
sterling. Whatever they wrote about the wider horizons of mankind, however far-ranging their thought on the imponderables of
human existence, the Victorian intellectuals very well knew that
the prosperity of England, and with it the immunity from social
anxiety of her leisured class, depended on the continuance of
successful trading and on the skill of all those hard-headed men
who did not read the quarterly reviews and who, like Baron
de Reuter (or Anthony Trollope's impression of him as Augustus
Melmotte in *The Way We Live Now* [1873]), remained unknown
to the dinner tables of fashionable London.

A straighter view of this matter was taken by the officials of empire who, although they knew almost nothing of commerce and kept aloof from its devotees, knew in what context their business belonged. When presenting the Indian budget to the Viceroy's Council in March 1877, Sir John Strachey attacked those who liked to fancy that even a sense of duty could subsist on air, independent both of circumstance and of that larger duty to preserve oneself and one's own interest. "We are often told," said he,

that it is the duty of the Government of India to think of Indian interests alone, and that if the interests of Manchester suffer it is no affair of ours. For my part, I utterly repudiate such doctrines.[10]

It is unlikely that Strachey had ever visited Manchester, the capital of England's textile North; but he knew that the Indian market was a highly profitable part of the imperial world over which it ruled, and that it was to the interest of England that it should so remain. The British Empire was not some mystical structure, rooted (according to one's taste) in geology or in metaphysics, above and beyond mundane matters of money, whose officials were devoid of self-interest. It reflected the social gradations of England, and repeated the assumptions accompanying them. The entire English connection with India, with all that had sprung from it, was the direct product of commercial imperialism. No reading of the record could make it otherwise, however much it irritated the civilian and military officers of the *Raj* to have this drawn to their attention. As a detached member of this group was doucely to remark in the latter, self-questioning days of the Empire, "Criticisms of the British *Raj*, though often ill-informed and ill-natured, are not on that account ill-founded."[11]

Although a dislike of commerce and its world was common among *bourgeois* who had become isolated from their own origins, its remarkable achievement forced itself on everyone's attention. Whether it was industrial capital or finance capital which was responsible was something that might be left for posterity to debate: what was plain was that a revolution in both technique

[10] Lady Betty Balfour, *Lord Lytton's Indian Administration* (London, 1899), p. 477.
[11] Penderel Moon, *Strangers in India* (London, 1944), p. 5.

and communication, and consequently of life itself, was under way. Commerce and capital with it would indeed never have got itself so bad a name had it not become so all-pervasive, leaving its proper habitat of the countinghouse to become the touchstone of men's attitudes to society and to their own place in it.

Lenin like Hobson before him was to observe this process of pervasion, but neither interested himself in the revolution it was generating. They drew attention to the impact of the superior European technology upon the backward countries of Asia and Africa, but because they objected to the whole process and more particularly to the social aims of those who were operating it, they made no serious attempt to evaluate it, reserving their powers of analysis for the capitalistic motivation of the metropolis only. Lenin did not concern himself with the end product of imperialism since he believed that imperialism was a self-destroying agency which could not in the nature of things have a product at all. It was not dynamic, it was only so much dynamite. For imperialism was literally about to explode, taking the works of capitalism, all the world they had made, with it. He saw in imperialism what Marx had seen in industrialism: a train of powder.

But in the European empires overseas, and more especially in India, "that garden full of ripe mangoes,"[12] the capitalism that had promoted the work of colonization was in turn upheld by it. The one process heartened and rejuvenated the other. The expansion of capitalism did not prove lethal; it gave it fresh force and a much larger capital to work with. Under its modern name of imperialism, it was therefore less a "phase" of the capitalist drive than an integral part of its impetus. Tin and rubber and tea and coffee and oil built as great an empire for themselves as wool and wheat had done in the previous era, while increasing the market for wool and wheat as well. While Lenin still lived, the technological revolution begun in the West was spreading fast into the "undeveloped" countries, an adjective that refers to a standard they imposed on themselves, despite its alien origin and tone. Their leaders, once educated to grasp the nature of what was happening, welcomed it. They have continued to do so whatever

[12] Majumdar, *British Paramountcy*, p. 12.

their ideological attachments, and often despite their devotion to the doctrines (also alien) of political self-determination. In all the extra-European world, only one nationalist hero has arisen who set his face against the pervasive industrialism of the West, seeing in it not a rescuer but a destroyer. This was Gandhi, who has had, to date, no successor.

Japan, like Italy, was a latecomer to the imperial field. She had no capital to export. Again like Italy, she tried to reverse the process. She hoped to utilize colonies to increase the economic power of the homeland. Her eye always on western models and motivation, she was convinced that the possession of colonies would increase her prestige, her military strength, resources, and power. This done, she would convert her "have-not" status to a "have" status. She would attain the desired position of equality with the great powers. The Japanese name for her imperial arena, the "Co-Prosperity Sphere," sums up this hope. Japanese power would weld together, to mutual benefit, Manchuria, lower China, and the Pacific archipelagoes into one economic unit. The ownership of so much property would breed prosperity. Prosperity would beget profit. Profit would beget power. Power and profit were the twin pillars of empire. There was no durable power that did not rest on a solid economic base. No prosperity could endure without a corresponding power to protect it.

It needed no startling insight to discover these platitudes, nor any rigid doctrine to propound them. In these affairs no one spoke another language, for there was no other language to speak. Although men in general might shy from the profit motive and agree, with Tolstoy, that man should not live by bread alone, few of them were prepared to argue that man would ever be born into the world without worldly ambition, or that, base creature though he might be, he was able to live without bread at all. To raise the standard of living (as though it were some kind of banner) was everybody's aim. The slum-dweller in the West, the beggar in the East, alike had his eyes fixed on this goal.

But could the one achieve it except at the expense of the other?

Here was a question whose shadow has fallen far into the twentieth century and clouds the future now. The intra-European imperial rivalries, the contests between those who had more and those who had less, were converted into a racial struggle between those who had something and those who had nothing; for, as a result of the imperialist exercises, the men who commanded the world's economic resources were white in color, and the men who did not were not. As population "exploded," more and more swelled the number of those who went without; and since these explosions mainly took place among the non-white, the basic situation showed no signs of change. The competition for profit, to which the privileged had long been accustomed and which in one sense they had enjoyed, was threatening by the twenty-first century to turn into a scramble for survival, governed by the insecure ethics of the frontier. Yet a continuation of this competition seemed inevitable, since opportunity is not a commodity that men are willing to share.

Those with a position to conserve cannot share either the present or the future. The two are in fact one: for a shared present may cancel out the future altogether. They do not see it as a matter of choice, but rather as one of prescience: it takes skill to know what is significant, now. Hence the value, and the name, of *avant-garde* ideas. These may only just maintain their footing in the present, but who is to say that they will not colonize the future? It is for just such an imperial task that any *avant-garde* that deserves the name is fitted.

In England at the turn of the twentieth century, when yellow and other colored perils were first being heard of, and the diagnoses of Thomas Malthus[13] were winning further reluctant attention, *avant-gardes* of both Right and Left took much the same stand. The Fabian socialists, in a pamphlet *Fabianism and the Empire* (1900), edited and largely written by Bernard Shaw, used the language that Joseph Chamberlain had already popularized. The Fabians, doctrinaires to a man, felt compelled to draw up a blueprint for the future, since shapelessness and imprecision were their chief enemies in the present. They agreed with Chamberlain that if she did not formulate a plan for her own future career, England would lose herself in an *impasse*, would not survive to face the world in any shape that any patriotic citizen would either recognize or want. Was Great Britain to be

---

[13] The Rev. Thomas R. Malthus (1766–1834), author of *The Principles of Population,* first published in 1798.

the nucleus of one of the world empires of the future? Or would it be reduced to its actual geographic location of two islands in the North Sea?—a tract of water which might by then be appearing on maps other than German as the German Ocean.

No one was capable who was not also strong. For Fabians it went without saying that the British Empire would be incapable of taking the necessary positive action if its heartland, England herself, were not rescued, by Fabians, from the net of capitalism, class strife, and private interests in which it was just then engulfed. But the ultimate success of their own doctrines, the establishment of the socialist creed as the basis for domestic progress, was not intended to preclude the continuance of England's influence on the affairs of the world at large. The paternalism that had for so long and for the most part so wastefully been expended upon colonies abroad must now be brought home, but the doctrine of paternalism itself did not come under attack. Socialist doctrine was nothing if not paternalist: what had to be striven for was efficiency. Only by this, insisted the Fabians' chief mentor, Sidney Webb, would England be able

to exercise her proper weight in the councils, and consequently in the commerce, of the world.[14]

Thus, the English voice was always to be heard, the English weight felt, whoever ruled the domestic roost. The Left, trained to fight the tory world, at heart belonged to it. If national empires were to pass away, to be replaced by world empires, then England must be the heart of one of these, a moving force, and not a satellite far out on the rim of decision, moving indeed but in someone else's orbit. No Englishman who took an interest in public affairs at all ever questioned the propriety and validity of these axioms. He had no doubt that it would be for the world's own good that English counsels and ideas should everywhere distribute themselves—so ingrained had the imperial idea, with its paternalist tradition, become.

Since the commerce of the world was England's business, and would remain so, so was the state of the world itself. The socialists,

[14] Quoted in Bernard Semmel, *Imperialism and Social Reform* (London, 1960), p. 73.

whose hopes were set on the betterment of the human condition, whose dream it was to attain the state of social justice, who were determined to raise the standard of living of the workers, were certainly the last men to take a hostile view of commerce. Far to their own Left, even Lenin at the last, when Bolshevism had stormed the ramparts of capitalism only to find itself stranded in a wasteland, was driven to adopt a "New Economic Program" remarkably similar to many an old economic program, whose scope and aim would not have been unfamiliar, for example, to Colbert in the France of Louis XIV. Socialist doctrine insisted that commerce, like everything else, had got into the wrong hands, and that capitalists were assuredly the last people to be entrusted with capital. But that capital was itself the necessary foundation for success and power was something not worth anyone's while to deny.

A latter-day Fabian, in 1947, had seen no reason to change his mind on this point. Sir Stafford Cripps, as Chancellor of the Exchequer in the British Labour government, told a conference of colonial governors that the ultimate solution of the difficulties which the sterling area was then facing was to be found within the colonies. The United Kingdom therefore intended "to increase out of all recognition" the tempo of colonial development in Africa.[15] Such a development would justify the continuance of the paternalist imperial relationship. Capitalism and colonialism were still looked upon as essential partners in an association beneficial to both, and Britain's most doctrinaire socialist saw nothing to complain of in this state of affairs. If this was imperialism, it had the hallmark of social justice stamped upon it. The brotherhood of man, yet to be achieved, was still its first principle. That this was perhaps a white man's idea only, born of his liberalism and his success, had not occurred either to Cripps or to his Cabinet colleagues, who were just then promoting a companion idea of "multi-racialism" in a British Commonwealth emancipated from the old-fashioned imperial bonds.

Cripps' remark supplies another proof that mercantilism and its derivatives were not economic fashions that lived only in the

---

[15] Quoted in W. R. Crocker, *Self-Government for the Colonies* (London, 1949), p. 128.

pages of the history books. Colonial development had always played a large part in the habit and thought of "economic man." The mercantilist of the eighteenth century had seen the world as an oyster, and had set to work to build a foundry for making the tools best fitted to open it up. Colonies had one *raison d'être:* to produce raw materials which the mother country could not. She would then utilize them, market them, and invest the profit of the transaction in the expansion of her manufacturing potential. The mercantilist therefore put a premium on "precious metals," worked to promote foreign over domestic trade, and developed industry at home. He acted exclusively in his own interest and, like Hilferding's finance capitalist, tried to reinforce his commercial ventures with the power of his own State. He approved of monopoly and hoped to establish it wherever his enterprise took him. He imposed high tariffs on imports from his neighbors, who were naturally (since they were pursuing identical aims) his competitors. Since a struggle for power was the context of his existence, he approved the efforts of his diplomats to balance power, in order to preserve that context. On the whole he managed to achieve what he wanted, for it was he who bequeathed to posterity that condition of economic security from which alone his own exertions could have been denigrated.

The English free trade doctrinaires in particular, for whom the world market lay open, regarded the works of mercantilism as contemptuously as they did the feudalism from which it had originally escaped. They exclaimed their surprise that anyone should still believe that one nation could profit in trade at the expense of another. What was this but a degraded superstition? Members of the Manchester School of economics, whose music was the whirring of looms, were very apt to think they were richer than their fathers because they were better men: the reading of the Good Book and the keeping of good books, as Professor Asa Briggs has pointed out, went together.[16]

Their competitive forebears had thought that political dominion existed for the sake of drawing off tribute. But this doctrine had been punished by the American colonists, once they had become

---

[16] Asa Briggs, *The Age of Improvement* (London, 1959), p. 27.

citizens of their new Republic. The young United States of America, by providing the British manufacturer with a far less restricted and more profitable market than the thirteen colonies had ever done, fueled the contempt of the Free Traders for a protective system of empire. They tended to assume that because they were virtuous, there need be no more cakes and ale; that because it was no longer profitable to preach mercantilist doctrine, it was no longer possible to do so. They supposed that others would share this opinion, and that therefore no one would ever preach it again. Yet it is a very natural notion, that the main point of establishing a political dominion is to exact a tribute. Why trouble to exert dominion at all, as Mary Kingsley asked, if one is not going to reap whatever benefits accrue? Administration always has a high cost: revenue to balance it has to be got from somewhere, someone, or something. In fact, everything costs: the sensible and statesmanlike thing to do is to make certain that the price is worth the paying. Monopoly might seem wicked to the merchants and traders of a country which, like England, thought it had outgrown the need for it; but it was still serviceable to others throughout the nineteenth century, and the twentieth century was to see it become serviceable once more to England herself.

Monopoly moreover had never worn moral trappings. This was another reason why Victorian opinion found it hard to condone. When men indulge what Adam Smith called their human propensities they are only a step away from converting them into human rights. For example, since man has a propensity to eat, he thinks it his due that he should have food, perhaps someone else's, if there is not enough to go round. But even in the worst pinch he has never had any warrant for believing that there is any right to trade. Few people have in fact bothered to assert this. The record shows many cases where tribes of men, with no wish to truck or barter, have none the less been forced to do so by another tribe strong enough to get its own way. The middle-class merchants of the East India and China Association of Liverpool, who sent a robust memorandum to the Foreign Office in February 1857, indeed sound like a cohesive, policy-forming *bourgeoisie,* or at least prove their ambition to become such. In their opinion, the British government failed in its duty if it did not insist on the right of opening to foreign trade any port on the coast of China, or on the banks of any navigable river, at any time they may think fit, and of placing consuls at such ports; [and] that our ships-of-war should have the free navigation of and access to all the rivers and ports of China.[17]

Devotion to the principle of free trade did not preclude, rather it encouraged, the growth of a moral conviction that wherever trade was not free it should be made so, and the recalcitrants who kept it unfree pushed aside. The long, sad history of the "Open Door" in China, and its attendant problems—whose door it was, how to open it, how to keep it opened—illustrates with a glaring clarity the impact of these opinions. Consular officials themselves, not beset with mysteries of high policy, shared them. "Far better would it have been," mused the British consul at Shanghai in 1873,

both in the interest of China and in ours, had the earliest blow been struck home while she was comparatively strong, and had her rulers and people been taught . . . that intercourse with the foreigner, if accepted at all, must be accepted on conditions of entire equality and universality.[18]

The promotion of trade by the waging of war, by the dispatch of gunboats and punitive sorties, was reckoned a natural and laudable enterprise. Once the unprogressive barbarian had been crushed, he would be made welcome within the arena of civilization—and even clothed, if that were necessary.

In 1835 Richard Cobden, still waging his campaign for that free trade which was to triumph fourteen years later, looked back into the record of the nations and traced the strain of violence and cupidity:

The policy of nations, *then*, if judged by the standard which we apply to the conduct of individuals *now* . . . was, to waylay their customers, whom they first knocked down and disabled, and afterwards dragged

[17] Cobden referred to this memorandum in a speech on 26 February 1857: J. E. Thorold Rogers, ed., *The Speeches of Richard Cobden* (London, 1870), II, p. 144.
[18] W. E. Medhurst, *The Foreigner in Far Cathay* (New York, 1873), p. 12.

into their stores and compelled to purchase whatever articles they chose to offer, at such prices as they chose to ask.[19]

But whether matters were so different *now*, in the 1850's and 1860's, was just the matter for contemporary argument. It was just their conviction that Lord Palmerston was still enamored of this knockdown policy that made Cobden himself together with Bright so hot in the Foreign Secretary's pursuit. And even if England had mended her ways, other nations had not, and probably would not. Both Spain and Portugal, together with the Empire of Brazil, had to be hounded into abandoning the transatlantic slave trade by those very gunboats Lord Palmerston so liked to employ; while the author of a study of *The Dutch in Java*, written seventy years after Cobden's analysis of international behavior, considered that the Dutch government in that island had, at least until 1875, been merely "an armed instrument for extracting wealth."[20]

But in these bad old times (whether or not they still subsisted) the question was less whether the strong had a right to oppress the weak, than whether the weak had any right to expect any better treatment.

Privilege, by its nature, belonged to the powerful. Men sought power in order to become privileged; and a privilege shared was no privilege at all. Security itself was also reckoned a privilege, one that many generations of men thought of as unobtainable save by divine aid. Security was certainly seen as something to be earned, not owed. The weak could make no valid claim to immunity, to noninvolvement, in ages of fierce competition among those who were seeking to become strong.

The efforts of Spain and Portugal in the sixteenth century to divide the as yet undiscovered globe between them, although buttressed with the support of a pliable Papacy, were judged invalid by outsiders less because of the dubious propriety of so monstrous an assertion than because of their well-founded suspicion that these two powers, with a truly Greek *hubris* descending on them, had bitten off more than they would ever be able to chew. But the Iberian nations, since they were in the van of a

[19] Cobden, *Political Writings*, II, p. 221.
[20] Clive Day, *The Dutch in Java* (London, 1904), p. 16.

vast reconnaisance movement into the extra-European world, set up principles for others to ponder and pioneered practices that others were to improve upon. From the two papal edicts of 1493 a fundamental doctrine was deduced: that all lands, discovered or to be discovered, that were not already the property of a Christian prince, became the property of the discovering prince. This situation provoked envy and emulation; so that, where Spain protested a proprietary right, others were quick to serve an equal claim. Competitors crowded to a starting line and entered the race under their own starters' guns.

In a short time the international air rang with strictly meaningless charges of justice and injustice, with definitions of what was lawful and what was not: and, in order to keep the civilized world from breaking apart at its center, the threatened state of anarchy was warded off and held at a distance, beyond the bounds of Europe itself. There was tacit consent that the imperialist rivalries and the bloodshed they caused should wage and spill out of sight, behind God's back, beyond the "line": *les lignes d'amitié*, between the tropic of cancer and the prime meridian passing through Ferro in the Canary Islands.[21] Every chartered joint-stock "Company of Adventurers" promoted and financed by European merchants expected indeed to have adventures. It expected to have to battle for its life, and it was right: in 1630, as one example, Portuguese and Englishmen were fighting one another without quarter and with Indian auxiliaries at Surat in western India, while peace reigned between their two nations at home. There was no point in protesting against this state of affairs, since there was no one before whom any such protest could effectively be brought: Grotius' *On the Law of War and Peace* was then five years old, and the masters of Portuguese, Dutch, and English "East Indiamen" sailing for Asian waters never learned to con it as a text.

No one, then, had any right to anything beyond what he had the strength to get and hold. This was a basic tenet of the doctrine of profit—effectively removing from it any "body of principle" as

---

[21] For the controversy concerning "The Line," see Garrett Mattingly, "No Peace Beyond What Line?" *Transactions of the Royal Historical Society,* fifth series, vol. 13 (London, 1963), p. 145 ff.

its terms of reference. The early efforts of Brandenburg-Prussia to find a place in the sun display the acceptable acquisitiveness of the era. In 1647 the "Great Elector," Frederick William, was doing his best to found an East India Company on Dutch and English models. In 1650 he bought two towns from the Danes in India. He sent an expedition to West Africa's Guinea Coast in 1676. He founded an African Commercial Company in 1682 and built a headquarters for it at Gross Friedrichsburg in 1683. He was in fact the model of mercantilist activity. In his time there was still room, between the interstices of the other European empires, for such interloping projects; but this condition of things ended with the seventeenth century. Thereafter the lists were set for the conflict, blazoned with the names of the dynasties of Europe but fought all round the world, between the two great imperial rivals, France and England.

That there is more cupidity than dignity in the record of the efforts of the nation-states to better themselves, and to put down durable stakes for survival not only into their own soil but into whatever areas their mariners and commercial adventurers took them to, is recognized even when it is not directly confessed. The book on imperial history that refers to "The *Struggle* for North America" will usually have a chapter entitled "The *Scramble* for Africa"—a distinction that makes plain the modern disenchantment with the procedures of empire and the practices of imperialists. The expert socialist attack on capitalism and commercialism has probably influenced those who have not read Marx and Engels as deeply as those who have. The contempt expressed by the communist ideologues is natural to men who consider themselves citizens of a world that is struggling to be born, and who, since they are therefore free of history and all its verdicts, cannot be accused of their contemporaries' transgressions. But Marx saw a utility in this expansive, if squalid, period of *bourgeois* dominance. It was a necessary and inevitable part of history, necessary because its task was to create the material basis of that new, classless, and far better order of society on which Marx had set his hopes and plans.

But although it was a useful and essential phase, which made "the barbarian and semi-barbarian countries dependent on the civilised ones," it deserved no one's congratulation. Brute force had established the colonial system and would keep it operating. What were its aims? Profit and power, both of which the capitalists would forever misuse. Marx's contemporary, the English political scientist Edward Gibbon Wakefield, had propounded a scheme of "systematic colonisation," which had in the 1830's and 1840's impacted heavily on the settlements in New Zealand and South Australia. It brought down Marx's thunder. Systematic indeed!—since its main aim was to make a profitable equation from the three elements of land, labor, and capital. The masters of capital would always be masters of the system and of the colonists as well. Spread beyond the antipodes, this same systematization was just that which, in Lenin's diagnosis, was to create imperialism—the process by which the capitalists take and thrust their system from one end of the earth to the other.

The nations and their annexes created by these *bourgeois* who were determined to accumulate all wealth and property within their own grasp were bound to act selfishly also. Marx pointed out that John Bright's indignant picture of India ruined by the fiscal follies of the East India Company was very well as far as it went, but how far did it go? For it did not, of course, "receive the supplement of India ruined by Manchester and Free Trade."[22] Had not India, "the mother-country of cotton," been inundated with cottons? Nationality (nationalism) and patriotism with it were only the cloaks woven by these same cotton-spinning capitalists to conceal their true aims from their dupes. Their imperializing was designed simply to enable them to capture all the means of production and distribution within the home market. This in turn would give them control over all aspects of their nation's economic life. Whoever commanded the economy commanded everything and everyone else, since there was no social or political power that was not at base economic. Thus, by continuing their predatory career, these *bourgeois* would be assured of perpetuating the empire of their own kind and their sway over generations to come.

Although the very idea of the nation was part of this sinister plan, some nations were better (of more service to the dialectical process) than others, since their aspirations might assist that

---

[22] 7 June 1853, *Daily Tribune*, New York: Marx and Engels, *On Colonialism*, p. 30.

greater movement (of which these narrow nationalists knew nothing) towards the achievement of the revolution of the proletariat and the founding of a communist society at large. *Bourgeois* industry and commerce were creating these material conditions for a new world in the same way as geological revolutions had created the earth's surface. When the great social revolution had mastered the results of the *bourgeois* epoch, had taken over both the market of the world and its powers of production and had subjected them to the common control of the most advanced peoples, ah then,

. . . then only will human progress cease to resemble that hideous pagan idol, who would not drink the nectar but from the skulls of the slain.[23]

Stirred by such apocalyptic visions, aware only of human greed and the tragedy of existence when confined within the wrong bounds, Marx did not investigate the nature of imperialism, leaving it for his followers to identify. In his turn, Lenin did not attend to the nature of internationalism. It was left to Stalin, no moralist and unstirred by any vision whatsoever, to argue in his *Problems of Leninism* (1924) that in some cases the Union of Soviet Socialist Republics should support nationalist movements, those in particular that were likely to weaken imperialism and to bring it down. He added that the question of the rights of nations was not an isolated, self-sufficient question: "It is part of the general problem of the proletarian revolution."[24]

So it is indeed, and it may be left to the examination of its own doctrinaires. But even in the non-communist world, since everyone has sat for a century if not at the feet of at least in the same room as Marx and Lenin, the terms *bourgeois* and "capitalist" have become so identified with the communist ideology, so impregnated with a value judgment, that a gap has been left in objective speech. But under whatever name they go, and even when not named at all, the economic imperialists, pursuing their profit, are found in every age; and if Marx's *bourgeois* industrialist, wielding weapons greater than he knew, is in fact responsible for creating "the material conditions of a new world," he did it

---

[23] 8 August 1853: *Ibid.*, pp. 90–91.
[24] Quoted in R. Conquest, *The Last Empire* (London, 1962), p. 14.

by applying the same imperialist principle that had been handed down to him, and by taking advantage of a strength that grew upon what it fed.

The imperialism of commerce, with profit as its purpose, and with security, influence, and even an accumulation of surplus finance capital waiting in the wings of its future, is an old story. Imperialism and colonization are modern names for ancient activities of assertion and movement. Every settled area, Europe included, is the product of colonization: every colonization is the product of an imperialist drive. Industrialism may indeed have increased the strain of cupidity, since it so vastly extended the field in which profit could be taken. It did something else also that was bound to have a revolutionary result: it multiplied the number of opportunities available to the enterprising. The older world had extended itself by a similar practice of enterprise, but the generations that followed on the heels of its pioneers were granted the time to consolidate their fathers' gains and to build what seemed to them a static society, run by the right people, with all its gates well manned, and all its doors of opportunity closed fast against the outsider. They laid a solid foundation for the future.

Marx and his followers, agreeing that the foundation was necessary if the world was to make progress, objected only to the kind of progress it would make under its present commanders. They objected in fact to continuity in history, and deduced a style in historical progression that broke free from the tyranny of a consecutive process, with the same race going always to the swift, who would always be the same type of people. Because they objected indeed to human nature itself, they·devised an environment for it such as it had never yet known. In such, all those acquisitive propensities to which Adam Smith had so good-humoredly drawn attention would never again have an empire of their own.

.   .   .

Yet the human propensity to truck and barter, and to exchange one thing for another, lies at the core of all the civilizations that men have made.

It has been a prime factor in the building of cities, the centers in which the idea of civilization itself has taken root and grown. Fairs, markets, and towns developed at places easy of access. Their business was, as it still is, to exchange ideas and information as well as goods. They were founded, and are still to be found, at the crossroads and termini of routes of trade: Alexandria and Constantinople in one age, Glasgow and New York in another, have their materials made of the same stuff, the concrete quest for security and profit.

When men came to think of the sea not as a barrier but as a thoroughfare they were able to transfer themselves as well as their commodities, and set themselves down in "colonies": Europe's earliest sprang up at serviceable harbors around the middle sea, the nontidal Mediterranean, and by the seventh and sixth centuries B.C. Greeks from the southern peninsula of the Morea had established themselves in southern Italy and eastern Sicily. As it progressed, colonization laid a heavy responsibility on the parent State, which had to maintain the line of communication to its distant settlement. Since this involved keeping that line open by means of a sea police, such a State came early to appreciate that doctrine of sea power which the American Admiral Mahan was to lay down as axiomatic for imperial success.

To maintain control over sea-lanes required more skills than men, more science than sailors. This was not true of overland colonization. The very nature of this altered the map, imposed arbitrary frontiers, disrupted entire communities, and could very quickly empty a treasury that did not have or did not speedily find for itself a regular means of replenishment. A chain of garrisons required a mass of men to keep them. These men were, at any one time, either idle or dead. Whatever their fate, they were at all times absent, not available to the domestic labor market. Their upkeep drained the resources of the State, and only if a soldier was kept fully, that is to say gainfully, employed could any portion of this outlay be recouped.

A project of Empire thus needed an efficient funding service, and such funds were best got by taking advantage of the human propensity to truck and barter: there comes, however late in the evening, a limit to loot. The great Alexander (356–23 B.C.) as he moved eastward founded a chain of cities as strategic and com-

mercial centers for the Greek culture which he hoped was a part
of the baggage train of his army in Asia; and the better to cement
their security, he lavished on all of them the bullion of the defeated Persians. This was certainly an inflation of their economy,
but their economy was sound enough, otherwise the three Greek
kingdoms which he imposed on Macedonia, on Syria, and on
Egypt would not ultimately have been thought worth the con-
quering by Rome. Rome's own brand of Hellenism, filtered
through these channels, naturally owes more to the influence of
Alexandrian capitalism than it does to the philosophies of
Periclean Athens.

In Europe thereafter the idea of empire, like that of civilization
itself, was essentially urban. However widespread its frontiers,
empire centered on a metropolis; and, as does a town, it needed
always an efficient system of communication and protection, with
a headquarters to oversee it. If western Europe after "the fall of
the Roman Empire"—that is, after the metropolis of Rome was
no longer able to act as such, since it had lost control over its
provinces and, with that, the presidency of their civilization—
experienced a "dark age" some five centuries long (*circa* A.D.
476–976), it is because the absence of good communications, by
preventing the movement of men and ideas, gradually eroded the
will to move at all. The darkness was one more of the spirit than
the mind. For empire, like all emanations of power, depends on
will: and it was a loss of will, it appears, that was the major
casualty, the most important consequence of the barbarian in-
cursions. (This pattern was to repeat itself in the twentieth century). Barbarians entered the Roman service without imbibing
the ideas of duty that were supposed to accompany it. Barbarians
became senators, even emperors, without falling heir to the ideals
of *Romanitas* prescribed by an earlier day. Roman citizenship, in
the time of Paul, in the first century A.D., had been a sought-after
privilege and status: but after the Emperor Elagabalus had made
everyone a citizen (A.D. 219) no one minded the idea of the city.
New cities did not spring from the old towns, for the towns
themselves did not grow.

Since civilization was no longer organized from a center, in
many places where the organization had been broken civilization
itself died. Romans had once met and traded with Chinese at

Yarkand in high Asia, but the world of their posterity was a world contracted, one that had lost its earlier geography. From the fifth century to the thirteenth there is no record of anyone from western Europe reaching central or southern Asia. Geography itself lapsed into the realm of fable, producing Prester John in one era and El Dorado in another. The Church, drawing upon the surviving prestige of the Eternal City, held together the European community under the name of Christendom; but, seeing itself as the agent of the world to come, it was content to act as a patient in the world that was. It was no friend to adventure either of mind or spirit and was content to conserve its authority within narrow confines. It was hostile to the secular aims and practices that grew up too easily in towns. It condemned profit and proscribed usury; and so gave to the capitalist, the manipulator of money, that bad name which still strikes so deep a chord in Marxist and in puritan, and in every combination of both.

Post-Roman Europe was thus an agricultural estate in a pre-capitalist age, feudal and monastic in its habits. Where communities were self-sufficing, the volume of internal trade was small. Europe indeed had its external commerce, but this it did not control, for the terms of trade were not in European hands—an experience which, although there is no direct evidence, must have left its mark on the attitudes and ambitions of the mercantile group in all western countries. What specie the merchants could command (and since internal trade was so limited they never commanded much) was drained away to pay for goods whose source they did not know. This problem of "drain" or fiscal reciprocity was perpetually to crop up. Rome in the second century, the states of Europe in the eleventh century, Britain in the nineteenth century, all found themselves writing a chapter in the same story. They all had an identical "balance of payments" difficulty to contend with. How were they to establish a genuinely reciprocal trade in goods, not in cash, with the rich, self-sufficient countries of Asia? In the nineteenth century the passage of opium from India to China survived all moral attack because here at least was one article of western commerce for which the Chinese were prepared to pay in silver specie: otherwise, the much-boosted China market remained the despair of all the commercial imperialists of Europe and the United States, since these teeming millions seemed not to want to truck or barter in anything that the West had to exchange.

Medieval Europe, without any such reserves of capital, was baffled also by its own geographical ignorance. The merchants of Europe had no clear idea whom they were dealing with in the first place. What could they, dealing principally in furs, hides, wool, and timber, offer in return for what Asia had to sell: for the pepper, rhubarb, ginger, mace, cinnamon, cloves, sugar, rice, Barbary lead, Indian cotton, calico, saltpeter, coffee, Egyptian corn, African ivory, Guinea gold, damasks, gauze, muslin, lemons, syrup, silks, pearls, diamonds, oranges, figs, perfumes, camphor, ambergris, gum, wax, and all the catalogue of civilized living whose items were commonplaces among the men of the East?

Between the ninth and the twelfth centuries Europe was the commercial colony of a mysterious Asia. It lived barbarously while the world of Islam flourished. It was from this alien world that Europe, "a giant fed through the chinks of a wall,"[25] learned the principle and practice of an ordered commerce and something at least of that ease of life which is part of its gift. Even in the "darkest" of times papyrus, silks, and textiles were always available to the clerks and nobles of "the West" (a term worth more attention than it gets, since it emphasizes that Europe enters the world stage as an appendage, a peninsula of Asia). Oriental merchants had advanced headquarters in such "Far Western" towns as Cordoba in Spain, Orleans and Marseilles in France, and they employed Jews, Greeks, and Syrians, men who literally knew their way around, as their frontier agents and commercial travelers. For Islam, although politically decentralized, was linked by chains of religion and commerce of equal strength. It governed a world whose merchants were its princes—a world in marked contrast to Christendom, where the merchant was despised. The Prophet himself had declared that merchants were the couriers of the world and the trusty servants of God on earth; and had thus given to the man of commerce a profound conviction both of his own worth and of the necessity of the commercial empire over which he presided and which he always wanted to extend. It was a world whose tenets imposed on every good Muslim at least one

[25] The phrase is R. H. Tawney's.

journey in his lifetime, his pilgrimage to Mecca; and thus the Muslim, unlike the villager in Europe, grew up with the horizon in his mind.

Along the same routes as his commerce, the "Saracen" brought also into Europe, into its best minds, his own brand of intellectual imperialism. His knowledge of geography, astronomy, and medicine was, as Europeans gradually discovered, more accurate and useful than their own. Moreover, Arab scholars had preserved more of the Hellenic culture than had survived in the European memory, or was now within the compass of European thought. A comparison of the literary catalogues of the West with the lists of books available to Muslim scholars, writes R. W. Southern,

makes a painful impression on a Western mind; and the contrast came as a bombshell to the Latin scholars of the twelfth century, who first had their eyes opened to the difference.[26]

The Europeans accordingly found themselves drawn within the orbit of a society that was the enemy of their religion, the master of an indisputable culture, and the monopolist of most of what was profitable in their own commerce. The very existence of Islam presented a baffling and disheartening moral problem to the mind of Christendom, which was not privy to its counsels and could find no explanation for its immense success. Co-existence with Islam might well mean contamination by it, as the fate of the Spanish Christians was there to show. It was not oppression, to Christians an honorable legacy, but assimilation that was feared. Christians had their own context, but its promises were not of this world. Islam it appeared had all this and heaven too. The magnetism of success, the magnetism above all of the riches, the profits, and the power that displayed themselves as massive pillars for the economy of the Saracens, was always a more probing danger to the security of Christendom and to its hopes for salvation than any army of Saladin and all his kin. Yet it was just these secular attractions that Europe had no sure means of countering.

As Africa was to Europe in the nineteenth century, so was Europe to mid-Asia in the twelfth.

[26] R. W. Southern, *Western Views of Islam in the Middle Ages* (London, 1962), p. 24.

It was a colonial area, still resistant to, but unable totally to reject, a cultural and technological penetration by aliens. It was an outlying part of a greater world, a world whose nature and resources were known intimately by Muslims but scarcely at all by Christians, who were still unable even to hazard an intelligent guess at the configuration of the earth east and south of Alexandria in Egypt or arrive at any inkling whence came all the wealth of eastern commerce. "There was a period—during which the traveller could pass from the confines of China to the pillars of Hercules, from the banks of the Indus to the Cilician gates, from the Oxus to the shores of the Adriatic, without stepping outside the boundaries of the territory ruled over by the Caliph in Damascus or Baghdad."[27] Such a traveler was inevitably a follower of the Prophet. Ibn Battuta (1304–78), journeying from Tangier, met in the western Sudan the brother of a man he had known in China.

Thus was a vast, rich world, unknown to the true God, the Christians' God, paced, measured, and enjoyed by the children of Ishmael.

It is when this predicament, long recognized as such, becomes thought of as intolerable that the Europeans' pattern of imperialism first takes recognizable form. An imperialism of their own is their remedy for their own state of colonialism. The whole story is one of colonial rebellion. Like all such, it is a rebellion against narrow bounds, against the circumstances that confine not commerce only but life itself, that keeps intelligence stagnant and enterprise still. The motivating force is a wish to break free, to break out. This need to assert converts easily into a determination to dominate, and from that unascertainable moment when a state of liberty has been imagined, a revolution gets under way that leaves no part of the context of European life unchanged. This new era begins with the Crusades; for this series of "punitive expeditions" contains the embryo of every species of European imperialism that was afterwards to seize and shape the lives of all the peoples of the world.

The Crusades gave gainful employment and a sense of social

[27] A. P. Newton, ed., *Travel and Travellers of the Middle Ages* (London, 1926), pp. 89–90.

utility to the European aristocracy. They promised to all its ranks and degrees unlimited profit in this world (and not only mere baronies or manors, but kingdoms, kingdoms) and assured salvation in the next. They allowed kings to give positive and effective illustration to what had been an academic doctrine of divine right. They made action and movement a test of virtue. They made the Church militant, and by doing so made it attractive to men of serious purpose. They nourished the idea of the Christian community and gave it heart. They made the fortune of a myriad of camp followers. They mapped new arteries of commerce and brought to splendor and success the dominant republics of Venice and Genoa in Northern Italy. On behalf of all Christians they cast Jerusalem in the role that Mecca played for Muslims; and *partant pour la Syrie* was long to remain a French imperial dream in honor of Frankish forebears.

The Crusades introduced for the first time the idea of the horizon into the mainstream of European consciousness. They quickened the tempo of life and broke the chains of acceptance. They gave to the Papacy a foreign policy, which, again for the first time, a majority could respect, and helped make it a European power, one which was, in time, to become the agency of a highly successful imperialism. They canalized what had hitherto been sporadic and personal adventures against the forces of Islam, like that of the town of Pisa against Arab Sardinia (1016) or of the Normans against Arab Sicily (1060–90), and set them into the wider, sweeping context of the armed pilgrimage, blessed by Holy Church: for Pope Urban II, when launching the First Crusade (1096) on French soil, spoke of delivering from their infidel bondage the Christians not only of Palestine but of Asia Minor as well.

This context, once established, was never lost sight of. Henry prince of Portugal, known to history as "the Navigator," first made contact with the outside world, which was the world of Islam, at the siege of Ceuta in 1415. This event was of a type and purpose that could have taken place at any time during the past three centuries, and it stimulated him, as it would have any Frankish hero, to thoughts of further venture, farther afield. (Henry was himself the Grand Master of an Order of Chivalry of Our Lord Jesus Christ, itself founded by the Knights Templars, or Poor

Knights of Christ and of the Temple of Solomon.) The Crusades had in fact incubated ideas of action and purpose that were to take many different and contradictory forms. During them, actual physical contact was made with the states and statesmen of the East. Their mysteries had been revealed as so much politics, of a type perfectly familiar to the West and diligently practiced by the oligarchs who, in establishing security for a Christian Levant, found they could often call on Muslims to help them do so. Muslims were men like other men; and if the Cross was ever to displace the Crescent, the matter might be less one of divine providence than of political tactics. Force with faith, even force without faith, would suffice to loosen the grip of Islam on the rich places of the earth.

Even when, in 1291, the Franks evacuated Syria and brought the Latin Kingdom to an end, and with it both the era and the enthusiasms of the Crusades, the lessons learned were not forgotten. Thereafter Europe returned in upon itself, but it was an active Europe, whose rulers busied themselves with the construction of national States: neither France's Philip the Fair nor England's Edward I were men likely to interrupt this arduous task in order to go on pilgrimage. Edward III of England, in company with the Holy Roman Emperor Charles IV, promised to join a crusade in 1359, but neither did so: it was only a polite genuflection towards the accepted concept of a royal duty. England's Henry V, as antique in mold as his contemporary Henry of Portugal, might have shone forth as a hero of Christendom had he lived longer; but as it turned out the Ottoman Turk was temporarily stopped not by crusaders from the west but by the barbarous Tamerlane from Transoxiana in the north, the conqueror of southern Russia and India, and a territorial imperialist of the simplest kind. Although in the West the demands of religion were becoming subordinate to the loyalties of national sentiment, nations whose rulers continued to seek out means of reinforcing their power did not forget the horizons that had been opened up by their ancestors.

This national sentiment, bred in men who were now better informed of the state of the world and its inhabitants and better able to calculate how much might be got from the new knowledge, was ready to establish a condition of change. Once Europeans were in a position to assess the nature of "the East" and its economy, it was but a short step to making plans what routes would best take them there. "Cathay and the way thither" summed up a vision that magnetized both Marco Polo in the thirteenth century and Columbus two hundred years later. Schemes were put forward how to take Islam in the flank, and the belief grew that Europeans had only to reach those hidden sources of wealth to monopolize them. By their means they could equip themselves with the powers that would serve, in God's good time, to fill Asia with Christians while filling Europe with spices.

Here was an attitude far removed from the previous acceptance of that state of affairs which apparently it had pleased God, in His mysterious way, to decree upon His own children. The old feelings of envy were now fully converted into an ambition to emulate. The fact that, geographically, things had changed very much for the worse made no difference to the new sentiment in Europe: rather it increased its intensity. When the Crusades began at the end of the eleventh century, the Seljuk Turk had reached Nicaea in Asia Minor. When they had become a memory, yet a stirring part of several nations' patriotic history, the Ottoman Turk was overlooking the Danube. But the degree of tolerance had also changed. Acceptance was gone. The sense of subordination, of being caught indeed in some kind of trap (of just that kind which is completely familiar to the "emerging" nations of the twentieth century) had finally proved too much for the self-respect of the subordinate to endure.

These ideas, these emotions, were given meaning and movement by an awakening of the European spirit and by a renaissance of its mind. An awareness of the horizon promotes unrest and question in other areas than geography. Ideas so nourished were bound in no long time to issue a challenge to all the doctrines of conservatism, particularly those imposed by the Church whose rule it was that containment bred contentment.

The Church was right to see herself in the role of Christendom's preserver; but in order to play it effectively she had to bind the minds of men within an intellectual chrysalis of her own devising. The question was now to be put, whether it was to the interest of mankind that there should be any such chrysalis at all. The thunder of the ferocious battles that were the direct result of this question have not yet died away: for what "interest" can men have that, since it is by definition mundane and self-seeking, does not obstruct the life of the spirit? There was a "New World" in European minds before ever America was heard of. The attack on feudalism, the attack on the authority of the Papacy, the attack on the Oriental hegemony in commerce, are all aspects of a cumulative movement, stirring each generation, that was to take Dante (1265–1321) and Erasmus (1469–1537) as two of its seers and Machiavelli's *The Prince* (1513) for its political guidebook; while also producing, in the world of action, a race of explorers and mariners whose fame has never been allowed to dim. A sense of liberty, once got, does not compartment itself or operate only within a particular sphere.

In commerce Europeans want to quit the role of patient. They intend to become an agent. They determine to make their own mark on that great unknown world, ruled by others, all so vastly rich. They must first find out more about it. Where, for example, do the spices come from? This resolve to discover, and to know (in order to compete) is the force that galvanizes the era a modern Asian scholar calls "The Age of Vasco da Gama,"[28] the age that lasted some five centuries and will leave its shadow on an age as long again. In such times the unexpected finds an instant place in men's understanding. Marco Polo at the end of the thirteenth century had come home to tell tales of China and high Asia that no one believed: Pedro Cabral's voyage from Lisbon in 1500 revealed to Europe three places so disparate as Brazil, Madagascar, and Somalia, and was a remarkable money-maker besides. The existence of the money proved the truth of what he said. Between 1492 and 1502, nine voyages from Spain traced the configuration of the American coasts between Honduras and Pernambuco. Vasco da Gama himself, on reaching Calicut in western India in 1498, defined his aims as "Christians and spices!" But hinterlands filled with Christians, holds filled with spices, were only the means to an end. The end was physical dominance, a complete political control that would encompass every privilege and profit a particular area had to give. This is the aim that

[28] K. M. Panikkar, *Asia and Western Dominance: a Survey of the Vasco da Gama Epoch of Asian History* (London, 1959).

governs the efforts first to trace and then to command the communications to the East, to perfect the ocean-going ship and the
haven-finding art, and to make accurate maps and charts (only
to conceal them immediately from the prying eyes of competitors,
so that to this day mysteries obscure the emergence from obscu-
rity of some island groups of the Pacific).

Sebastian Cabot, when pilot-major to the Emperor Charles V,
was dispatched in 1526 to three actual places and to two that
were fictitious,

to discover the Moluccas, Tarsis, Ophir, Cipango, and Cathay; to
barter and load his ships with gold, silver, precious stones, pearls,
drugs, spices, silks, brocades, and other precious things,

and found when at Mecca that the citizens of that holy place did
not themselves know the sources of the goods that came to their
market, a natural center for distribution. In these circumstances
it was clear that the world was to be discovered afresh. Its secrets
could be scanned by the fortunate, by the enterprising, and by
all who could call the true God to their aid. In the process the
technology that had been born in the East was to be expanded
by Europeans out of all eastern recognition.

This is the revolution that begins in the twelfth century, which
reversed a wheel of fortune that had once put Muslims into
Cordoba but was now to put Christians into Calicut.

The turning of the African flank of Islam was slow work. It
took two centuries and the lives of many pioneers whose names
are not now known. Yet the Cape Verdes were probably the only
island group in the Atlantic not discovered before the time of
Portugal's Henry the Navigator, whose own ideas on the nature
and extent of the flank to be turned were limited, since his immediate objective in sending out his expeditions "was the discovery of Guinea, and the capture of the rich desert trade which
kept the ports of Barbary filled with Christian galleys."[29] If this
Guinea coast bore, as it was thought to do, on the Indian Ocean,
so much the better. Pioneer generations had to accustom themselves to surprise, as Columbus bore witness; but even the Amer-

[29] See J. W. Blake, *Europeans in West Africa 1450–1560*, Hakluyt Society,
second series, vol. 86 (London, 1942), I, pp. x, 3.

icas, that entirely unexpected and unwelcome obstacle on what ought to have been the short route to Cathay, were speedily brought within the pale of Europe by acts of colonization and settlement. Asia, because of her vastness and numbers of population, was neither colonized nor settled; but her civilizations were pervaded and her politics subverted none the less. Africa in contrast was for centuries thought of as a warehouse from which everyone in every other continent was entitled (since Africans themselves did not combine to force them to any reconsideration of this idea) to draw commodities, animate as well as inanimate; and, until the middle of the nineteenth century, appeared on maps only as a series of coastlines, all of them itemized by European or Muslim names.

The pattern and fashion of the commercial rivalry between the competing nations of Europe, as this revolution got under way, were early established. They were to repeat themselves from one century to another; and, though the means by which capital was accumulated underwent a revolution of its own, the process that Lenin commented on in the twentieth century was one that any Grand Master of the Templars in the twelfth well understood.

It was not a specifically European pattern either, for the Chinese in fifteenth-century Ceylon, or in the Majapahit Hindu Empire in Java, followed it faithfully. Men, wherever they came from, were true to their human propensities, wherever they found themselves. The Portuguese who in the early sixteenth century established their walled "factories" in Timor and Macao and Malacca knew nothing of Chinese practice but a great deal of Venetian. The Venetians had perfected the pattern in the Levant over five centuries previously. The Dutch when they arrived in eastern waters at the turn of the seventeenth century copied the Portuguese model. The English followed the Dutch. In India, the French, Dutch, English, and Danish factories were distinguishable only by the dominant language within them (and sometimes not always by that, since a pidgin Portuguese was a bastard *lingua franca* among them all). It is not surprising that to Muslims throughout the world all foreigners were Franks, *feringhi*, blood brothers to those original Franks who had stayed them at Tours (A.D. 732) and clashed the Cross against the Crescent in Syria; and forever after the distinction between, say, Spaniard and Dutchman was never so clear to their eye as it was to Philip the Second and William the Silent. Similarly, the Chinese of the nineteenth century were unable to distinguish between one brand of foreign devil and another. All were barbarians, it went without saying. For once the world beyond Europe had been caught up into a commercial and military network, it was of no moment, to its inhabitants, who it was who had woven the mesh of their particular part of the net.

Because it was the Venetians who first established a commercial frontier in Asia, it is they who have been singled out as the precursors of "the *bourgeois* revolution." The Republic that described itself as the bride of the Adriatic was the pioneer who set up the base from which others were to operate, who wrote the book from which others were to take a leaf, or who, as Marx has it, were the agents of the historical process of bringing the ultimate triumph of the proletariat one step nearer its accomplishment. The Venetians indeed adapted procedures already at hand: the great monastic Orders relied on remarkable systems of communications and finance, in particular the Templars, whose strongholds spanned from Armenia to Ireland, and who had made of their Paris "Temple" a money market whose efficiency gradually increased their power to the point of mortal danger to themselves. But it was, certainly, the Venetian Republic that in 1174 devised the two *bourgeois* institutions, sanctuaries never yet relinquished by capitalists, of a National Debt and a State Bank.

The Republic's doctrine of profit was as clear to its own contemporaries as to its critical posterity. In the tenth century the Venetians' trade with Egypt and Syria was the agency for the supplying of the Saracens with arms from Europe; and thereafter no amount of Christian shock or Papal thunder could for long break them of this habit. They remained as tolerant of infidel customers and their needs as were the Muslims themselves. When England's "Black Prince" Edward arrived in the Christian outpost of Acre in Syria in May 1171, he was scandalized to find Venetian merchants there busily exporting arms and provisions to Alexandria in Egypt. In one treaty, made in 1297 with the ruler of Egypt, the Venetians were granted the accustomed protection for their commerce and their merchants, together with a permission to visit under escort the Holy Sepulcher in Jerusalem.

A provision added that Venetians bringing to Egypt "objects prohibited by the Christians," a category that certainly included both munitions and slaves, should be exempt from duty on the products they took in exchange. Although in 1308 Pope Clement V issued a bull prohibiting all trade with the infidel, Venice throughout the fourteenth century (in company though not in collusion with the cities of Genoa, Pisa, and Marseilles) maintained her *fondachi* (special trading posts, *fondouks,* or factories) in the port of Alexandria. There is a particularly modern flavor of co-existence about this: a parallel might be drawn with the role of Hong Kong (1965), a British "factory" on the skirts of a hostile ideological Chinese Empire.

This type of pragmatism, which is the lynchpin of all successful imperialisms, denies the utility of formal doctrine. The value of the precedent Venice set was quickly appraised: Francis I of France, when he allied himself in 1536 with the dangerously rising power of the Ottoman Turk, could (and did) plead in response to Papal fury that he was following *raison d'état* of the kind that the Venetians, good sons of the Church like himself, had always favored. Their doctrine of profit was not subterranean at all. It needed no excuse. It needed indeed no formulation. Wealth was ostentatious: a rich man lived in a palace and was despised if he did not. The Venetians' motives were entirely and openly mercantile, and the leaders of the Republic from one generation to the next stayed untroubled by other, deflecting ambitions: the one Doge who did not, Marino Faliero, was executed (1355).

Venice, the landless city, became a metropolis of empire less by conquest or extension of herself than by playing a successful political game among those who had just those ambitions. She linked together by means of a sea power unrivaled in Europe the *fondachi* and commercial clearinghouses she had been allowed to establish at Antioch, Tarsus, Ephesus, and elsewhere in the Byzantine Empire. (The "Golden Bull" of 1082 of the Emperor Alexius had granted the Venetians exemption from import duties and taxes in the Empire as a reward for their naval contribution to the defeat of the attacking Normans from Sicily.) Although the Republic's relations with the Empire continually fluctuated—they were not improved, for example, when a Venetian fleet on its way to rescue the Holy Land from the infidel in 1122 paused to seize the Byzantine stronghold of Corfu at the mouth of the Adriatic, together with other Greek islands—no Emperor at Constantinople could afford to dispense with the services of Italian middlemen. Two years later, "quarters" in the towns of Tyre, Askalon, and Jerusalem, which had been regained by the Crusaders, were granted to the Venetians, the Genoese, and the Pisans. In these Syrian markets the Italians established themselves on the terminus of the trade route from India and China, whose exports were brought by Arab and Persian traders to Baghdad and thereafter taken up the valley of the Euphrates to the caravan routes that joined the desert with the sown.

Saladin took Jerusalem in October 1187. The "Third" Crusaders regained it in July 1191. And the Italians returned to their business and its privileges. Among these was the right to exercise their own powers of jurisdiction within their respective "quarters": and thus was founded that system of "capitulations" and extraterritoriality, preceding the arrival of the Ottoman power in the Levant and destined to fall with it eight centuries later.

Such success fomented rivalry. Just as Bismarck sought advantage in the late nineteenth century for the German Empire by promoting jealousy between the French and the British Empires in regard to the "rightful" control of Egypt, a Turkish possession, so in the mid-twelfth century the Greek Emperors of the Eastern Roman Empire at Constantinople sought to curb the power of Venice by promoting that of Genoa. Manuel Comnenus, Emperor from 1143, did just this, extending concessions to both Genoa and Pisa and ultimately confiscating all Venetian property within the Byzantine dominions (March 1171). But the Empire had two frontiers to man. Facing a militant Islam in the East, it had an open backdoor towards Europe and could not long afford to defy the one power that had the surplus capital to finance all those there who had vague but strong intentions of imperializing at Constantinople's expense. By 1187 Venice had the satisfaction of making a treaty at Constantinople that granted that, in all lands which were to be conquered with the aid of a Venetian fleet, the Venetians were to have "a church, a warehouse, a bakehouse, a quay, and free trade."[30]

---

[30] F. C. Hodgson, *The Early History of Venice* (London, 1901), p. 334.

A church, a warehouse, a bakehouse, a quay, and free trade. All of these were simple enough requirements. All of them had great implications. Wherever the Venetians went, these were what they set down as the stakes of their power. Wherever in the future other Europeans went, whatever doctrines of imperialism they appealed to, however much the terms of trade were changed, and no matter how revolutionary the impact of industrialism and the accumulation of finance capital was to prove on the habits of producers and consumers alike, if the empires that they established did not rest securely on these simple stakes of power they had no insurance for the future, that future which above all things they wanted to command.

In the Venetians' simplicity of aim lay their strength. Living in a narrow corner, angled between the two very distinctive worlds of western and eastern Europe, the Republic could afford to limit its imperial ideas in ways not open to the Holy Roman Emperor at Vienna or to the Byzantine at Constantinople. The imperialism of Venice was always (to return to Professor Langer's definition) "a manageable concept," manageable not only by her own citizens but by others also. Their imperialism, like that of the Dutch who in the seventeenth century fell heir to their role of "carrier" in European waters, trenched on no one's ground and distributed goods that otherwise would not have been available at all. The "Flanders galleys" of the Italian republics, which throughout the fourteenth and fifteenth centuries served England and the Low Countries, built up the prosperity of both areas to the sound of the loom. Both were thus introduced to markets and horizons (and ultimately to an imperial future of commerce) which they could never, at that time, have found for themselves. The Italian style of commercial imperialism indeed did more for the civilization of Europe, by expanding its economy, and with that its range of possibility, than Europeans ever managed by similar practices to do for the civilization of Asia—since in extending their own horizons the Europeans narrowed those of the peoples whose economy they came to control.

England in particular owed a great deal to foreign middlemen and their experience. As late as the year 1600 the English owned no territory overseas. Their single area of colonization, Ireland, was in turmoil: already an old and disheartening story. England lay, as her King Henry VIII had put it, in an angle of the world, but, unlike Venice, it was an angle that projected beyond the world's rim. As Europe was served in goods by Asia, so was England served by the Italian carriers. Calais was her own particular, highly prized *fondouk* on the European coastline. Throughout the fifteenth century the Iceland fishery and the Gascon wine trade accustomed the west-country seamen to long voyages, but Cadiz was still as far as English merchants cared to send, and it was still cheaper to send goods overland to Venice than by sea. From the 1540's onward Englishmen began to follow Frenchmen, good Catholics all, on to the papally forbidden ground of the Guinea trade, and to enter Asia by the northern route through Russia; but in the subsequent Elizabethan era, a heretic England endured more loss than profit, more misery than glory.[31] Her turn at empire was still to come; and when it came, it was on Venetian commercialism and Dutch exclusivism that she built her imperial institute.

The Venetian experience included the knowledge that profit needed power to protect it. The Republic was early forced to promote a political imperialism to defend its own interest. It was one however of a negative kind. Italy was Venice's especial "sphere of influence," for she could allow no rival imperial authority to establish itself there. On the whole the Venetians preferred the rivalry of the Greek at Constantinople to that of the German in Vienna, since the Greek had and always would have other problems on his mind besides those of the Italian peninsula. The German saw life otherwise. Frederick "Barbarossa," elected Holy Roman Emperor in 1152, was a man of one idea, of a kind that was to make a powerful appeal to Germans in the nineteenth century who were continuing to search for a world-historic vocation. He saw his Holy Roman Empire as a great moral force for keeping the West in peace and for delivering the Holy Sepulcher from Islam. To carry out these schemes he had to crush the feudal barons, whose ideas of power were more localized; to bring to order (his own) the free cities of Lombardy;

---

[31] James A. Williamson, in his Introduction to George B. Parks, *Richard Hakluyt and the English Voyages* (New York, American Geographical Society, 1928), p. ix.

and thence to unite Italy, which would then serve him as a springboard for his eastern adventure. He found arrayed against him exactly those elements that had long hampered the free movement of the Venetians themselves: the Papacy, the Normans of Sicily and Apulia, the Byzantine Emperor, and the Saracens too. But where the Venetians saw these as people to bargain with, Barbarossa saw them only as foes, conducted himself accordingly, and found all his hopes frustrated.

From such a crusading spirit Venice remained inoculated, and had reason to congratulate herself on her commonsense. But she was very willing to put her temporal weight behind those whom it moved. Nothing had such great need of territory as a spiritual imperialism; and plainly such could never achieve its goals without money and supplies. Venice therefore acted as quartermaster and carrier to the Crusades and proved that what was stored in the warehouse on the quay had a striking power as great as all the conventional weapons in the armory.

The track of ambition followed by the southern Normans was taken also by Venice for purposes of her own.

The Normans were the most fervent supporters of the European foreign policy of the Crusades, and were to remain that policy's Frankish, driving force. It is their chronicler, Geoffroy de Ville-hardouin, who first speaks of *la terre d'outre-mer,* and he has Syria in mind. The Franks early decided that the main obstruction which blocked the road to a Holy Land restored to Christian keeping lay less in the military capacity of the Saracens now in residence there than in the tortuous diplomacy of the Byzantine Emperors. The latter's insistence that conquests made by the Crusaders at once became fiefs of the Empire poisoned relations between Frank and Greek. The Greek continued to consider even Sicily, the Norman base, as his own property and the Normans as renegade tenants. The allegiance that the Emperor Alexius had demanded in the First Crusade was therefore demanded again by the Emperor Manuel Comnenus in the Second (1147). Throughout its course he fought a running battle not only against the Saracens but with Roger of Sicily, who had no intention of handing over any trophies. During the Third Crusade (1189) the Emperor Isaac Angelus actually chose to ally himself with Saladin, so fearful was he of the imperialist ambitions of Frederick Barbarossa and his Norman allies.

Of this long-standing hostility Venice took full advantage. Her doctrine of profit carried her far. For her assistance in mounting and transporting the Fourth Crusade, Venice asked the Franks for a half of all the lands and property taken, together with a fee of eighty-five thousand marks. The Franks could promise the property but could not raise the fee. This gave the Republic an opportunity to use Frankish forces against both the Hungarians and the Greeks, under cover of a specious argument—for the Crusaders in 1204 entered not the Holy Land but Constantinople itself, nominally to deliver the Byzantine Empire from a usurper. This deliverance, which put Franks into the Emperor's palace for fifty-seven years, gave Venice a quarter in the capital, with valuable colonies in the Aegean, in the Morea, and in the island of Crete.

Thus by 1205 Venice, already supreme in the Adriatic, was firmly seated at the Golden Horn. Her chain of emporia ranged the Levant, and her links of trade with Syria and Egypt grew stronger. The single-minded pursuit of commercial privilege, which had built for her a sea power unmatched in Europe, had now put her into a post of eminence to which everyone, for three centuries to come, would pay suit. Profit and power had plainly no close kin with public scruple.

Venice's negative attitude to territorial power (that others should not have it) was now converted into a positive policy of conservatism. She was no longer able to play the part of a reasonably honest broker among the powers. She was a power herself. This brought to a point the long-smoldering enmity of her principal commercial rival, Genoa. Wars between the two Republics for the possession of the Levantine and Black-Sea trades were to drag on with varying fortune between 1253 and 1380, creating a situation whereby the Ottoman Turks were signally aided to consolidate their power in Syria and in Asia Minor, to the ultimate detriment not of Venice only but of all Europe.

These wars, fought in the Mediterranean and Adriatic, find later parallels in the waters of the Arabian Sea when Arabs fight Portuguese; in eastern waters when Portuguese fight Dutchmen;

and in the Indian Ocean when Frenchmen fight Englishmen—all
of them "trade wars," all of them fought under a banner of national monopoly, all of them matters of literal life or death and
continued until one of the contenders reached that political point
in the struggle for empire and came to a standstill: Genoa in 1380,
Portugal in 1580, the French in 1761.

And not only did Venice strain herself to defend her outposts
at sea, she was compelled also to expand on land, to obtain better
food supplies, trade facilities, and that degree of security which
was always to obsess conservatives who, having fallen heir to
empire, would go to the most radical lengths to conserve it. Thus
the landless city, bride of the sea, became mistress of a large *bloc*
of northern Italy, and hostess to the frontier problems that inevitably attach themselves to such a role—problems of the same kind
as were to beset, four centuries later, the English East India
Company's factors in Bengal, who found themselves the "country
power" in central and eastern India.

For when commercial empire has been established, territorial
imperialism of a definable kind necessarily begins. In the age of
achievement, every energy is taken up with the purpose at hand:
in the case of Venice, the planning of a system of commerce to
include East and West. The age of imperialism is properly the age
that follows the success of the purpose. What has been got must
be kept. Stockades must be built. The more distant the stockade,
the farther the horizon the metropolis commands, the better its
citizens sleep. But stockades require soldiers. Soldiers require pay.
Pay comes from a treasury. The treasury must be filled. Trade
must be promoted. Competitors must be outstripped or, even
more conveniently, ousted. So preserving the desirable *status quo*
turns out to entail a spirited imperialism, an active nationalism,
and, above all, success, which alone can satisfy everyone's need
to be reassured that these laurels will neither fade nor be snatched
away.

In the century that followed the establishment of the Ottoman
power in the Levant the Venetian Republic rose to its zenith of
prosperity. In the last years of the fifteenth century the largest
Venetian galleys were of twelve hundred tons and were bringing
to the European market over three and a half million pounds of

spices a year, two-thirds of it loaded at Alexandria, and nearly half of it pepper.

The territorial imperialism of the Ottoman Turks had not interfered with this traffic: five days after his army had captured Constantinople in 1453 the Sultan issued a *firman* confirming the commercial privileges of the Italians. Although Mohammed II went on in 1461 to take Trebizond and Kaffa on the Black Sea, this injured Genoa more than Venice; and this closure of the western termini of the Central Asian route to China certainly made the Mediterranean route, of which Venice was still mistress, of even greater importance and profit. (Central Asia had anyway been inaccessible to European traders for a century past. The famous passage to Cathay, which had taken first Marco Polo (1254–1324) and ultimately Christian bishops to Pekin, had been blocked since the mid-thirteenth century; and since the death of Tamerlane (1405) a state of impenetrable anarchy had set in, flanked by the policy of an antiforeign dynasty in China itself, which saw to it that Chinese ships no longer visited Ceylon or the ports of Ormuz and Siraf on the Persian Gulf.)

Yet the fact of Constantinople in Turkish hands marked the future with its shadow. For the new masters of the Levant were not content with these bridgeheads alone. The Egyptian-Syrian trade continued, to Venice's enrichment and without molestation for sixty more years; but when Sultan Selim II (1512–20) conquered Egypt, northern Mesopotamia, and Syria and received the capitulation of Arabia and the Caliphate; when his successor Suleiman the Magnificent (1500–60) attacked Baghdad and the states of the Persian Gulf, took Aden at the mouth of the Red Sea, and gave to the Algerian corsairs naval power in the western Mediterranean, the stability of the world to which Europeans had grown accustomed was totally undermined. A new age of confrontation had come in, guided by militant spirits.

Italian traders had thought it possible to coexist with Islam and had proved their point. Similarly, since Charles Martel's victory on the field of Tours, Islam had tolerated the existence of Europe, provided always that the Franks did not secure their infidel kingdom in the Levant. Both Europe and Islam had now produced men of a different policy. Other states in Europe were ready to catch up the Frankish gage. To no one was it clear, perhaps not even to the Ottoman Turk himself, how far his militance against the infidel would take him. It took him far enough. He besieged Vienna in 1529. By 1540 he had defeated Venice herself in a ruinous war and had joined with the French to attack Nice. By 1556 his Empire included the Balkans, most of Hungary, and northern Africa; and the tide of his movement, if not that of his ambition, was not finally to be turned until another century had passed, when he was held back from Vienna for the last time in 1683.

Europe's eastern marches had therefore to be held in strength against the Turk. But there was no profit in that exercise; rather the reverse. The days of a Latin kingdom in the Levant were plainly over. The Iliad of the barons now became an Odyssey of the merchants. Turning away from the Turk, towards the other horizon, the horizon in the West, peoples who were hardly known in the East were preparing to take with them the Italian techniques of economic penetration. The sophisticated Venetian attitude, which allowed for the idiosyncrasies of others, was replaced by something more direct. Policy was worked out by men with rougher ideas and of simpler culture; and applied with dire results for those of still another kind of culture whom they encountered *en route.*

Although the West never magnetized Europe as had the East, it had long had its obvious commercial uses. The Franks in particular were accustomed to facing both ways. Jerusalem had their heart; but they were not always in a crusading mood. Norman kings of Sicily had been the first to enter into formal treaty with Muslim emirs in North Africa. They were closely followed by Pisans and Genoese. From the tenth century commerce thrived, and Christians trafficked in all the ports of Barbary in goods that were quite obviously not products of the littoral, but came from mysterious realms to the south. Although the Christians had their *fondouks* in the coastal towns, no route into the interior was opened up for them as it was in Central Asia, and the great market of Timbuktu was as closed to them as Baghdad itself. Where the gold, the slaves, the malaguetta pepper, the ivory, the ebony, all the goods they shipped to Europe, came from, remained a standing challenge, symbolized by the Catalan maps of the fourteenth century which depict an African monarch sitting on a mountain of gold somewhere in the Sahara. The idea of turning Africa's flank was at the outset unconnected with any notion of a route to the East; but as the Portuguese slowly mapped the coast, colonizing the Cape Verdes in 1459 and finally arriving on the "Guinea" (gold) coast in 1481, it was already clear that the equator was not an impassable barrier and that somewhere beyond Africa must lie a way to the eastern world.

Da Gama made this quite manifest in 1498. Six years later the Venetians were reporting an alarming shortage of spices in both Alexandria and Beirut, for by then the Portuguese were dispatching a dozen ships a year from Lisbon around the Cape of Good Hope. From 1507 Portuguese fleets were blockading the mouths of the Red Sea and the Persian Gulf. By 1512 they had established themselves at Malacca in the Malayan peninsula and in the Moluccas, the Spice Islands themselves. By 1517 they had sent a fleet to Canton in southern China. They knew just what they were about and what its consequences would be. What their great viceroy Affonso d'Albuquerque said of Malacca (which had been in Muslim hands since 1450) was true of the "Far East" as a whole:

> . . . If they [the Portuguese] were only to take Malacca out of the hands of the Moors, Cairo and Mecca would be entirely ruined; and Venice would then be able to obtain no spices except what her merchants might buy in Portugal.

And Malacca in particular was a prize worth having, such great profits could be made there, where spices "cost five to seven times as much as in the islands where they grew."[32] If they cost that in Malacca, what could they not be made to cost in all the cities of Europe?

The Venetians had shown Europe how to trade and how to finance a trade. The Portuguese imprinted a deeper pattern on imperialism: they showed Europe how it might obtain the means of production itself. They built up a fund of experience on which others were to draw. They learned how, if never how best, to live in the tropics. They devised the way to deal with "natives," to build and sail ocean-going ships, to map the monsoons, and to plot and chart unknown coasts. Their pilots and their portolans

[32] J. S. Furnivall, *Netherlands India* (Cambridge, 1939), pp. 15–16.

and their rutters found their way into the service of every maritime nation. It was they who, by taking sugar out of Greece into the Azores in the Atlantic in the 1440's, and by transplanting it to Brazil in the 1520's, began the remarkable colonial career of that crop, whose story, with all its repercussions on the habit and emotion of the races of man, is not yet finished.

They found out also, faster than Venice had been required to, how dangerous is too single-minded a pursuit of profit. It was not Portugal only who had learned the Italian technique. It was therefore pointless for Portugal's ambassador d'Araujo to protest to Elizabeth I of England in 1561 that, since Portuguese merchants distributed the commodities of Africa liberally over all Europe in the natural course of trade, there was no necessity for the English or for anyone else to make voyages in search of them. If liberality meant plenty, this was true, but in no other sense was Portuguese trading free. Their prices were always high. Antwerp in the sixteenth century was an emporium one had to be affluent to enter; while in London cloves from the Moluccas cost seven shillings per pound. No wonder, then, that Venice, although relatively diminished, had no need to close its doors as a trading Republic. Venetian merchants were still using the Aleppo-Basra route, from Syria to the Persian Gulf, in 1564, that year importing nearly two and a half million pounds of pepper. In the 1570's they were pioneering new trade routes into India and Burma, taking full advantage of the fact that coffee, rice, and many other eastern commodities could not be carried around Africa, however speedy a Portuguese carrack, and survive in any condition fit for market.

Portugal had opened up half the world, and that the richer half, whose gates she had not the strength to keep forever shut. They were stout gates: a chain of them stretched from Aden and Ormuz to Goa in India, to Ceylon, to Malacca in Malaya and to Macao in China. One of these, Goa, was not to be taken from her until the mid-twentieth century (1961); and another, Macao, has not been taken from her yet (1965).

Although they could man these gates, the Portuguese never had the power to master a hinterland. They belonged to one of the poorer nations of Europe, with less than a million in population, whose own existence could not guard itself against the growing imperial ambitions of the Spanish monarchy. Not all the heroes

Camoëns sings of in *The Lusiads* (1572)[33] could prevent the strain of empire from weakening Portugal's grip on the East. She never, like her Dutch supplanters, developed the preponderant sea power that alone could have defended her position. As did Japan in these same waters four centuries later, Portugal spread her area of dominion too far. The Japanese had this made plain to them by their enemies only three years after they had made their greatest advances: the Portuguese were at least given the grace of a century and a half, time enough to fashion for themselves an epic story of empire, such as Japan would dearly have loved to own.

Moreover, unlike Spain in America, Portugal could establish no great base, honeycombed with mines of gold and silver. In the East geography favored the raider more than the settler: in the West this was never so. Francis Drake in 1585 took five thousand men into the Spanish Main[34] but never took an island; but in the East the "gadflies" could intrigue successfully with native rulers who saw no reason to honor an agreement with the Portuguese, since at any one time there were so few Portuguese present to keep it enforced. The day of the "interloper" was quickly at hand, with Frenchmen in the van. Francis I's agreement with Suleiman brought the French for the first time to the Egyptian market at Alexandria; and Portugal had even more reason to complain when they came to trade on the Guinea Coast, her own discovery (Liberia, for pepper). As the 1530's opened Frenchmen were interloping both in Sumatra in the East Indies and in Brazil, probing everywhere into all the areas that the Pope had tried to seal off from all other sons of the Church, and going far beyond them in the search for gold—as Jacques Cartier did in the valley of the St. Lawrence.

In the East a pattern of competition was already established. The Portuguese themselves were only interlopers. Although Islam had recoiled from the shock of this new infidel entry into their eastern paradise, and could not recoup their loss at the great sea

[33] Luis Vaz de Camões (1524–1580), *Os Lusíadas* (the Portuguese).
[34] Or, rather, beside it. The "Main" was originally *tierra firme,* the mainland, i.e. the coast of modern Venezuela. When or how it transferred its meaning to the sea itself—"comes silent, flooding in, the main" (A. H. Clough)—I do not know.

battle off Diu in western India in 1509, they did not retire. Da Gama reached India only twenty-eight years before the Mughals conquered that subcontinent; and farther east the Muslims reinforced their power by seizing the headquarters at Majapahit of the Hindu Empire in Java (1526). The Portuguese were able to retain their prized monopoly of cloves, granted them by the ruler of the island of Ternate in the Moluccas, for only fifty years (1522–75). By 1600 it was as doubtful as it had been in 1500 whether, if a territorial empire was to develop in the eastern seas, it would not be yet another extension of Islam.

But as it turned out it was not on that wall that Portugal's fate was written. Her monarchy was absorbed in Spain's in 1580: and it was Spanish control not only of Lisbon but of Antwerp that first set the Dutch of the Low Countries to thoughts both of rebellion against this yoke and of striking independently into the eastern seas to obtain the "carrying trade" of all the world.

To summarize: by the late sixteenth century, the course of commercial empire was well marked, the doctrine of profit well learned, and the techniques on which all later imperialism would thrive established. What the Dutch planned to do and actually carried out in the first forty years of the seventeenth century the French and the English continued to dream of; but both, when at last they went into successful imperial action, were content to use the proven methods of the Venetians, the Portuguese, and the Dutch. The propensity to truck and barter was everywhere as strong as ever.

In the East, however, it continued to meet exasperating obstruction. The Dutch who reached the Spice Islands and found no takers for their cloth faced a problem already centuries old but forever bewildering to whichever European trader was meeting it for the first time. In Java Jan Pieterszoon Coen, the Dutch equivalent of Portugal's Albuquerque in India, took it as an axiom "You cannot have trade without war, or war without trade"[35]—but the trade he spoke of was not trade in and with the countries of the East itself, but trade with Europe. Since western nations could not find customers for their own goods in the East, they became predators rather than merchants. They set out to monopolize

[35] Furnivall, *op. cit.,* p. 23.

the produce of the area. It was as if the East was a modern oil
well and the sea-lanes to Europe its pipeline: as the imperial history of the oil business plainly shows, both the well and the line
need to be protected.

As a result, empires in the East were of necessity military empires. The doctrine of profit which had brought in the interlopers
became inextricably entangled with the doctrine of power and
helped to hammer out new principles of foreign and imperial
policy. The imperial "interest," economic at base, became all-
encompassing. Although the colonial priest, the colonial soldier,
and the colonial merchant envied one another's sphere of influence, they all upheld the imperial structure and depended upon
one another's success. This was always more obvious to a subject
race than to any individual among the overlords, but it was
always true.

In such circumstances no one could afford to give a competitor
elbow-room. In European waters Venice and Genoa had long
competed for the same commercial trophies, but they had never
tried to expel one another from the Italian peninsula, and even in
an age noted for cynicism would have thought the idea improper
as well as impracticable. The carrying trade was anyway profitable enough for two to live on. In the East this was not the case,
so expensive was it to maintain, at so great a distance from the
European market.

The behavior of the Dutch made this clear. Elsewhere in the
world, wherever their enterprise took their seamen, the Dutch
acted as genuine commercial travelers and honest brokers. Their
ships and goods were always sure of a welcome in the ports of
English America or in the English and French West Indies: "the
Dutch have a proverb," as England's governor of Jamaica dryly
commented in 1673, " 'Jesus Christ is good, but trade is better.' "[36]
Even the Spanish colonial governors, although they knew well
how gravely they were breaking the rigid rules laid down both by
the Council of the Indies and the *Casa de Contratación* at Seville,
would look the other way when Dutch merchantmen entered the
roadstead at Carthagena or Vera Cruz. For America, unlike Asia,

[36] Sir Thomas Lynch to the Council of Trade and Plantations, 4 April 1673;
Public Record Office, London, Colonial Office Papers 1/30, no. 19.

was a continent settled and planted, and by the mid-seventeenth century the Spaniards and the English were too firmly entrenched there to be displaced by a marauding sea power alone. They presented no such weak front as did Portugal in the East. To Spain, the preservation of her American Empire, with its gold and silver, was a matter of literal life and death. The quip was quite true, that the king of Spain

looked on Portuguese Asia as his concubine, but on America as his lawful wife.[37]

He was determined never to let an interloper get his hands on the *frutas dessas Indias* (the riches of the Indies) that his conquistadors had won. And Spanish kings, although harassed over three centuries "beyond the Line" by European adventurers and by their insolent claims for an open trade, stayed faithful to this resolve.

Thus in America the Dutch had to be content to play interloper and to insert themselves between the chinks of a system of monopoly of just that same kind which they themselves maintained against all comers in the East Indies. Finding the slave trade peculiarly suited to the middleman's services, they made of their West India Company's Caribbean base at Curaçao a rich emporium for the traffic in Negroes from the West African coast. They made so much profit from this that they could afford to ignore their own original terms of reference. But this West India Company's charter, issued in June 1621, deserves notice, so piratical a document it is, and so abrim with the imperialist truculence of its time. It gave the Company a twenty-four year monopoly of the trade, navigation, conquest, and commerce in all seas and lands between the straits of Magellan and Newfoundland, between the tropic of cancer and the Cape of Good Hope. In the Pacific, its sphere of operations extended from the western coast of America to the eastern tip of the island of New Guinea. Its intention was

to colonise fruitful and unpeopled lands, and to do everything necessary for the service of the nation and for the profit and increase of its trade.[38]

[37] C. R. Boxer, *The Dutch in Brazil* (Oxford, 1957), p. 16.
[38] E. Sluiter, "Dutch Maritime Power and the Colonial *Status Quo*, 1585–1641," *Pacific Historical Review*, xi, pp. 29–41.

The Company had a paid-up capital of seven million florins and a conviction that it must fight to survive: for the States-General of the United Provinces gave it sixteen ships of war, which the burghers agreed to maintain if the Company's directorate would do as much. Looking for somewhere to conquer, this directorate (nineteen of them, the Heeren XIX, hopeful of finding the same route to power pioneered by the Heeren XVII who governed the sister East India Company) chose to strike at the weakest possession of the weakest of the American powers—and so began a long campaign for the conquest and exploitation of Portugal's colony of Brazil (1624–54). But Spain was another matter; Spanish America remained unassailable; Piet Heyn's exploit in 1628 of capturing the plate fleet, with fifteen million florins booty brought in triumph to Amsterdam, was not to be repeated; and at the general European settlement made in Westphalia in 1648, the Dutch by the treaty of Munster were content to have Spain recognize their independence as a nation in Europe and to allow them a trading foothold in America.

It was not so in the East. There no third party prevented the Dutch from overlaying the rival foundations of empire and making off with the *fumos da India* (the riches of the Indies). They did this with ruthless speed. They took Bantam in Sumatra from the Portuguese in 1598, Amboyna in 1605, Ternate with its sultan and spices in 1607. They destroyed a Portuguese fleet off Malacca in 1606, a Spanish fleet off Gibraltar in 1607. Their truce with Spain, concluded in 1609, was never honored in the East, which existed beyond a mental "line." The Heeren XIX sent out a war fleet in 1614, which defeated a Spanish armada off Peru in 1615 and penetrated to Manila in the Philippines. In 1623 the Dutch ejected the English from the Moluccas, since they seemed to think that they could sail into eastern waters with impunity, in the Dutch lee. The year 1624 saw the Dutchmen successful both at Bahia in Brazil and in Formosa in the north Pacific. They crowned this eastern enterprise with the capture of Malacca in 1641: "a rendezvous for our whole Indian navigation," and thought of as a permanent counterweight to the Spanish headquarters at Manila.[39] As Coen wrote home, to the delighted

[39] In fact Batavia, founded in 1619, constituted the main Dutch stronghold in the East Indies.

Heeren, "Something great can be done in India . . . and it can yield rich profits years by year."[40]

This it did. Something certainly remarkable was done. The Dutch East India Company was not anxious for territorial rule: as one of its historians puts it, "Its polestar was profit and its lodestone greed."[41] But if these were forms of happiness, they had to be pursued from a secure base. To get such a base, territorial rule had to be established. Commercial imperialism, different in degree from that which Venice had cultivated, now bred an authoritarianism of its own.

What the Dutch in fact established was a pattern of behavior, which the French essayed and the English carried to a conclusion in Asia a century later. Strategy must be geared to the protection of a commercial monopoly. When this is done, the status of security imbues in those who enjoy it a confidence that they are thus masters of their fate because they deserve to be so, because they come of superior stock, armed with superior ideas, and are not as these others among whom their lives are passed. Even if they are not what their subjects murmur in their ears—lords, kings, perfumed ones, sons of heaven, among the twice-born—they are assuredly the favorites of a benign, and wise, Providence. They have inherited what is, after all, their own, their due. The world is marked out as an area for the enterprise of Europeans, for who else has the enterprise so to mark it out?

In the East Indies the Dutch became the masters not only of an entire commerce but also of the economy that produced it and of the peoples which that economy upheld. A base was first laid in Java, from which the desired monopoly of trade could be organized. Around the base an area is required to act firstly as a stockade, then as a perimeter. So that this area may be supplied, "buffer states" beyond it, subservient to the central alien authority, have to be regularized or, if not in existence, created. Puppet princes have to be installed in these states so that they may continue to play their appointed role. Out of all these accumulated needs emerges what is to become another long-enduring pattern

---

[40] Furnivall, *op. cit.*, p. 27. The "India" referred to is Netherlands India, *Insulinde*, the chain of islands of the "East Indies."
[41] *Ibid.*, p. 34.

of imperialism: the establishment of a system of "indirect rule," wherein the local rulers, in return for the privilege of being allowed to rule, raise the taxes on and transmit the tribute from their own people in order to lubricate the imperial machinery. These native regents, appointed and salaried by the European authority, depend upon it and are responsible to it; so that in time their regimes become as conservative, and sometimes more so, as that of the imperial power itself.

Supported in this way from below, the European ruler can begin to take his ease. The problems he has are more those of administration than of policy. He does not think of the future. The sun must clearly not be allowed to set on the present, so delightful is its shape. It is radicalism verging on subversion to believe that the sun is not under control, that it will proceed on its own way, and that the future will inevitably not only differ from but may even cancel out the present.

Yet while the sun is still high these forebodings are faint. What began as a trading adventure, full of risk and effort, enjoys its meridian as an empire devoted to a static routine, officered by gentlemen who do not often choose to enter warehouses or keep ledgers, and who see the natives only on official occasions, the nature of which they themselves appoint. At all other times the natives are socially invisible. What aspirations they have remain unascertainable, since phantoms can hardly have desires. Since it is they who provide the manual labor of the economy, the laborer's status is reserved for them exclusively; and because manual work has a low prestige, so too have the natives who perform it.

It thus becomes literally impossible for a European in the tropics to work with his hands. He acts as manager and protector of the economy, and his success establishes both in his own eyes and in those of his subordinates what the French are the first to call *prestige*. The only sin he can commit is the single one that will stir the disapprobation of the entire society of rulers and ruled. He must not, he cannot "lose caste." He is the agent of the superior civilization, and his role binds him to a certain habit of thought and conduct.

What habit this is, may now be examined.

FOUR

The Doctrine of Civilization

Imperialism not only depends on national self-confidence, it is the crown of its achievements.

For nationalism realizes its full potential, develops its strongest emotional pull, only when its proponents export it to the world outside, there to measure their own attainments with those of the peoples of that place. As Hans Kohn has pointed out, "Inequality in the level of civilisation and civilising energy are of the very essence of imperialism."[1] What the Russians said about their task in Central Asia was repeated by Frenchmen, invoking their *mission civilisatrice* in Africa and in the Far East; by Germans, planning to implant their *Kultur* in a world that so plainly needed it; by Japanese, who wanted to westernize others as they themselves had been westernized; and by the British who, without asserting doctrine, took it for granted that their presence anywhere ensured more peaceful and prosperous conditions than those that had obtained before. Their governments, although often accusing one another of hypocrisy, agreed on their mutual role. It was they who, having fashioned the present, had the clearest right to command the future. They appealed to the authority given them by success and were ready to exploit the deference that was readily paid to it.

Success was its own justification. Since the extra-European world, which their imperialism controlled, did not because it could not order its own fate and therefore had no hope of success, it could be discounted in the drive for human progress. The in-

[1] Hans Kohn, *Nationalism and Imperialism in the Hither East* (London, 1932), p. 62.

154

habitants of that world were backward and inferior. This was not an aspersion, it was a fact—for if they had not been backward and inferior, would they have chosen to live in a world governed by fear and magic? They had fashioned their bondage by themselves, long before any European arrived to discover, exploit, and increase it. They were bound not only to the past, but in some cases (as among the Malagasy of Madagascar) actually to the dead, to ancestors who still conditioned their thought and action. Such people could have nothing of value to say about the future, either their own or anyone else's. They had no image of it: time itself meant little to them, and punctuality—as generations of European managers were to find out—nothing at all.

The people who were destined to inherit the future, according to Benjamin Kidd's *Principles of Western Civilisation* (1902), were those

who already bear on their shoulders the burden of the principles with which the interests of the future are identified.

Here was the real "white man's burden": his own knowledge and recognition of the problems that beset his quest for progress. The removal of the ignorance and darkness that blinded the world which still lay beyond Europe's civilization was a spur to his effort. So too was the fog that obscured his own path. Technology and purpose lay in the hands of the European: how he handled them was the challenge that faced his civilization, which could not survive unless he made a fitting response to it. While squaring to this task, he ought not to be bothered with matters essentially trivial, or by people essentially extraneous; for one of the most remarkable spectacles of the modern world, Kidd added,

is that of more tribal or local egotisms which have expressed themselves under the forms of nationality—claiming, in this respect alone, the rights and tolerance of our civilisation.[2]

Of what nature, then, was the larger egotism? What standards did the civilized, thinking themselves so, planning to remain so, apply?

One of their central principles declared that a civilized state

[2] Benjamin Kidd, *The Principles of Western Civilisation* (London, 1920), pp. 5–6, 99.

must possess a fixed organization and be capable of maintaining and defending it. Gorchakov's "circular" of 1864 contrasts a civilized state with a wandering tribe of "no fixed organisation," with a "nebulous political development." In such conditions men could develop no public conscience. The progress of civilization had no more efficacious ally than commercial relations, but to establish these at all implied "a revolution in the manners of the people." Only force could bring this about: it would never generate itself spontaneously. Asiatics had to be made to understand that trade was better than plunder. They must be compelled to take up an entirely new way of life. In bringing this about, European power would open new horizons for them: purged of their blindness, these enforced recipients of civilization would cease "to hang back from the movement of the world."[3]

Some stressed the means more than the end. Treitschke's remark that "the great strides which civilisation makes against barbarism and unreason are only made actual by the sword" is some distance from Napoleon III's plaintive assertion "L'Empire, c'est la paix"—but they are nevertheless milestones on the same route. Treitschke expressed a natural German horror lest the future be dominated either by the Russian knout or by English moneybags; yet the school of Darwinists was convinced that the sword's decision, whatever it might be and whomever it favored, would be biologically "just." Whatever was, was right. Darwin himself described natural selection as the doctrine of Malthus applied to the whole animal and vegetable kingdom, and the comment of his colleague Alfred Russel Wallace became famous: "The fittest," said Wallace in his book *Darwinism* (1889), "will survive." Society was a living, developing organism. Development and progress were synonymous terms. The Germans believed, while the English denied, that the good of the State and the good of society were also synonymous terms; but neither doubted their own condition of fitness and superiority, or doubted that the imposition of their ideas and habits on "lesser breeds without the law" (Kipling's phrase for those whose forms of social organization were rudimentary) could bring anything other than good.

---

[3] The phrase is the third Lord Salisbury's, Prime Minister: Lady Gwendolen Cecil, *Life of Robert Marquess of Salisbury* (London, 1932), IV, p. 385.

In his *Imperialism*, with a reluctance the reader can sense, J. A. Hobson admits another view of the scenes of exploitation he is describing. He allows "two tentative principles." These are,

First, that all interference on the part of civilised white nations with "lower races" is not *prima facie* illegitimate. Second, that such interference cannot safely be left to private enterprise of individual whites. If these principles be admitted, it follows that civilised governments *may* undertake the political and economic control of lower races—in a word, that the characteristic form of modern Imperialism is not under all conditions illegitimate.[4]

What Hobson conceded with caution, others seized on with gusto. For his countryman Joseph Chamberlain, the happiness of India lay in the continued security of British rule. He told the Toronto Board of Trade in December 1887 that the Anglo-Saxon race was infallibly destined to be the predominant force in the future history and civilization of the world. He told the London Chamber of Commerce the following spring that the extension of the British Empire in Africa was a necessary work of colonization and civilization, which would justify "our position as a nation." Eight years later, when he had become Colonial Secretary, he assured his listeners, in regard to the Sudan, that there was no idea "of handing back to barbarism such territory . . . as we may recover for civilization"; and in a review of the state of the world a year later he announced his conclusion that "the minor kingdoms—those which are non-progressive—seem to be destined to fall into a secondary and subordinate place."[5] In that place, they would be protected; but to any other place, they had no right.

The Chinese term for "rights" is one that illustrates their acclimatization to western modes of thought. It is two words which literally mean "power and interest."

British imperialists had no quarrel with this. Lord Salisbury, a statesman who disliked the noisier style of imperialism which painted the map red, still had no doubts, as a good Christian, that the civilized nations had a mission to perform in the world. Their paternalism was best expressed through an authoritative imperial

---

[4] Hobson, *Imperialism,* p. 204.
[5] Strauss, *Chamberlain,* pp. 60, 65, 69, 77.

rule. They had a responsibility to colonial peoples themselves—to protect, equip, and educate them. In doing this, a larger service was also performed, to the idea of civilization itself, since these new recruits to it, properly guided and guarded, would enlarge and enrich the area of the civilized life. Salisbury allowed that the African had a right to law, a right to protection, a right to education. But he did not allow that the African had a similar right to self-determination, and why? Because the African had not yet found a self to determine. Salisbury's generation had seen what "Africa for the Africans" could mean: pillage, barbarities, slavery.[6] Civilization did not lie at the end of that road. A similar, if less severe, case presented itself in Egypt. There, after the invasion of 1882, it was Britain's task to bring forward the people within the pale of the civilized world, under an ordered government approved of by the public opinion of Europe. And there were always those who said these same things about the Irish, denying them Home Rule because they would abuse it. And they at least were not surprised when the first thing the Irish did when presented with freedom in 1922 was to start a civil war.

But men do not allocate a secondary and subordinate place to other men without developing a contempt for them. They can justify their dominance only on the assumption that these others are not worthy to share it. The subsequent anti-colonialist campaigns have accordingly had as their principal objective the release of whole peoples from this contempt, which is the most searing of all forms of bondage.

Imbued with the notion that the European nations had won their respective places in the sun by the exercise of their own talents, that success was the reward of virtue, their nationals judged as unprofitable servants those who had never invested any talents at all. In a survey of the Dutch East Indies in 1911, the writer refers to a current, anti-imperialist theory—that the natives should be left to arrange matters beween themselves—only to dismiss it as "simply puerile." For what did the record show? The natives of Indo-China had arranged matters by subjecting the Shans and the Cambodians to the tyranny of the Annamese. The peoples of the East Indian archipelago had for centuries arranged matters

[6] Cecil, *Conservatism*, IV, pp. 341–343.

by means of Malay and Achinese invasions, chronic piracy, head-
hunting, ritual murders, incessant warfare, depopulation, and
mental degeneration on every side. To pretend, then, that

a European domination, even with its regrettable blindness and failures
of justice, is not for the good of such peoples, is to deny the past, to
deny the petition of the victims in favour of the complaint of the
privileged despoiled of their privileges.[7]

It is unnecessary to read between these lines to find the assumptions that govern them. The people who so "arrange matters" are
people who block the paths of progress, people who do not now
and who will never comprehend what progress is; people who,
since they cannot be bodily removed from the scene, must be
confined within strict limits, that they may do no further damage
either to themselves or to others.

For these are people who, in a word, are not members of the
same moral order as the civilized. They are people who, since
they are not equals, cannot be treated as such. They are people
who belong to the dark or the medieval age, whom time has left
behind, and whose ignorance holds in check that potential expansion of the world's resources that Providence gave to it so that men
of resource and energy, Providence's own children (who must at
some time have thus baptized their parent), might exploit them.

This view of their fellow men was not, of course, invented by
the nineteenth century's imperialists. It had long been a commonplace among the educated and the privileged. Political philosophers had the habit of confiding their philosophies to those who
were most likely to appreciate them. Dante in his *De Monarchia*[8]
builds on the same foundations that support Aristotle's *Politics*:
certain races are born to govern, others to be governed. Dante
follows his own hero, Virgil, in praise of the majesty of Roman
power. It was by combat of man against man that the Romans
gained their Empire: "therefore it was by right that they gained it;
and this is the principal thesis of the present book."[9] This is the
doctrine that has long upheld those who plead imperial necessity

---

[7] A. Cabaton, *Java, Sumatra, and the Other Islands of the Dutch East Indies*
(London, 1911), p. 369.
[8] *De Monarchia*, written between 1310 and 1313. Printed in 1559.
[9] *Ibid.*, II, c. 7–11.

as its own justification (the British most notoriously in their naval actions at Copenhagen in 1807 and at Mers-el-Kebir in 1940). It has heartened those who, sincere devotees of good government, have wished to reinforce its beneficence with a religious sanction.

The structure of the Holy Roman Empire was based on the idea that by virtue of his plenitude of power the Pope was entitled to create the universal Roman Emperor in the West by transferring the imperial crown back from Byzantium to Rome, in order to escape his own subjection to the Greek Empire in the East.[10] Holy Roman Emperors therefore saw it as their spiritual and secular duty to spread Christianity, the more so since it contributed handsomely to their own aggrandizement. Germanic "crusades" in Slav lands precede by some three centuries the Frankish movement against Islam. Germanization and civilization in eastern Europe were very naturally equated, and time did not diminish the attraction of the equation. Hegel argued that the Germanic nations' destiny was to furnish support for the Christian principle, as well as to aid the development of the human intellect. Germany, because it was the civilized people *par excellence*, was the natural, indeed the only proper, guide for humanity at large. In these latter days, was it not Prussia which had freed all Europe of Napoleon's yoke? Were not the Germans the true successors of the Jews—a failed people, a people who had not carried out the mission God gave them? Were they not Germans, with their celebrated capacity for work and concentration, who were best equipped for this task, one that demanded the kind of organization that only a "fit," God-chosen, superior people was able to shape and control?

On this score the Germans were more vehement, perhaps because more convinced, than other Europeans; but the latter subscribed to the same sentiments—saving always the German claim to incorporate a superior type of humanity, which of course they thought nonsense. Both Mohandas Gandhi and Marcus Garvey, two dissidents who were lucky in never having to cope with an Imperial Germany in full flush, underline the point. To Gandhi

[10] Walter Ullmann, "Reflections on the Mediaeval Empire," *Transactions of the Royal Historical Society*, fifth series, vol. 14 (London, 1964), p. 89 ff.

imperialism was a system that was inherently corrupt simply because it was based on the assumption of the inferiority of others.[11]
It corrupted both those who held power and those who suc-
cumbed to it. Garvey, the first articulate voice to be heard from
the West Indies, also saw to the heart of this matter. In his judgment, the prejudice of the white race against the black race was
not so much because of color as of condition:

because as a race, to them, we have accomplished nothing; we have
built no nation, no government; and because we are dependent for
our economic and political existence.[12]

Superiority was thus based on accomplishment, and the moral
prestige of white men in a position of imperial power depended
very largely on their own continuing determination to assert it.
White men in the Union of South Africa, whose domestic position
belongs to the imperialist context, have always recognized their
own responsibility here. In 1925 their Premier, General Hertzog,
insisted that the native Bantu would need the guidance of the
white man for many years. The eventual aim must be to develop
and train him so that he could take charge of his own affairs in
his own territory. Even so, it was plain that both the affairs and the
territory lay and would continue to lie within a specific context.
Apartheid or segregation was from the outset seen as a solution
of the native question along lines which, without depriving the
native of his right of development, would recognize as paramount
the essentials of European civilization.

In fact, one form of development only was recognized: the one
that brought the colored man out of his darkness into the white
man's light, but never into the white man's path.

Imperialists who distinguished between those who were part of
their own moral order and those who were not nonetheless recognized that their very status of superiority imposed a moral duty
upon them. There could be no question as to their right to rule;
but how *best* to rule was a matter for fair debate.

Humanitarian justice was seen as an essential part of the equipment of the superior civilization, if it was really to deserve the

[11] Gandhi, *Young India*, p. 351.
[12] A. J. Garvey, ed., *The Philosophy and Opinions of Marcus Garvey* (New
York, 1923), p. 18.

name. Although an imperial power must deal daily with secondary and subordinate races, it was not justified in treating them as so much cattle, or worse. Indeed, an imperial power best justified its authority when it used it to prevent its own nationals from running riot on some distant frontier. It was evidence of the lack of a strong imperial policy, not of its enforcement, when "uncivilized" behavior went unchecked. The natives of Tasmania had been shot down in droves and given poisoned food. The great classical scholar Gilbert Murray, writing in 1901, could recall his Australian youth, when drunken graziers had spent their wild Saturday nights picking off the aborigines like game.[13] This however had not happened without arousing the indignation of colonial officials, one of whom, Herman Merivale, in lectures before an Oxford audience had argued that in no case ought a colonial legislature be allowed control over the natives in its own territory, since so much evidence proved that it would inevitably abuse it. That such authority belonged only to the imperial government was—surely?—a principle in which "even the most jealous friends of colonial freedom must acquiesce." For every native must be envisaged as, potentially, a citizen; but, until he realized that potential he must be protected, as a dependent. Plainly this was in his own interest. No doctrine of democracy or equality could confute this, for a state of fictitious equality was far worse for Kaffirs in southern Africa or Maoris in New Zealand "than one of acknowledged inferiority, with its correlative protection."[14]

What kind of protection should this be? What end should it have in view?

Throughout the nineteenth century high-minded men argued this out, far from the arena of democratic opinion. One voice comes from the mountains of Nepal. We profess to leave the Nepalese entirely to govern themselves, wrote the British Resident in 1843, and the only cases in which it is incumbent upon us to advise, demonstrate, or dictate, are when our own interests require such interposition. But the British government would be ill-represented (in Nepal or anywhere else) if every valuable

[13] Gilbert Murray, "The Exploitation of Inferior Races," *Liberalism and the Empire* (London, 1900), pp. 153–154.
[14] Herman Merivale, *Lectures on Colonies and Colonization* (Oxford, 1860, reprinted 1928), pp. 495, 522.

opportunity were not used to prompt to that which is good, and to deter from that which is evil; to express abhorrence of acts of cruelty, perfidy, and injustice; and to give full approbation of all that is benevolent, honest, high-minded, and just.[15]

Another voice comes from the waters of the central Pacific. The Governor of Fiji insisted in 1879 that it was of the utmost importance to seize, if possible, the spirit in which the native institutions had been framed, and try so to work them as to develop fully the latent capacities of the people for the management of their own affairs—and to do this without exciting their suspicion or destroying their self-respect.[16] The essence of this theory of indirect rule was that it did not seek to impose western values upon a primitive society. The duty of the imperial government was to hold the ring. Within that ring the natives' capacity for development would be given full scope, under the guidance of their own chiefs—who would in their turn remain under the surveillance of the imperial authority.

Yet that authority must not try to become a social agency. It must not act as a catalyst of change. When the Arab Sudan was finally taken under British control in 1899, the English Sirdar[17] saw to it that Friday, not Sunday, was the weekly holiday for everyone, and that no official permission was ever granted to any Christian body that sought to establish a mission within the northern half of the territory. Here was a straight reversion to eighteenth-century practice, carried out, with relief, by men of much that turn of mind. Warren Hastings had himself remarked that in Bengal it might indeed be a grievance to deprive the people of the protection of their own laws, but it was assuredly a wanton tyranny to require their obedience to others of which they were wholly ignorant, and of which they had no possible means of acquiring a knowledge.[18]

---

[15] Thomas Thomason to Sir Henry Lawrence, 18 November 1843: Sir Herbert Edwardes and Herman Merivale, *Life of Sir Henry Lawrence* (New York, 1873), p. 322.

[16] John Bastin, *The Native Policies of Stamford Raffles in Java and Sumatra* (Oxford, 1957), p. 43. The governor was Sir Arthur Gordon (Lord Stanmore).

[17] Hindu, from the Persian: a leader or commander.

[18] Bastin, *op. cit.*, p. xv.

But to later generations, quicker to analyze their consciences than Hastings', this begged a very large question. The imperial government might declare itself as trustee for the happiness of the backward and the uncivilized—but could it truly be asserted that men who were backward and uncivilized were in any state to pursue happiness, or capable of even knowing what it was? (A replete cannibal was, doubtless, happy enough). Should such not be wrenched out of, rather than preserved in, that condition? The Shanars in the district of Travancore, who were devil-worshippers, worshipped an Englishman as such for many years and on his death sought to placate his spirit with offerings of whisky and cigars.[19] Surely, there was a limit to what was allowable?

Long and hard, accordingly, was the battle fought between those who wanted to preserve the context of native life and those who were determined to get rid of customs which at best they looked on as totally useless and at worst as a set of odious superstitions. Everything monstrous and abominable in India, remarked the historian of the East India Company, J. W. Kaye, had the sanction of some puerile or obscene legend to recommend it to the superstitious and the depraved.[20]

When, for example, a British expedition from India in 1811 took the island of Java from the Dutch, Lord Minto, the Governor-General of Bengal, found that "the whole system of property [was] vicious and adverse alike to the interests of government and people."[21] His disciple, Stamford Raffles, setting to work to order the life of the Javanese under a better principle, enunciated that of native welfare, but found out that one man's view of another's good was always likely to prove controversial. He later wondered whether the policy of gradual pervasion, of setting a "good" example rather than of imposing a definite program of behavior, really served anyone's interests; whether

instead of continuing as heretofore to mould our government according to the vague and childish notions of an uncivilised people, we

---

[19] Kaye, *East India Company*, p. 652.
[20] *Ibid.*, p. 357.
[21] Bastin, *op. cit.*, p. 11.

ought not to act at once on the broad and enlightened principles which are recognised by all civilised countries.[22]

This debate, and the dilemma it set before those who took part in it, was never to be fully resolved. Authority, having begun by putting to question its own methods, ended by questioning its own rights, and so opened a gate into its own citadel.

They fared best in the battle who took up and held to their stand on moral superiority, since they presented but one front to the foe. John Lawrence remarked that in India, of all places, it was hopeless to try to do one's duty and at the same time to please the multitude. But he saw no dilemma here: clearly, duty must take priority over pleasure. "We are here by our moral superiority . . . in doing the best we can for the people we are bound by our conscience and not by theirs."[23] The conscious imperialists had thus the clearest consciences. Rationalists, they saw no need to have patience with the irrational. Utilitarians, they refused to dignify the futile. Civilized, they saw no point in pandering to the uncivilized.

The evangelical Christians, of whom John Lawrence was one, founded and staffed the school of thought that wished to purge in order to purify. They would not abide those who asserted that the task of government was to guide and protect society, but not to shape it. The pragmatic advice that Robert Dundas gave Minto in 1808 offended them deeply. It was desirable, wrote the East India Company's chairman, that a knowledge of Christianity should be imparted to the natives—but the means to be used for that end should be such only as were free of any political danger or alarm. He added that British paramount power imposed on it the necessity to protect the native inhabitants in the free and undisturbed possession of their religious opinions.[24] This could only strike those who were acquainted with these opinions as a form of blasphemy: and "John Company" was anathematized in evangelical circles as "the Churchwarden of the Idol."

Charles Grant, the Clapham "Saint," thundered against all those

---

[22] *Ibid.*, p. xix.
[23] R. Bosworth Smith, *Life of John Lawrence* (London, 1885), I, p. 440.
[24] C. H. Philips, *The East India Company* (Manchester, 1961), p. 164.

who took up this position, in a work whose very title epitomizes the "new broom" school: *Observations on the State of Society among the Asiatic Subjects of Great Britain, particularly with respect to morals; and on the Means of Improving It* (1797). For a Christian nation deliberately to say that it would prohibit the communication of that religion which came from God, to fifty millions of men, sunk in idolatry, superstition, and vice, was a proposition so monstrous and shocking, so contrary to the most rational and probable cause to be assigned for the conduct of Providence in committing so vast an Empire to England's care, "that I tremble at the thought of it and the consequences it would be likely to produce."[25]

The Company's historian was right in saying that Grant's sentiments were looked on by his contemporaries as those of an amiable fanatic, since they took it as an axiom that no method existed of introducing an alien religion into a deeply religious society which was free of political danger and alarm. But, writing in 1853, when there were over four hundred missionaries at work in the Indian field, Kaye could also rightly say that these sentiments were now, by *his* contemporaries, "looked upon as the language of calm and authoritative reason." The calm and authoritative Whig who was just then in charge of the Colonial Office, Lord Grey, displayed no evangelical fervors in his public conduct, but he was quite of Grant's opinion that a Christian nation would not be justified in throwing off the responsibility that Providence had placed on the British government. That government could not, therefore, turn its back on the white settlers and the Kaffirs in southern Africa while they struggled for possession of the soil, for that would both leave to the devil's care the hindmost, and cast the Kaffirs in the hindmost's role.[26]

It was not enough, therefore, to own an Empire. One had also to formulate a policy to deal with it—and that policy must be based on Christian doctrine. That this was duty, was clear.

The foremost propagandists for this doctrine were naturally the churches themselves. The Catholic weekly *The Tablet* sum-

[25] Quoted in Kaye, *op. cit.*, p. 639.
[26] Earl Grey, *The Colonial Policy of Lord John Russell's Administration* (London, 1853), II, 254.

marized an extreme form of it on 9 September 1933, with a
sublime disregard of every political consideration whatever. The
Eternal Word of God, it observed, might have chosen to become
incarnate in the womb of a black or yellow or red or copper-
colored mother, but He did not so choose. The Angel of Annun-
ciation delivered his message to a white maid in a white man's
land, and therefore it was no arrogance, but a reverend and
dutiful obedience to the course marked out by divine Providence,
which required white men to wield hegemony of Christendom.
The choicest of non-whites knew this, and were content that it
should be so. It therefore followed that the maintenance and
enhancement of the whites' moral prestige among those who wore
other skins was of inestimable importance to Religion, and not
only to imperial and secular interests.[27]

The wearers of other skins were not likely to distinguish between the religious and the secular outlook of the European, since
the European did not make such a distinction himself. It was anyway a tradition in "the Far East" that missionaries were the
advance agents not of a higher but of a foreign power. The
"Christian century in Japan" (1540–1640) was long gone, but not
forgotten; while in China toleration of Christianity had been
withdrawn in 1724 and was only reauthorized under duress of a
concert of foreign powers in 1860.

A superior attitude towards the alien culture was an intrinsic
part of the missionary's equipment: he could hardly have claimed
a vocation had he not possessed this. Time altered his methods
but not his outlook. Francis Xavier had been free with his opinion,
offered in praise, that Japan was "the finest of uncivilised nations,"[28] while Alessandro Valignano the Jesuit director had noted
of the Japanese that they would not suffer being slapped or beaten,
nor imprisonment, "nor any similar methods commonly used with
other Asiatic Christians," nor would they endure, like the inhabitants of Portuguese Goa, being marched to church in squads of

[27] Quoted in George Padmore, *How Britain Rules Africa* (London, 1936),
pp. 389–390. I owe this reference to Dr. Gabriel O. Olusanya, of Ahmadu
Bello University, Nigeria, whose Ph.D. thesis (Toronto, 1964), "The Impact
of the Second World War on Nigeria's Political Evolution," deserves publication.
[28] K. G. Jayne, *Vasco da Gama and His Successors* (London, 1910), p. 219.

fifty.[29] But in China Christianity met with a more deeply entrenched and authoritative ideology than it did either in Japan or in many parts of India. Confucianism was the state religion as well as a personal ethic, and the officials and *literati* of the Middle Kingdom opposed the European religion in much the same spirit as they had, centuries before, opposed that other foreign and corrupting influence, Buddhism.

They particularly distrusted a religion that assured its followers happiness after death. Persons who fixed their eyes on the next world might well prove hostile to the constituted temporal authorities of this. (West-Indian planters in the eighteenth century had vetoed the Christian instruction of their Negro slaves for exactly this reason.) They marked the pretensions to Christianity voiced by the leaders of the Tai'ping movement between 1851 and 1864: Hung Hsui Ch'uan, the Tai'pings' rebel "Emperor," described himself as a messenger from heaven and referred to Jesus Christ as his elder brother. They noted the missionaries' practice of granting annual stipends and other favors to their "converts," and they very readily transferred their contempt for these "rice-Christians," the riffraff of the ports, to those who were so easily fooled yet who still proclaimed a higher standard of conduct and a deeper insight into the ways of the world. They reckoned the Catholics, who employed a Chinese priesthood, a more insidious enemy than the Protestants: but in fact the Chinese intellectual could make no distinction between Protestants and Catholics—to the mortification of both, who naturally responded by a redoubling of their respective missionary effort. But as the Manchu dynasty weakened, and as the skirts of its Empire were ever more easily rent by the European powers, China was compelled to give ground before these spiritual *condottieri* of the invading ideology. In 1858, after a half-century in China, the total number of Protestant missions amounted to eighty only, confined to the five Treaty Ports and to Hong Kong. But by 1905 that number had been multiplied forty times, and the missionaries were working where they pleased throughout the Empire.

By their regular appeals to their own governments for protec-

---

[29] C. R. Boxer, *The Christian Century in Japan 1549–1650* (Berkeley, California, 1951), p. 79.

tion, the French and British missions, later reinforced by those from Germany and the United States, continually fueled the charge of imperialism brought against all aliens in China. One of Karl Marx's few uses of the word refers to events in that country during 1857, in a passage that also includes the term "civilisation-mongers."[30] The missionary was the first foreigner permitted to travel into the interior. He was a privileged person, not because of his calling but because he could, if checked, spark the wrath of the Christian powers who had looted and burned the Summer Palace in Pekin.

In his own eyes, the missionary was the messenger at once of the gospel of Christ, and the gospel of progress—yet what was progress to a cultivated Chinese, mused a European consul, "but the free introduction of a pushing, self-willed, and eccentric race?"[31] But detachment of that kind was not possible to the Chinese. Nor could the missionaries, equally committed, who saw themselves, in good faith, as the true friends of China, reconcile themselves to the obstructions that were put in their way without vehement protest. One British Foreign Secretary, Lord Clarendon, indeed remarked in 1869 that really the missionaries required protection less against the Chinese than against each other, since they seemed to live in a state of perpetual bickering and mistrust;[32] but, as an aristocrat, he had no love for what his class termed "enthusiasm," or for the vulgarities of "Exeter Hall." Neither had Rutherford Alcock, a consular veteran: China, in his view, was right to see in Christianity yet another sword in her flank. In the end, he noted, the whole question of the missionaries' difficulties resolved itself into one of peace or war; for the propagation of Christianity could continue at all only under the menace of forcible intervention by one or more foreign powers against the will of the rulers of China, and in defiance of the moral convictions of the Chinese people.[33] This indictment of Christianity, that it was a white man's religion, to be tolerated only so long as the white man was powerful, was never to be withdrawn.

[30] Marx, *On Colonialism*, p. 127.
[31] Medhurst, *Far Cathay*, p. 194.
[32] 9 March 1869: Paul Cohen, *China and Christianity* (Harvard, 1963), p. 195.
[33] *Ibid.*, p. 199.

Thus imperialism, whether it was spiritual or lay or an amalgam of both, effectively expressed the purposes of the belligerent European civilization. It did not often pause to assess whether it was making a durable impression on those whom it physically controlled: only the missionaries took this issue to heart. So long as energy was abundant, its authority would be secure. Imperialists, the accredited agents of their civilization, intended to promote peace, order, the prevention of crime, the redress of wrong, the enforcement of contracts, the development and concentration of their own military forces, the construction of public works, and the collection and expenditure of the revenue required for all these objects "in such a way as to promote to the utmost the public interest." There were always officials who knew that the imperial coinage, the imperial medals, had their other side. One of them categorized the items listed above as "somewhat grim presents" for one people to make to another—but none the worse for that.[34] Henry Lawrence, like his brother John a faithful servant of the Indian system, who was to die in its defense at Lucknow during the Mutiny of 1857, commented in 1843 how erroneous it was to reckon on the attachment, in any crisis, of the peoples of India:

. . . as if any Hindu or Mohammedan *could* love his Christian lord, who only comes before him as master or tax-gatherer; as if it were not absurd to suppose that the chiefs of Burma, Nepal, Lahore and the like could tolerate the Power that restrains their rapacious desires and habits—that degrades them in their own, and each other's, eyes.[35]

But there were always, too, a great number of imperial officials who saw no need to trouble themselves with this kind of analysis. It was also in 1843 that Sir Charles Napier conquered the province of Sind in northwestern India: and he made a riposte to some brand-new subjects of the Company's *Raj* that became deservedly famous. They came to plead before him for permission to retain certain of their time honored social customs. Be it so, said Napier magnanimously,

This burning of widows is your custom. Prepare the funeral pile. But my nation has also a custom. When men burn women alive, we hang

[34] Sir James Fitzroy Stephen, *A History of the Criminal Law in England* (London, 1883), III, pp. 344–345; Stokes, *Utilitarians and India,* p. 285.
[35] Edwardes and Merivale, *Henry Lawrence,* p. 313.

them and confiscate all their property. My carpenters shall therefore erect gibbets on which to hang all concerned when the widow is consumed. Let us all act according to national customs.[36]

This forthright language is a measure of the depth of contempt felt. It was an attitude that the English were sometimes to mute but seldom entirely to lose. In India their eyebrows, from the outset, remained raised. Lord Cornwallis, Bengal's Governor-General in 1792, declared his belief that every native of Hindostan was corrupt.[37] A century later Lord Roberts, on his retirement as England's foremost "sepoy-general," testified in his autobiography *Forty-One Years in India* (1897) that in that country evidence on almost any subject could be had for the buying. He added that, however well-educated and adept a native might be, and however brave he might have proved himself, it was his own belief that no rank that the government could bestow on such a man would cause him to be considered as an equal by the British officer.[38] This opinion died hard. An official committee, examining in 1921 the problem of "Indianizing" the Army, thought the business would take forty years, and considered segregation as a possible solution to the difficulty of getting white officers to serve under Indian officers.

The overriding problem, as seen by India's masters, centered on the matter of "character." By this was meant the qualities of energy and initiative, probity and loyalty, with the self-respect that was their natural accompaniment. Prestige rested upon conduct; and Macaulay had declared that English valor and English intelligence had done less to extend and preserve England's Empire in the East than English veracity. Throughout the nineteenth century public schools were founded in England with no other purpose than to inculcate these qualities in the young. No institution in India was thought likely to do as much for the Hindu, whose character had been formed, and continued to operate, within a very different context. The misappropriation of

[36] Sir William Napier, *History of General Sir Charles Napier's Administration of Scinde* (London, 1851), p. 35.
[37] Quoted in L. S. S. O'Malley, *The Indian Civil Service 1601–1930* (London, 1931), p. 16.
[38] Lord Roberts, *Forty-One Years in India*, thirty-fifth, one-volume edition (London, 1905), p. 248.

public funds, remarks one twentieth-century commentator, was generally regarded more as a subject for mirth and envy than reprobation;[39] while another records his discovery that an enlightened ruler of a princely State, the founder of many schools and other useful institutions, a nobleman highly eulogized by Lord Curzon himself, held no greater place in popular memory or esteem than his successor, who had to be deposed for drunkenness and riotous living, have squandered the State's resources on merry-making, fireworks, and colorful debauches.[40]

Earlier observers took a severer tone. James Mill's *History of India*, a six-volume bible which every aspiring Company cadet took with him on his first ship out, describes the natives of India, and the Chinese for good measure, as dissembling, treacherous, mendacious, cowardly, unfeeling, conceited, and unclean, the victims of despotism and priestcraft.[41] (Mill never visited either India or China, and there is no record of his ever having met a native; but Robert Morrison, the London Missionary Society's solitary representative in China, had written home in 1817 urging his superiors that they should henceforth tell all future missionaries to the Chinese "that of this people it is true—'All men are liars.'")[42] Young men who arrived in Asia with these preconceptions grew to be old men without having found any occasion for changing them. In 1876 a distinguished senior remarked that executive government posts demanded qualities other than intellectual, such as energy, decision, self-reliance, power of combination and organization, of managing men, "and so on."[43] No Indians qualified under those headings: in 1870, of the 325 candidates who applied for 40 vacancies in the Indian Civil Service, seven were Indians, and one passed.

Sir Walter Scott once commented how the lesser gentry of Scot-

---

[39] L. S. S. O'Malley, ed., *Modern India and the West* (Oxford, 1941), p. 156.

[40] Penderel Moon, *Divide and Quit* (London, 1961), pp. 101–102.

[41] James Mill, *History of India*, Second Edition (London, 1820), II, p. 195.

[42] I owe this reference to Mr. Lawrence Kitzan, whose Ph.D. thesis (Toronto, 1965) deals with the first years of the London Missionary Society in India and China.

[43] Sir Richard Temple, 5 June 1876: quoted in Majumdar, *British Paramountcy*, p. 789.

land sent their younger sons to India, as automatically as they sent their black cattle to market in the south. G. O. Trevelyan's *Letters from a Competition Wallah* (1865) tell how boys brought up in "Anglo-Indian"[44] families looked upon India as their birthright. Here was Tom, for example, at the age of thirty-one in charge of a population as numerous as that of England in the reign of Elizabeth. How could any member of the Service, with so broad a horizon stretching before him, feel any misgiving concerning the dignity and importance of his work?[45]

Few did. But the thought of young Tom, turned loose to dispense high, middle, and low justice in the Deccan or Rajputana with what assistance his character could give him, disturbed some commentators. On the one side an attractive image was presented of the fair-haired Saxon youth opposing his well-trained intellect to the new difficulties which crowded around him. Alternatively, as the same historian points out, this same youth might be assessed as

an ignorant upstart, slenderly acquainted with the native languages, and not at all acquainted with native feelings, laying down the law . . . and committing errors of the most irritating kind with an incredible amount of assurance and conceit.[46]

But this assurance was in fact the key to any situation; and the system, the machinery of the *Raj*, was reckoned flexible enough to circumvent the consequences of anyone whose assurance turned out to be ill-founded.

The older school of officialdom felt anyway that it was the competition-wallah himself, product of the examination system, who was likelier to make a fool of himself, since his intelligence had been trained without reference to the quality of his instinct. Henry Lawrence's biographer commented, admiringly, on that hero of the Punjab and the Mutiny, that he would have been

---

[44] In Victorian dialogue, "Anglo-Indian" signified an Englishman who had an official position in the *Raj*, past or present. "Eurasian" signified a man of mixed European and Indian blood. In the twentieth century, and particularly after 1919, the Eurasians adopted the term "Anglo-Indian" to describe themselves, without however the approval of the original Anglo-Indians.

[45] G. O. Trevelyan, *Letters from a Competition Wallah* (London, 1865), pp. 113, 120.

[46] Kaye, *East India Company*, p. 260.

failed by the examiners for a cadetship in the Indian Army, "a fate which, under the circumstances, must have befallen Nelson himself, and about three-quarters of the heroes to whom England owes her glory."[47] At the turn of the century in the Sudan, its new British masters were still anxious to recruit to the ranks of government not intellectuals but tent-and-saddle men, men who "fitted in," men who had for example the social grace to prefer Turkish to Virginia cigarettes.[48] A competitive examination was in almost any case an absurd method of selection for administrative personnel, "where character is of the first importance."[49] This dogma lodged itself in far places. When the Japanese set up their National Foundation Training Institute in Java in April 1945, they insisted on character, not scholastic ability, as a prerequisite in their students, and were forever seeking "sincerity" in their relations with the various nationalities of their Co-Prosperity Sphere.[50]

An exported civilization looked for its own reflection where it could find it: not an easy task, but easier than setting up courses in perpetual schoolmastering. The kind of character that the English appreciated was to be found in India, they felt, far oftener among hillmen than among plainsmen, among hostile Muslim tribesmen than among servile Bengali clerks. In the hills could be found, in Lord Curzon's phrase, the common bond of manhood, a type of outdoors comradeship (reminiscent of school playing fields) among men who respected one another. An instinct for recognizing this "was the secret of the success of every great frontier officer that we have ever had."[51] It was a misfortune for both sides that the earliest conquests in India took place in Bengal: for had the English encountered sooner in their imperial career the Hindu warrior-races—Marathas, Rajputs, Sikhs—they would not have formed so harsh a stereotype of the "native

---

[47] Edwardes and Merivale, *Henry Lawrence*, p. 450.

[48] Sir Ronald Storrs says so in his *Orientations;* and see R. Wingate, *Wingate of the Sudan* (London, 1955): "There was a time when cynics criticised the Sudan Civil Service as composed entirely of 'Blues' [i.e. Oxford or Cambridge men who had played or rowed for their University]," p. 135.

[49] *Ibid.*, p. 135.

[50] W. H. Elsbree, *Japan's Role in South-East Asian Nationalist Movements, 1940–45* (Harvard, 1953), p. 105.

[51] 7 November 1898: Curzon, *Speeches in India*, I, p. 11.

character." Much in contrast was their instinctive reaction to the world of Islam. This had a long pedigree. It perhaps began with the eastern odyssey of Lady Hester Stanhope (1810–39). It gained strength from Eliot Warburton's *The Crescent and The Cross* (1848). It borrowed an aura of mystery from Disraeli's *Tancred* (1847). It attracted the satire, even at this early stage, of Thackeray, in his personification of "young Mr. Bedwin Sands." Its principal misconception, one that would have puzzled the medieval Crusaders, Tancred included, was that Christian civilization had a lot in common with that of Islam.

The nature of this sympathetic fallacy (which in popular fiction was to make of the *sheikh*, pre-eminently a tent-and-saddle man, a figure of high romance, and in reality helped to detach T.E. Lawrence from the world of the practicable entirely) was early grasped by the Hindus, who accurately judged the estimate in which their masters held them. It led them to popularize the cry that the British were holding India not by the exercise of justice but by expediency, by means of the old Roman method of "divide and rule." It was also a leaf taken from the book of imperialism in Ireland; for, as that country's first modern nationalist, Wolfe Tone, had discerned, the English maintained their ascendancy there "by perpetuating the spirit of internal dissension grounded on religious distinctions."[52] In Ireland, too, did not the English use the weapon of contempt? Had there not been "a systematic defamation" of the Irish character ever since the Act of Union in 1800?[53]—with the result that few Englishmen took either the Irish or the Irish Question seriously, or saw it as a matter to be discussed between equals?

Whether it was policy or merely instinct, "divide and rule" certainly suited the book of the Indian Muslims, since there was no doubt, if ever they had to choose between a British and a Hindu *Raj*, which could expect their support. They kept in mind the precepts of their first leader, Syed Ahmad Khan. Think for a moment, he had urged in 1887, what the result would be if all government appointments were allocated by competitive examination; "there would remain no part of the country in which we

[52] W. E. H. Lecky, *A History of Ireland in the Eighteenth Century*, New Edition (London, 1892), III, p. 222.
[53] Erskine Childers, *The Framework of Home Rule* (London, 1911), p. 23.

should see at the tables of justice and authority any face except those of Bengalis."[54] It was a thought not then, and not ever, to be borne.

Thus, although the British denied the charge that they were dividing in order to rule, their sympathies in fact lay at no great distance from their policies, as two Viceroys of the same era bear witness. In 1893 Lord Lansdowne's government in India reported on a resolution previously passed by the House of Commons in England, to the effect that examinations for entry into the Indian Civil Service should be held simultaneously in England and in India (and not, as heretofore, in England alone). The report declared that a material reduction of the European staff then employed in India would be incompatible with the safety of British rule, and that any system of unrestricted competition would also practically exclude from the imperial Service

Muhammedans, Sikhs, and other races accustomed to rule by tradition and possessed of exceptional strength of character, but deficient in literary education.[55]

In 1906 another Viceroy, Lord Minto (more tory than his ancestor a century back), cordially welcomed a Muslim delegation led by the Aga Khan. They justly claimed, he said, that their position should be estimated not merely on their numerical strength but in respect to the political importance of their community, and the service it had rendered to the Empire: "I am entirely in accord with you."[56] It is thus not surprising that one of the aims of the All-India Muslim League, founded that year, was to promote feelings of loyalty toward the British *Raj*. This contrasted remarkably with the drive of the Hindu National Congress towards self-government.

To inculcate the principles of one's own civilization in men in whose company was felt at best a deep bewilderment, and at worst as deep an antipathy, was a task always too great for the pragmatic, nonphilosophic rulers of India, who assumed that their

[54] C. H. Philips, ed., *Select Documents on the Evolution of India and Pakistan 1858–1947* (Oxford, 1962), pp. 187–188.
[55] Quoted in Majumdar, *British Paramountcy*, p. 790.
[56] V. B. Kulkarni, *British Statesmen in India* (Bombay, 1964), p. 263.

own degree of civilization was so self-evident as not to need any propaganda in its behalf. As a result, an English authority on eastern religions doubted that Christianity would ever make much progress in Asia, since what was commonly known by that name was not the teaching of Christ but a rearrangement of it made in Europe and, like most European institutions, practical rather than thoughtful.[57] The British Empire also was practical rather than thoughtful. In it the formulation of policy depended not so much on any philosophy of empire as upon the economic and social conditions that existed in the colonial field, and upon the economic relationship between the colony and the metropolis.[58] But even British pragmatism was hard put to it to accommodate both the doctrine that dependencies should eventually graduate into self-governing status, and the conviction that in the Indian case this would never be practicable.

For the Hindus were simply not to be trusted within the arcana of the *Raj*. Their "character" was too faulty: or the structure of their personality was too different. Whatever the terms of the verdict, the consequences were clear. It was not safe to acquaint men so innately unreliable, so unaware of Anglo-Saxon codes of civilized behavior, with state secrets on military and foreign affairs: as late as 1942 Stafford Cripps on his mission to India was authorized to accommodate the Congress on many points, but *not* on the immediate creation of a Ministry of Defense, with a Hindu in charge.

It was Lord Lytton, the only Viceroy (1874–80) who was also an intellectual and a poet, who put on record the true nature of the dilemma in which the officers of the *Raj* found themselves. Such phrases as "religious toleration," "liberty of the press," "personal freedom of the subject," "social supremacy of the law," and others, which in England conveniently summarized ideas of long standing and broad appeal, were in India, to the vast mass of the natives there, only the mysterious formulae of a foreign and uncongenial system of administration. They produced bafflement. By enforcing these principles and establishing these institutions,

[57] Sir Charles Eliot, *Hinduism and Buddhism* (London, 1921), I, p. xcviii.
[58] Bastin, *Raffles in Java*, p. xii.

We have placed, and must perpetually maintain ourselves, at the head of a gradual but gigantic revolution—the greatest and most momentous social, moral, and religious, as well as political revolution, which, perhaps, the world has ever witnessed.[59]

The western-educated Hindu was putting forward many claims. He was nursing many expectations. But they were claims and expectations of a kind that never could or would be fulfilled. Believing this, the rulers of India

have had to choose between prohibiting them and cheating them—and we have chosen the least straightforward course.[60]

For what future lay before the "babu," the English-educated clerk, who had learned to simulate but had not the capacity to emulate? He represented nothing but the social anomaly of his own position.[61]

What Lytton could discern in 1878 became much plainer to the sharply critical eyes of the next generation. Mary Kingsley deduced from her West African experience that the white race would never "drag the black race up to their own particular summit in the mountain range of civilization."[62] Cecil Rhodes declared that the missionaries were wrong, for they were civilizing in the wrong direction. When they turned out men who were capable of administering the telegraph and postal systems, and of doing carpentry and managing machines, they would be doing their job: for these were the men who would get the franchise without any difficulty. Who wanted Kaffir parsons who knew Latin and Greek?[63] Gilbert Murray, all his long life a liberal, was also a convinced paternalist. White men were superior to black, brown, red, and yellow men; "that is to say, that on the whole the first mentioned colour tends to rule and the other colours to obey."[64] Hobson's *Imperialism* stressed the disappointment that lay at the end of the road, one to confound both the ruler and the ruled:

[59] Balfour, *Lytton's Administration*, pp. 511–512.
[60] Quoted in Majumdar, *op. cit.*, p. 787.
[61] Lady Betty Balfour, *Personal Letters of Robert Earl of Lytton* (London, 1906), II, p. 21.
[62] Kingsley, *Travels in West Africa*, p. 680.
[63] Vindex, *Cecil Rhodes*, pp. 366, 383.
[64] Murray, "Exploitation," p. 134.

We are incapable of implanting our civilisation in India by present methods of approach: we are only capable of disturbing their civilisation.[65]

And this civilization, whether disturbed or left to stagnate, still commanded no respect from the aliens in its midst. Very few of the able, energetic officials who administered the British Empire from Downing Street, or in the field, either believed that the populations they ruled were capable of being trained for effective free self-government, or geared their policy to accommodate such a contingency in the near or remote future. They were certainly committed to a policy of educating natives along western lines, but they remained pessimistic as to the results of this process. Men who distrusted intellectual development when they encountered it among their fellow Englishmen were no more inclined to welcome it in their subordinates.

One bad omen was the indolent sophistication of the *effendi* class in Egypt, French in culture but not in action: for here again was emphasized the usual result of a European system of education on the Oriental mind: a mind that absorbed learning quickly but superficially and, of course, "without the stability of character that learning should bring."[66] Egypt accordingly, in the opinion of the imperialist periodical *The Round Table* in December 1918, provided an example of those countries of the Near East for which there was at present "no hope, except in the guardianship of some civilised state."[67] In India the guardians remained resolved to entrench themselves. They neither wished nor hoped that native officials should one day become the servants of a free Indian nation. "We do our humble best," said the Viceroy, Lord Curzon, in 1905, "to retain by justice what we have won by the sword."[68]

The sword might be acceptable: but the humility, the excellence, and the justice were not. In the East the arbitrament of the sword had always been better understood than a concept of justice whose terms of reference belonged to an alien tradition.

[65] Hobson, *Imperialism*, p. 266.
[66] Sir Archibald Wavell, *Allenby in Egypt* (London, 1943), p. 37.
[67] *The Round Table*, no. 33 (December 1918), p. 23.
[68] Curzon, *Speeches in India*, I, p. 5.

Similarly with all other forms of action in India, since the context was mysterious, the action was unintelligible.

Englishmen in the East, wrote a distinguished jurist with Indian experience, Sir Henry Maine, came into contact with vast populations of a high natural intelligence, to which the very notion of innovation was loathsome.[69] The very fact that such populations existed suggested that the true difference between the East and the West lay in the fact that in western countries there was a larger minority of exceptional persons who, for good reasons or bad, had a real desire for change. From the English proconsul in Egypt, Lord Cromer, came the same testimony. When the European once stepped outside of the influence acquired by the power of the sword and looked for any common ground of understanding with the subject race, he found that he was, by the elementary facts of the case, debarred from using all those moral influences which in more homogeneous countries bound society together.[70]

The western-educated saw this problem from another angle. They saw it from below. Intelligent aliens could gauge the breadth of the gap that lay between ruler and ruled; but the ruled knew its nature and the humiliation engendered by living a life at secondhand. Gandhi when on trial in March 1922 said that he was satisfied that many English and indeed Indian officials honestly believed that they were administering one of the best systems devised in the world, and that India was making steady, if slow, progress. What they did not know was that a subtle but effective system of terrorism and an organized display of force on the one hand, and the deprivation of all powers of retaliation and self-defense on the other, had emasculated the people and induced in them the habit of simulation.[71] But Cromer, too, had noticed this: "the common oriental habit of endeavouring to say what is pleasant to the interrogator, especially if he occupies some post of authority."[72] And it was with this same diagnosis that Southern Rhodesia's Lord Malvern shocked the more sensitive

[69] Sir Henry Maine, *Popular Government* (London, 1885), p. 97.
[70] Lord Cromer, *Political and Literary Essays 1908–13* (London, 1913), I, p. 252.
[71] Gandhi, at his trial on 23 March 1922; *Young India,* p. 1053.
[72] Cromer, *op. cit.,* p. 83.

ears of the 1950's when he said it out loud: "All Africans are liars." There was, therefore, a particularly vicious circle here. The rulers despised the ruled because they lacked character. But the system of government that the rulers imposed was such as to prevent the ruled from expressing any character worth the name. A mutual bewilderment and exasperation thus persisted.

This, it appeared, was the upshot of what a governor of Bombay had called, in 1860, the perilous experiment of continuing to legislate for millions of people, with few means of knowing, except by a rebellion, whether the laws suited them or not.[73]

Within the context of domestic law and order, and an external *Pax Britannica*, in touch with a higher civilization than their own, native societies *should* have been content, should have thrived, should, above all, have *changed*. The British were not alone in feeling this. The French, squaring to the same tasks with a better logic and a firmer agenda, met with the same disappointments. The French doctrine of assimilation, the making of Frenchmen out of non-French materials, was one for which the English had an instinctive dislike: the more another people acquired the English culture, one official noted (and in a published report), the wider became the gulf between. That he was right, the exclusively white membership of India's Byculla Club, and all its progeny throughout the colonial tropics, attests. British colonial policy indeed set its face against cultural integration. A paternalist philosophy could not accommodate any such notion. Imperialism included no melting-pot in its equipment. Natives must live in their own, native world, purified by benevolent authority. It was a cardinal principle, declared the maker of modern Nigeria, at whose feet policy makers were later to sit, that the interest of a large native population should not be subject to the will either of a small European class of settlers or of a small minority of educated natives who had nothing in common with them and whose interests were often opposed to theirs.[74]

Such ideas were perhaps the product of English insularity of thought; but from that fault Frenchmen were, by definition, free.

[73] Sir Bartle Frere; quoted in Majumdar, *op. cit.*, p. 757.
[74] Sir Frederick Lugard's "Report on the Amalgamation of Northern and Southern Nigeria, 1912–1919" (H. M. Stationery Office, London, 1920, Cmd. 468), p. 19.

For France saw herself not only as a warden of civilization, but as its founder. We have not come to Algeria to oppress and exploit the people, Napoleon III insisted, "but to bring them the benefits of civilization."[75] The Emperor styled himself King of the Arabs as from 1863—but if he deluded himself on France's role, he was in good company. The historian Michelet, Lyautey the founder of French Morocco, Hanotaux the imperialist official, all spoke the same language:

France was the heir both of Rome and of the Christian Church in *la terre d'outre-mer*. She could not avoid her responsibilities: Michelet said that "tongs of necessity" held France in their grip.[76] France was therefore, by her own nature, *une nation doctrinaire*. Colonies were a part of the indivisible Republic, and France could do no other than assimilate them and the lives that were lived within them to the life and culture of the metropolis. She was prepared to scan British methods and ideas concerning the administration of territories overseas; the English were a hard-headed and adaptable race, and on anything pragmatic and practical they were safe guides. But, trameled to their doctrine of individual right, they had worked out no philosophy of the state and could take nothing beyond their own borders other than the talent, or lack of talent, of a particular generation of colonial officials. France in contrast lived by a political philosophy; and even Jules Ferry, "English" in his approach to the colonial question, warmed to the romance that was its essence. It was necessary to find new markets for French manufactures, yes: but there was more to it than that. Higher races had a duty to civilize lower races; and this he maintained before the uproar of deputies in the Chamber, who thundered at him "Rights of Man! Seventeen Eighty-Nine!" To withdraw or to abstain from the task was simply to take "le grand chemin de la décadence!"[77]

The universe, which French philosophy included and which indeed in one sense it had invented, contained a great many of these lower races. They posed a problem. How noble was the

[75] R. F. Betts, *Assimilation and Association in French Colonial Theory, 1890–1914* (New York, 1961), p. 19.
[76] Jules Michelet, *Le Peuple* (Paris, 1846), p. 246.
[77] Quoted in Delavignette and Julien, *Constructeurs*, p. 297.

savage was still a racking question. The confident answer given it by the eighteenth century's philosophers did not, a century later, convince those who faced it. To say the noble savage existed meant only that he was capable of existence: that, guided by a civilized power, that is to say France, his latent nobility, his whole potentiality for life, would show forth.

The policy of *assimilation*, which aimed at this result, has been defined as "that system which tends to efface all difference between the colonies and the motherland."[78] It was a form of seduction—and it could boast many gallants, among them the Jesuits of New France who sought at their great peril to make Christians, even if they could never make Frenchmen, out of the most unpromising human material on earth. But it posed its own problem. Were these lower races ineluctably stratified, as Gobineau in 1852 had described them? Were they incapable of graduation to higher levels? Were they destined only to be the drawers of water for the engineers of progress? Gobineau had convinced many thoughtful Germans that civilization, as such, was, to such, incommunicable. Was he right? For if he was right, assimilation was a vain hope.

The French anthropologists Emile Durkheim and Gustave Le-Bon did not believe in it, or in racial fusion either. There were laws of evolution which refuted it, were there not? They and their disciples founded a school of colonial sociology which no other nation ever matched—LeBon wrote on *Les Lois psychologiques de l'Evolution des peuples* (1891), his pupil Ernest Seillière on *La Philosophie de l'Impérialisme* (1903–07)—and from which came much news of *négritude* and *l'âme noire*. Was not, then, the policy of *association*, equivalent to the forms of indirect rule practiced in many diverse territories by the empirical Dutch and British, a better answer to the problem? If it was really impossible to make every *noir* into a *blanc*, was not the alternative to keep him close by, within the security of his own society, in the faith that its contact with French civilization would lead it gradually to take a place in the great world? One of the great weaknesses of the Roman Empire, surely, had been that the masses were not

[78] Roberts, *French Colonial Policy*, p. 67.

touched by any concept of *Romanitas,* by Roman culture at its best. Whatever method of colonization was adopted, this must not happen in any Empire worthy of the French name.

These *savants* could call on support from the martial ranks of the empire builders themselves. Louis Faidherbe took with him into western Africa much the same view of Islam as that of the crusading Franks in Syria. It was an obstruction to all that passed under the name of progress. In 1859 he was already convinced that Senegal would have to be united with Algeria, with Timbuktu as the lynchpin of a great French African Empire, a *champ d'honneur* indeed: the idea became a government policy twenty years later, save that its new pivot was Lake Chad. Joseph Galliéni, ranging France's domains from Senegal in 1877, to Tonkin in 1892, to Madagascar in 1896, also did not believe in philosophical formulae or imported principles, and his successes ensured that his successors mirrored his views. To him also the Muslim presence in Africa was something that must be expunged: and when he made treaties with the Islamic states of Samory and Ahmadou in the Niger basin it was only to forestall the British; he had no intention of honoring them. He advised his successor as *Commandant-Supérieur du Soudan* to consider all Muslim chiefs "comme des gens à faire disparaître et à ruiner avant peu d'années."[79]

These soldiers preferred to act as benevolent despots, *les bons tyrans.* They presented more *faits accomplis* to irritated civilian governments than ever British soldiers did, and the doctrine that "the man on the spot" was bound to be right was always also more French than British. The civilian "colonialists" were accordingly dubious about the nature of military expansionism, which did much of its work through African *tirailleurs,* native troops which served in hope of plunder and women; and no French government ever intended the military to carve out so vast an empire. Yet it was so carved, and it made its mark on French pride, even in Paris: those who had ejected Ferry for too much imperialism in Indo-China in 1885 were hounding Ribot in 1890 for not being imperialist enough in West Africa and the Sudan.

[79] "People who will be lost and gone before very long": I owe this reference to Mr. A. Kanya-Forstner, whose Ph.D. thesis (Cambridge, 1964) deals with French military imperialism in western and equatorial Africa.

Frenchmen who were not imperialists continued to see the whole task as grandiose and unnecessary. If crusades were to be mounted once more, there were places nearer home than Dahomey where they might do more good. Had not Ernest Renan diagnosed, once for all, that rural France itself lay as far from any knowledge and practice of French culture as any island of the New Hebrides—"a vast Scythia"? They objected to the romanticism, clerical, military, and lay, that was bred and nurtured within the hothouse confines of Empire. To the Radical Georges Clemenceau imperialism was only a policy of national chauvinism. Yet it lived on. And it did not, at the last, die: it was killed, by the pragmatism of the metropolis, whose civilians could never trace the outlines of any *champ d'honneur* amid the guerillas and atrocities of Indo-China and Algeria. In the mid-twentieth century the last agents of European imperialism and its doctrine of power were officers of the French Army, who manned its bulwarks with a bitter tenacity and did this not in allegiance to the Fourth Republic but in loyalty to a doctrine of superiority which was rooted in the nature of the task.

It needs imagination to devise and promote a doctrine.

But it needs very much less to follow its tenets. Assimilation in practice demanded a uniformity of treatment, which in turn bred a vast petty bureaucracy, as suspicious of imagination as of action: in 1902 Guadeloupe, in area five hundred eighty-four square miles, supported over eleven hundred officials. The essential differences between Morocco and Senegal were shrouded by the fiction that both were now French. Colonial areas were supposed to differ neither from one another nor, ultimately, from the metropolis. They were distant suburbs of Paris. Since the Empire was an organism for which France herself supplied both spirit and motive power, no Colonial Office *à l'anglais* was needed, with separate "desks" to cope with separate problems. In India, for example, the British encouraged the Muslims to arrive at a sense of their own distinctive identity within the imperial structure: but the French, since officially they lived for the day when Muslims, like everyone else, would be made over *à l'ouest*, could not admit that they had an identity. They made no distinction between Arabs and Berbers, and as a consequence their success with the broken and detribalized societies of Negro Equatoria was not repeated among the close-knit fraternities of the Maghrib. Islam could never divorce its culture from its faith, however seductive the French doctrine.

Algeria, wherein the resentment of Islam against this new Frankish invasion was fiercest (to the degree that the aims of its dissidents in 1860 and in 1920 and in 1960 remained identical) was the principal scene for the ruthless French tactic of *refoulement:* irreconcilables were driven out, and segregated, beyond the civilized pale. That this had to be done was a severe blow to the school of assimilation, which even before the First World War realized the impracticabilities of their task. For they had to confess that those within the pale were often as unsatisfactory as those without. The *évolué* had been created: from what he had evolved was plain enough, since every day he rubbed shoulders with it in the street, but where had he now reached? Too often he stayed suspended between the two worlds, deprived of the confidence of both.

This condition, which they described as an artificial chrysalis, was what the rival school of policy, the associationists, wished to destroy. They urged that a leaf should be taken from England's colonial book. Advisory local assemblies should be established. Native suffrage should be granted and extended. Not Paris, but the local capital, should be made the goal of local political ambition. But they had scarcely any more success. The magnetic field that rayed from Paris, whose force the entire civilized world acknowledged, reached also into the other world beyond its confines. As a British observer noted in 1950, while in British West Africa everyone who was politically conscious at all was a nationalist of some kind and recognized London as the sinister center, indeed the natural habitat, of every colonialist plot, in French West Africa there was a profusion of Catholics and anticlericals, Communists and Gaullists, socialists, syndicalists, and existentialists.[80]

This compliment to St. Germain and Montparnasse proves that both assimilation and association could congratulate themselves on victory, that the local capitals could indeed focus something of France, trap at least some of its essence, for others to distil. But it illustrates, too, how often imperialism in the tropics displays itself as a policy of extended urbanization. Only in towns could

[80] Lord Hailey, *An African Survey,* Second Edition (Oxford, 1957), p. 1226.

any notion of civilization be grasped. Where European standards succeeded at all was in Dakar or in Brazzaville—or in the case of the British, in Accra or Singapore. It is contestable that civilization recognizable as such ever made successful settlements in, as distinct from forays into, a continental interior. "Upcountry," to the colonial townsman, was a third world.

It is also contestable that the imperialists, seeking to civilize, were ever able, anywhere, to do more than establish a lodge in the wilderness. Cultural imperialism is the process that describes the permeation and pervasion of one culture by the thought, habit, and purpose of another. Before asking how this can be done, it is right to ask first whether it is done at all, as a conscious act. Civilization can be defined as the machinery of culture, as the aspect a culture takes on when it wants to accomplish something. But this definition, or any other, may not take an individual very far. For it is men who make contact with other men, not one civilization with another.

The doctrine of civilization is in fact one that has always been short of doctrinaires. The sociologists who so often invoke it are not themselves colonizers or colonials. They study the works of colonization. They judge the pressures that beset men in the colonial situation. They then return to the metropolis to issue their reports, which are seldom of such a nature as to assure them a welcome on any return visit to the colony they have anatomized. They are spokesmen for their own culture, for they suppose that theirs is the language of all their fellows. But the number of Englishmen, enterprising overseas, who could have passed an examination on the mind and thought of Shakespeare or Milton, has surely always been few: hence the general sympathy with the doctrine that it is "character" that counts. Similarly, not every Frenchman is the spiritual son either of Bossuet or of Voltaire; or every Dutchman the heir of Grotius or Rembrandt; or every Portuguese a devotee of Camoëns; or every Spaniard an expert on Cervantes; or every American a brother to Jefferson. Civilization has its high peaks of achievement, but most men are born within their shadow. The majority of us are plainsmen.

A colonizer thus may have some, but equally he may not have any, of the spiritual equipment that belongs to his own culture and society. Every European who sets foot on an unknown shore or crosses a range of hills for the first time, there to meet with strange peoples and customs, is not, by definition, opposing a world of fear and magic with the world of science and morals. It may be only a case of mediocrity meeting with superstition. Since there are so many unknown factors, each is likely to be suspicious of the other. The pioneer may have brought with him some sense of mission, but his first mission is to secure his own position, and sometimes this remains the only mission he ever finds time for. He has to find out whether the natives are hostile or friendly. If they are hostile he has to defeat them and then hold them permanently in check. If they are friendly he has to use them as best he can to reinsure his own dominance. Either way they are not his equals, to be treated as he would treat his own kind. They have no rights, as he has. He has a right to survive: and if this is his right, it cannot also be theirs. The idea that their lives are of as much value as his does not and can never occur to him. For he is a man who has a great enterprise afoot. He is a careerist; and the measure of his career, both in his own eyes and in those of his own society, is reckoned by the success and continuing stability of the colony his energy has founded.

This stability is at once the prize and purpose of the colonial or *colon*, the "Creole" or colonial-born European who is the heir of all this enterprise. His main aim in life is to keep what has been bequeathed to him, together with whatever his own efforts have added to it. All his thought and action are conditioned by this. The original colonizer was compelled to study the habits and gauge the ideas of "the natives" in his own interest, in order to survive; but the colonial, already secure, sees no point in doing this. He stays indifferent to the nature of the society in whose midst he spends his days. David Livingstone once remarked that in five hundred years the only thing the Africans had learned from the Portuguese was how to distil bad spirits with the help of an old gun barrel.[81] In Shanghai no European merchant knew the Chinese language, a fact to which many "Old China Hands" were to refer with pride. In Rangoon, as a traveler reported in 1941, there is a famous temple-pagoda, called the Shwe Dagon:

[81] Quoted in Cromer, "The Government of Subject Races," in *Political Essays*, I, p. 12.

It rises gold to the sky. Luncheon conversation was about it. To my surprise no one had ever been inside it. "Footwear," was the explanation. "You have to enter barefoot. An Englishman can't do that."[82]

The colonial sees all this as a backcloth, or simply does not notice it at all, which accounts for his shock and irritation when some outsider indicates its actual nature. Told that he is a member of a plural society, the colonial's likeliest response is to strengthen his resolve to preserve the partition that divides his own kind from the company of those beyond its pale.

If he does this, the colonial easily becomes an isolate. He cuts himself off not only from the native society but from the understanding of his countrymen of the metropolis, the Europeans of Europe, who have anyway got their knowledge of the colonial world not from the self-absorbed colonial (unseen till retirement and then out-of-date) but from the sociologists. It is these Europeans who propound, and often believe in, the liberal doctrines by which the Creole European is supposed to be guided. But he will not often be guided by anything except his own commonsense, of whatever kind that may be.

In 1864 Gorchakov's circular in regard to Central Asia spoke in terms of which it could be said that there was nothing in it which was not at the time generally believed. Generally believed, that is, by the educated opinion of Europe. But they rang hollow in the city of Tashkent, where its conqueror, Tchernaiev, governed according to native law through native officials. His entourage consisted of a Russian military society, the members of which continued to live the life they remembered, or imagined, having lived in St. Petersburg. But, as the inevitable observer primly observed, many allowed themselves liberties of conduct which elsewhere they would not have ventured upon or even thought possible. The rejects of the Imperial Army were posted to Central Asia: those who were volunteers were the wild ones, men "in desperate mood."[83] A Russian report of 1871 calculated the result:

In the eyes of the natives we are far from being on the moral height on which we ought to have placed ourselves as soon as we arrived in

---

[82] Diana Duff Cooper, *Trumpets from the Steep* (London, Penguin Books, 1964), p. 100.

[83] Boulger, *England and Russia in Central Asia*, I, p. 65.

Central Asia. . . . Our civilising mission has been limited up to this time only to the propagation among this people of our paper money—and in return we appropriate all their faults.[84]

The mysteries of administration confounded the resultant confusion. A Tashkent taxpayer told one of his Russian overlords that the people could understand it if the Russians tormented them in order to get money out of them, but they were baffled by a situation wherein the Russians spent their own money for the purpose of tormenting their subjects without getting any advantage for themselves.

Metropolitans with no intention of enterprising overseas have long used this kind of evidence to support their contention that all colonial societies are second-rate, since from the outset they are manned by second-raters. The type of civilization and culture which they disseminate, supposing them to do it at all, can only at best be third-rate: "culturally inert," says J. S. Furnivall of European colonies in general and of *Netherlands India* (1939) in particular.[85]

This body of opinion, naturally disliked in Batavia and Kuala Lumpur, has recruited the crowd-psychologists, tracing the neuroses of "the group," and taking a short line with the sociologist's concepts of "culture-impact," "culture-shock," and the like. For what is a culture? It is the complex of the distinctive beliefs, attainments, and traditions of a particular society, which in action assert themselves under the name of a civilization. It conditions the men who grow up in it. It forms their personalities. It does this so conclusively that they do not understand, sometimes do not even recognize, that there are other types of personality, other brands of reason, produced by environments of which they know nothing, and will never discover much. They will not discover much, not because they lack intelligence, but only the will to understand. Perception is always the product of an effort of will, and it is just this effort that the colonial will not make. The missionary with a true vocation may, with Gandhi himself, believe that all men are *harijans*, children of God, and so discover a way through this wall: but laymen find themselves in the realm of the

[84] E. Schuyler, *Turkestan* (London, 1876), I, p. 225.
[85] Furnivall, *Netherlands India*, p. 458.

incomprehensible and are content to accept the position—since, after all, never the twain shall meet.

It is, therefore, an obvious oversimplification to think of two cultures as two vessels unequally filled, and to suppose that they have only to be connected up for their contents to find a common level. Yet this, says O. Mannoni in his *La Psychologie de la Colonisation* (1950), published in English as *Prospero and Caliban* (1964), "is the schoolmaster's philosophy which has ruled Europe with a rod of iron."[86] Sociologists, the schoolmasters of our time, sort certain human situations into patterns and then comment not on the situations but on the patterns they prefer. To claim an attitude of scientific objectivity is merely to claim yet another white man's privilege. They categorize both the native and the colonial and assume themselves involved with neither. To be sure, these self-appointed appraisers of the colonial scene see themselves as fulfilling a genuinely liberal function. Liberals are men who believe all men are equally endowed with reason, but they have nonetheless their own definition of reason, and a particular habit of recognizing it. They are accordingly baffled when they meet with people whose own brand of reason does not translate into the liberal terms they understand.

Where, then, two different structures of personality impact upon one another, two things are likely to happen. The native's personality is eroded. The colonial's personality is intensified. The native's environment has been invaded, and therefore his personality, a product of that environment, has also gone down to defeat. Deprived of his cultural terms of reference, he becomes literally a nobody, not only in the invader's eyes but in his own.

The colonial does not change; he merely becomes more of what he already is. And what is he? The psychologist says that he is a colonial because he wants to be. In the civilization of Europe, it is the sense of inferiority, of talent as yet unrecognized, that drives a man upward. He competes in order to succeed. But, suppose he does not succeed? Suppose his talents are few? He wishes a superior status, but others who do not consider him their equal will not grant it. Why not, then, transplant himself to a place where equality is not a factor, where he will be surrounded by

86 O. Mannoni, *Prospero and Caliban* (New York, 1964), p. 84.

dependants, where his superior status will not be questioned? Life as the white man lives it in a colonial dependency will reassure him as life in Europe never will. Status need not be won: it is, instead, owed. The colonial is by definition "somebody," natural overlord of the nobodies. He may be permissive, but he is not genuinely paternal. He does not want to change the native's state of docility and dependence. To him all men are, and are called, "boys." He is not at all anxious to take up the white man's burden. He wants, instead, to drop it, to be free of its weight. The white man's burden is himself.

The colony, in this view, is part of an unreal world, wherein the colonist believes he can marshal the facts of life to his own perpetual convenience; where there is, for example, no such thing as racial prejudice, only a commonsense calculation as to respective merit. Mannoni illustrates from fiction the magnetism of this appeal, the universality of the dream. William Shakespeare presents a factual account of unreality in *The Tempest* (1611); Daniel Defoe repeats it in his *Robinson Crusoe* (1719). Both imagined a colonial situation and analyzed its essence. Shakespeare's Prospero has had the worst of a palace quarrel. He has immured himself from his contemporaries on an island and looks on mankind as his natural enemy. He has mastered the arts of magic. He seldom speaks without criticizing someone or complaining of his own condition. He is a bully. He bullies the "good" native, Ariel, whom he constantly asks for gratitude. He bullies the "bad" native, Caliban, whom he once made much of and sought to educate and civilize, but whom he has now rejected because Caliban tried to rape his daughter Miranda. He also bullies Miranda. He tricks and cheats the castaways whom the tempest, of his own making, sets upon the island. He enslaves one of them, Ferdinand, to whom very plainly he has no wish to yield up his daughter. He attains maturity when he relinquishes his magical powers, but it is not a full adulthood: for although at the play's end Prospero realizes that he can no longer rule his private world, he has no wish to return to the real world to take up his responsibilities. He will return, but only to retire, as a privileged and protected personage. He returns to Naples as Shakespeare's posterity will one day retire to Cheltenham or Bath.

Robinson Crusoe's story also tells "of the long and difficult cure of a misanthropic neurosis."[87] Crusoe is afraid because he is alone, and his fear is the fear of other men. Like Prospero's, his solitude is broken: but Crusoe has no magic with which to defend himself, and it takes him *two weeks* to recover from his first sight of Friday's footprint. But Crusoe too attains maturity: he learns to accept and then to master his condition, to control Friday, to outwit hostile cannibals, and to govern the island. He ultimately returns to the real world, fully healed, and much the richer because of some successful ventures in slave-trading.

In both tales, the desert island symbolizes the colony. It is peopled with one's own ideas and wishes. It is decked with the cloud-capp'd towers and gorgeous palaces which are our fitting homes, were our merits only recognized. Their inhabitants do not belong to themselves, but to us. Ariel and Friday are willing spirits, for they recognize and reflect our virtue and our superiority. Caliban is unwilling, for he sees our vice and reflects *that*. Ariel and Caliban are kin to each other, to Prospero, to Shakespeare, and thus to oneself. They represent man's divided nature: R. L. Stevenson was to name them Jekyll and Hyde (1886).

Crusoe is of course the "colonial" aspect of his creator Defoe; and when he published his dream, as Mannoni says, "all Europe realized it had been dreaming it"; and the story of Crusoe on his island has fascinated men from that day to this. For men must recognize their own several aspects if ever they are to grow up. Mannoni does not however suppose that the majority of us ever will; and chief among these retarded spirits are the colonials, for

The same unconscious tendency has impelled thousands of Europeans to seek out oceanic islands inhabited only by Fridays, or, alternatively, to go and entrench themselves in isolated outposts in hostile countries where they could repulse by force of arms those same terrifying creatures whose image was formed in their own unconscious.

The enemy, the barbarian, the savage, is feared not because we know anything about him but because we know too much about ourselves. Jekylls, we live in terror of Hyde. He is the Id, or image of the instincts: "The negro, then, is the white man's fear of himself."[88]

[87] *Ibid.*, p. 100.
[88] *Ibid.*, pp. 103–104.

To grant such an image "independence," or even to allow that it has a separate identity and volition at all, is of course to open the door to anarchy and violence. Hence the dogged attachment of the colonial to the *status quo*, the context of his dominant position. The sun must not set on his empire, which is all-inclusive, encompassing the world of idea and habit as well as the world of fact. The rights of man are properly viewed only through a prism made in France. Accordingly, the result of the much-vaunted French dream of assimilation, itself the produce of the doctrine of *la mission civilisatrice*, was the destruction of the native personality; and, not content with this ruinous result, *les civilisés* promptly betrayed him whose spirit they had pervaded, since they never in fact admitted him as one of themselves. The colonial relationship did not change merely because both parties to it left the physical bounds of the colony.

What, in essence, is a colonial relationship? It is one in which the captor is held as firmly by the chain as his captive. When the chain is broken, as it now is in this present age of decolonization, he suffers consequences as traumatic. For colonization could never have existed at all had there not also existed a willingness on both sides that it should. It has always required "the existence of the need for dependence"[89]—and there is, therefore, something too sweeping in the *Encyclopedia Britannica*'s definition of imperialism, which declares it to be the policy of a state aiming at establishing control beyond its borders "over people unwilling to accept such control." England absorbed an Indian Empire by force of Indian arms. Imperialist agents in Africa refused as many tribal treaties as they signed. Traditions linger in places as distinct from one another as Angola and Borneo of white men arriving from the sea, to be hailed as gods. White men, with superior *juju*, had more than magical weapons: they were thought to have a surer grasp of life and its problems. They could not be understood, but their power was clear—and, as obviously, it was underwritten by even more powerful forces that were unseen. They were men to be followed, men to be accepted, men to be placated, men to be feared.

This bond of dependence, particularly heartfelt among the

[89] *Ibid.*, p. 85

Malagasy, effectively excluded any growth of a feeling of inferiority: for dependence, like independence, is a status, which can
have its own dignity, as the achievements of centuries of feudalism
(which always distinguished between service and servility) stand
to show. It was the fear of abandonment, more than any urge
towards "nationalism" or self-government, that in Mannoni's view
precipitated the revolt in Madagascar in 1946. How could a notion
of self-government occur to a people whose lives, customs, and
emotions were governed by the dead? It was the European *colon*
who, swayed by his own sense of insecurity and fear of its
increase, communicated these things to the natives. They in
turn experienced a sense of loss that mounted to a pitch wherein they were ready in their panic to use violence, of a kind
that stranded them even farther out of reach of any reasoned
approach. None of their own educated leaders' talk of democratic right could heal their feeling of alienation from all that
was safe and known.

There is, of course, heresy here. Is not this, at base, a Frenchman's denial that any civilization worth the name exists beyond
France's own borders? Is it not an assertion that anyone who
voluntarily quits that splendid scene to live in earth's outermost
limits is not a voluntary at all, but an unfortunate who is in the
grip of some darkly irrational compulsion?

These subjective questions can find their own subjective
answers. Certainly the liberal tradition, which has sapped and
mined the colonial structure for over a century, which made imperialism a byword, and which today surveys the ruins of empire
with a deserved sense of achievement, holds it as an axiom that
all peoples wish to be independent, to stand firmly on their own
two feet. The educated leader, the "Brown Sahib,"[90] was this tradition's proudest product. That the imperialist agencies and the
colonial situation could never have survived if they had not represented the very reverse of a desire for independence; that there
are people who feel secure only when surrounded by customs
that are at once familiar and authoritative; that if such rise to
their own two feet they are put to it to stand still with success, let
alone walk—these are opinions which, since they have never be-

[90] Tarzie Vattachi, *The Brown Sahib* (London, 1962).

come part of anyone's political currency, nobody has wanted to circulate. Mannoni remains classified as an impressionist, whose entry into a field of study manned entirely by a representational school of scholars has caused surprise, but not much discomfiture and little change of heart or approach.

Yet this Freudian account of the motive and product of imperialism at least defines a context in which can be set both the doctrine of civilization and those who have preached it. The Christian missionaries valued only that kind of "culture-contact" whose ultimate outcome was the disintegration of the native culture. It was their plain duty to lead those in its thrall towards the light. How far they succeeded, whether or not they ought to have tried at all, has been subjectively debated: for the missionary has met the fate of yesterday's hero. Mary Kingsley wrote that although the missionaries in West Africa certainly did not intend to turn out skillful forgers and unmitigated liars, these were very often what they produced.[91] Conversion was a matter of the heart: Mannoni would remark that very few of us know our own hearts; Miss Kingsley asked only how many were equipped to look into the hearts of men with whom they had neither intellectual nor spiritual points of contact.

The white culture, for example, assumed that its own social instincts were instinctive among all men, expected the African to think more of his wife and children than he did of his mother and sisters, "which to the uncultured African is absurd."[92] In his turn, the colonial suspected the missionary as a radical in disguise, undermining for the sake of the next world the social order of this. The missionary reciprocated, charging that gin, rifles, and venereal diseases were the only gifts of civilization that the average colonial was willing to grant. Yet they shared a wider agreement than they admitted. Colonial settler or missionary, they were "the men on the spot." They lived among these natives. They were assured that they *knew* them as no imperial official, far away in an armchair, could know them. And they agreed together that the native, wherever encountered, was not of the same moral order as themselves. The settler as a result called him a savage. The mis-

[91] Kingsley, *West African Studies*, p. 661.
[92] *Ibid.*, p. 377.

sionary called him a lost soul. But he was, in either definition, an outsider.

If there is no common moral order there is no basis for human sympathy.[93] Benevolence, paternalism, protectiveness: all these can come into play, but not the understanding that comes from fellowship. In such a situation bodies meet, not minds. A proof of this is the status, or lack of it, allocated throughout colonial society to the man of mixed race, who has collected more wounding nicknames in the English language than in any other. This mingling of blood may not have been always, but it was certainly often, "the result of a brutal temperament which refused to be guided by anything except its own desires."[94] The privileged colonial was free to translate into his own terms the social conventions of a fast-forgotten Europe. Women were willing spirits, female Ariels, a compound of comfort and service, yet their very docility could sometimes establish an empire of their own over the Europeans who fell under what was often indignantly categorized as a spell. But white men have cohabited with women of another race for three centuries in the West Indies and in the American South without finding the time to reassess the moral order, or to promote them to a status of equality. In these areas the racial frontier has been continuously and devotedly manned by the "poor whites," a group constituting a separate caste, tenacious of a place and an identity in the social scheme which their own lack of energy and ability would otherwise have lost them.

Whatever its doctrine, no imperialism in practice ever broke free of its own insistence on the social superiority of its agents.

This it was that effectively prevented the transmission of genuine ideals that were conceived by genuinely civilized men. This was why Gilbert Murray for one preferred the imperial officers as a civilizing agency: they might often be ignorant and unsympathetic, but at least they would always be free from the "disastrous bias" of the colonists themselves.[95] For in the average European dependency, the native races were never admitted to the mental life of their masters. They thus could have no inkling into their

[93] E. F. Frazier, *Race and Culture Contacts in the Modern World* (New York, 1957), p. 46.
[94] Cabaton, *Java and Sumatra*, p. 187.
[95] Murray, "Exploitation," p. 155.

hopes and plans, no understanding even of the meaning and purpose of the daily routines of *bwana* or *sahib*. This was the true barrier. All other forms of segregation were flimsy compared with it.

As a result of its perpetual presence, the subjected came to value civilization not as an idea but as a provider. Its visible props were money and power and energy and techniques, all the things that gave the white man his social status and personal prestige. It was what the white man had, not what the white man was, that owned a magnetic attraction. It was because he knew this that the average colonial set his face against the emancipating trend that was forced upon him by the sophisticated liberals. He too had a personality to defend, an identity to preserve. He could not retreat from the position that he had what he had because he was what he was. And what he had he deserved; and it was this worth, this essence, that was not communicable, whatever the schoolmasters said. He would not admit that natives, however exhaustively educated in western fashion, would ever attain that degree of civilization which alone could entitle them to the money and the power and the social ease and all the etceteras of life, the "what-not" of Professor Langer's definition. These things were symbols of a superiority already possessed. What they symbolized could never be transmitted. Some things indeed could be transmitted, but these were only images, reflections. To take one example, a European language was the instrument of an imperialism of an especial, cultural kind: for it bred in those who learned it as a second tongue (but ultimately as the only one they could use in the modern world if anyone was to understand what they were saying) a loyalty to long and abstract words, and a corresponding wish to live that sort of life, political and social, in which such words were commonplaces of the day.

But who had the power to grant this wish? As liberalism advanced its own imperial frontiers, the blunt references to higher and lower moral orders, to silk purses and sow's ears, to superior and inferior civilizations, became unacceptable, and the writ of the ten commandments was now supposed to run, as it had not in Kipling's experience, "east of Suez": but the ideas that had bred these categories and stereotypes still lived. In 1860 Herman

Merivale, drawing on his official experience, could make the point plain:

To infer that, because what are termed free institutions have produced certain qualities in certain nations, therefore by giving the institutions you secure at once the qualities, is as if a geologist were to expect to make slate or coal by creating those geological conditions which have produced slate and coal in the laboratory of uncounted ages. The establishment of political liberty, where the national character has not the requisites for its reception, cannot succeed.[96]

Conceive, he added, the grant of liberal institutions to a community of Chinese! Conceive, chimed his contemporary J. S. Mill, representative government for Bedouins or Malays! A century later, Chinese, Bedouins, and Malays have all a political experience of representative institutions: but that this is a proper end product of western imperialism, a diminishing band of colonials and all their unidentified kin at home still doubt.

Empire, then, proved stony ground for the dissemination of a doctrine of civilization. It scattered itself among tares, many of which were of its own sowing.

But something was accomplished. What was it?

Karl Marx, although contemptuously dismissing the motives of imperialism, had seen the revolution it was bringing about. "Civilization-mongers," in China and elsewhere in Asia, would despite themselves and their curious theories create history's necessary "body of officers and sergeants,"[97] who would dragoon that backward and absurd world into the fold of western industrial society. It did not matter what doctrine they appealed to. They were not, as they so fondly thought, building anything; and the future they had in mind was not the future that was due to be born. Their real occupation, their true *raison d'être*, was in demolition work. They were destroyers. They would create a heap of ruins wherever they went. And quite rightly. England in India was the unconscious tool of history: for did not India (and here Marx agrees with both James and John Mill, whom he despised)

---

[96] Merivale, *Colonies and Colonization*, pp. 657–658.
[97] Marx, *On Colonialism*, p. 125.

live an undignified, stagnant, and vegetative life, one of barbarian egotism, caste- and slave-ridden, where men were never the sovereigns of circumstance, but remained worshippers of monkeys and cows?

Surely, then, there was a doctrine of civilization at work in the world, if Karl Marx, the bitterest enemy of its professed principles, admitted that it was at any rate *better* than anything that had been produced elsewhere? Marx, like all imperialists, looked forward to a future of his own devising, which he had convinced himself was history's own decree or, as the Rabbis of his original faith would have put it, was the law of Providence. Marx consigned the future to the proletariat and assumed that *their* imperialism, when they came to exercise it, would be right and just. The more orthodox imperialists had their own convictions, equally strongly held. They were mistaken, and so was Marx, for we are none of us prophets. The liberals found out that the world at large did not choose to travel the liberal path, that liberalism was in anti-colonialist circles looked on as just as suspect as any other equipment that belonged to the imperialist. The communists discovered that they did not hold a key to the ways of the world either. But both made their impact: both established a context in which others had to work. Both made "the West" the image that "the East" was determined to reflect, and made it inescapable that men in the extra-European world had to make a choice between these two forms of western ideology.

It remains, then, as an epilogue, to take a view of the world these imperialists and all their doctrines brought into being.

FIVE

Undertones

Practitioners of empire had no forum to preach it from after the twentieth century's First World War. The length of the casualty list that this clash of empires had produced was too notorious to be explained away. It could not even be adequately explained. The most resolute devotee of the doctrine of "strategic interest" could not pretend that anyone's strategic interests had been served by the slaughter and maiming of some ten million young men. The vanquished Germans were rounded on and accused of "war guilt," and of course they denied it: but that there was guilt attributable no one troubled to deny. If not the Germans, then the armaments manufacturers: if not these, then secret diplomacy. If not that, then the theory of the balance of power. Or the "war of steel and gold." Or the "international anarchy." And all these could be encompassed within the word "militarism"; and what was that, but the child of imperialism?

If this was not an adequate explanation, it was certainly satisfying. The critics of imperialism, those English and German socialists who had first discovered it, therefore became the accepted analysts of this later time. They were so clearly right. Sages and seers, they alone had truly divined the self-destroying nature of the world they lived in. In 1901, Koebner and Schmidt tell us, "there was as yet no general theory of imperialism in existence,"[1] but the nature and course of the war in South Africa, embattling simple farmers against capitalist machination, made imperialism an international slogan. The subsequent war

[1] Koebner and Schmidt, *Imperialism*, p. 248.

of 1914–1918 made it an international platitude. Under the concentrated attack of those who found in it the author of Europe's destruction, no doctrines of power or profit could hold their ground. The stage was presumed to be filled with dupes and villains, consistently below the level of events in the tragedy they were acting out.

At one side of it, surveying the debris from an eminence of idealism, stood the American President Woodrow Wilson, who had issued in January 1918 fourteen rules for the proper conduct of international affairs. At the other, a crowd of Bolsheviks, the founders of a far superior theatre for the world's action, continued to twist Lenin's knife in capitalism's wounds. They themselves followed a road to empire that denied the guidance of any imperialist theory at all. As they rushed along it they issued a series of diagnoses and verdicts on the world they had quit and which they now hoped, for its own good, to subvert. What were the new states of Czechoslovakia and Yugoslavia but part of the imperialist-capitalist nexus? Who were the "Young Bokharans" of 1920–23, but the gulls and lackeys of outmoded doctrine, *bourgeois*-nationalists whose petty ambition blocked the route to progress? Who could better clear that route than the Red Guards, the harbingers of the classless Utopia, who in February 1918 sacked Khokand; who brought down the "Kurultai" movement in the Crimea; and who settled a final account with the stoutest of all the enemies of the imperialism of the Tsars, the Circassians of the Caucasus? Who dared declare, chiming in with the tropes of the Wilsonian liberals, that Bashkiria belonged not to the proletariat, not to the future—but to the Bashkirs? What, anyway, was this new doctrine of "self-determination," but a cloak for self-seeking and a licence to greed? Destiny was already determined: how could any assertion of the self alter the march of history or produce anything but illusion and ultimate despair? Everywhere the truth, and the way to it, was masked and clouded by tradition, by custom, and by that very doctrine of acceptance which had for so long been so battened on by the strong. What (to take only one example) was the Arabic script, common to all the Turkic languages in use in Central Asia, but a vehicle of cultural imperialism? For was it not, as the Soviet Encyclopedia made clear, "the alphabet of the Muslim religion and one of the instruments for the enslavement of the masses through the medium of the priest-hood"?[2]

Russian Bolsheviks, in promoting their rigorous discipline and dogmas, did not do so in the name of Russia, which was not allowed to appear in the new title for their country: the Union of Soviet Socialist Republics. "Pan-Slavism" was only another veil, woven from vision and dream; and no one irritated the true communist ideologue more than the visionary and the dreamer. "Russia," one such dreamer, the novelist Feodor Dostoevsky, had cried, "at the head of the united Slavs, will utter to the world . . . her new, sane, and as yet unheard-of word!"[3] Whatever word he had in mind, it was not that which history, with the help of its devoted agents, was resolved to issue. Marx himself had declared Pan-Slavism to be an anti-historical movement, which if encouraged to any degree of success would betray the revolutionary cause for the shadow of a nationality. Lenin had found it stained with an "imperialist and autocratic connotation."[4] Modern communism therefore could not treat with it: its own doctrine of power must be made of different stuff. With history encamped at its side, it would set out to marshal the facts of the future, and whip everyone within reach along the only true path to progress and civilization.

The older doctrine of civilization was meanwhile enduring not only this appalling onslaught from without but a certain sensation of shame from within. As time passed the realization became widespread that the war of 1914–1918 had been, in essence, a civil war between the races that had for so long chosen to display themselves before the eyes of Asia and Africa as the trustees of civilization. As Lugard remarked of his own particular African bailiwick, the Nigerian now knew how to handle bombs and Lewis guns and Maxims, and had seen white men budge while he stood fast; "and altogether he has acquired much knowledge which might be put to uncomfortable use some day."[5]

This sense of discomfort, the suspicion that the future, by which the committed imperialist had long been fascinated, might betray

[2] Conquest, *Last Empire*, p. 95.
[3] John Erickson, *Pan-Slavism*, Historical Association Pamphlet G. S. 55 (London, 1964), p. 28.
[4] *Ibid.*, p. 20.
[5] Quoted in Michael Crowder, *The Story of Nigeria* (London, 1962), p. 224.

rather than crown his achievements, was to develop in intensity. The profession of the civilized, that it was their inescapable duty to spread the values of civilization wherever their agents' enterprise might take them, was now said to have provided only a further arabesque to the façade behind which imperialism carried on its essentially antisocial activities. Not everyone lost heart: but the first symptom that the heart was threatened was a failure in energy and will. A contemporary of Lugard's noted of *his* bailiwick, in this case Mesopotamia (Iraq), that the British Empire had won the war indeed, but in doing so it seemed

to have lost faith in its mission and belief in the obligation, imposed on it alike by duty and self-interest, to uphold the principles of authority and good government for which it stood.[6]

In other words, that "belligerent civilization," from which not even Marx had been able to withhold admiration, had lost its belligerence, and in expending it had spent also the moral capital on which all imperialists had so confidently drawn. Without its support, their authority stood ready to be revealed as a usurpation.

That "the West" was the guardian of civilization had always been taken for granted, since they were the powerful and successful nations of the West that had declared the principle in the first place. It was part of their imperialist equipment. This equipment had now to undergo a close inspection. After 1919 the physical ability of the European powers to control and defend their empires was very seriously diminished. No longer could imperialists believe that, as a reward for the exercise of their strong right arms, the Golden Age was just around the corner. Journey's end for that hope had been reached somewhere in the mud of the Somme, and was mirrored still in the disenchantment of those who came out of it. In 1900 Prince-Chancellor Bülow had asserted that in the coming twentieth century the German Empire would prove to be either hammer or anvil; but before its second decade was over neither hammer nor anvil could be confidently identified as such in the rubble that littered Europe. In such circumstances the old imperialist assurance—which had been to subject races its main attraction, since men are inclined to admire and envy other men

[6] Arnold T. Wilson, *Mesopotamia 1917–1920: A Clash of Loyalties* (Oxford, 1931), p. x.

who announce they know exactly where they are going and when they plan to get there—could not be upheld. Words such as England's Milner had used in South Africa, at the time of the Boer War (and even then a little plaintive)—

British influence is not exercised to impose an uncongenial foreign system upon a reluctant people. It is a force making for the triumph of the simplest ideas of honesty, humanity, and justice[7]

—were no longer relevant to or even sensible in a world that wearily allowed so shallow an arrangement as the Treaty of Versailles to crown four years of upward struggle towards honesty, humanity, and justice.

The years that followed were paced by paper tigers. If the European empires did not display their weakness, that was because no one openly exposed it. Their equipment was indeed inspected, but the general belief was that these emperors still wore clothes. In the seventeenth century the reputation of the imperial Spanish monarchy had far outstripped its capacity to assert its power, yet European states had continued to organize their foreign policy to cope with an expected Spanish initiative, as if Philip II still ruled. History now repeated itself. Once the Washington treaties on limitation of armaments had been signed in 1922, the Far-Eastern Empires of the United States, Britain, France, and the Netherlands existed under sufferance of a closely deployed Japanese navy. Twenty years passed, however, before this point was driven home, and very cruelly. In that interim, empire remained an accepted fact; accepted more because of the tradition of acceptance than because it brought with it anything immediately acceptable. Although the "unrest" in India (always called by that name) was a standing embarrassment to Britain, her politicians could and did treat it as a domestic, not as an international, problem. The rebellious Indian Congress movement of the 1930's, unlike its more fortunate predecessors in the American colonies of the 1770's, could find no outside assistance, and had not itself either the physical power or the self-assurance to unseat the British from the imperial saddle.

But imperialism, without a dynamic policy, made no more vic-

[7] Quoted in Edward Crankshaw, *The Forsaken Idea* (London, 1952), p. 37.

tories and could not even keep its own practitioners in good heart. The *status quo* was its temple: and *All Quiet on the Western Front* its prayer. Like Manchu China in the nineteenth century, it hoped to deny the movement of the years. Before 1939 none of the imperial powers bothered themselves making any calculation how to build some radically different future for their colonies: world policy as a working concept was always left to the innately romantic Germans to proselytize. The great initial mistake of the colonizing powers, Tunisia's President Bourguiba has pointed out, "the mistake which lies at the root of all the others,"[8] was that when they took over a country they never envisaged that they would one day have to leave, to pull out. In the interwar years, colonial officials did indeed reckon that such a day might be coming, but they saw no need to speed its arrival and made no effort at all to educate public opinion how to cope with it. Few educated Europeans could have accurately found on a map, let alone given a brisk account of the current problems of, Indo-China or the Gambia or Surinam. Matters were best left alone. Before 1914 the English socialist H. G. Wells had issued book after book filled with schemes and plans how best to organize the future: but *Mind at the End of Its Tether* was his diagnosis of man's condition in the world of 1945.

For, if the century's first war had weakened, the "gale of the world" that blew through its second exhausted the European nations involved in it. Six years of effort were this time crowned not by any peace treaty, however bad (for no one was capable of making even a bad treaty), but by two international revolutions. In the East the forcible imposition of a Japanese Empire, although short-lived, made any resuscitation of the former European empires there impossible. In Europe any hope of balancing power disappeared when Germany, the European center, was destroyed and partitioned. In one sense Europe itself disappeared, for it soon became a zone of strategic maneuver between the power of the United States and the power of the Soviet Union.

Accordingly, Europeans who were no longer able to balance power on their own continent had no chance of being able to retain it in their colonial territories overseas. The strain on their

[8] Bourguiba, "Outlook for Africa," p. 427.

moral and material resources was too severe. In the last days of the British Empire, that old enclave of power and its accompanying paternalist assumption, this process of strain can be most clearly traced.

In the circumstances of the post-1945 era no British Government either of the Left or of the Right could afford to defend the Empire against the surging tides of colonial nationalism. To do so would have required the mobilization of a standing British army in India and the marshalling of flying squadrons of military police, ready and willing to hold down restive colonies the world over, for an unforeseeable length of time. Britain would have involved herself in a bitter and probably irreconcilable quarrel with the United States, for whom she was physically no match; and she would have been forced to withdraw from any participation in the United Nations' Organization, a body whose hostility to the continuance of empire was plain from the outset. She would also have been forced to spend untold sums of money—money which she did not have and which certainly no one would have lent her; and she would have had to drain the country of the man power it needed so desperately to set the lurching domestic economy back, if not on its feet, at least on its knees. In direct consequence, she would probably have had to cope with mutiny in a conscript Army that had been promised peace, or at the least demobilization, when the war with Japan was over. Not one of these things could be afforded. Politics was still the art of the possible, and this no longer included the possibility of preserving an empire by force, in an age when its prestige had gone.

It was an unpleasant pill to swallow, and the Fourth French Republic would not swallow it. It faced the world with more deeply rooted preconceptions: it had honor to redeem, "face" to preserve. The French Army fought long and hard to maintain the French Empire, first in Indo-China, then in Algeria, and in doing so, had anyone cared to notice, effectively exposed the hollowness of the argument that all imperialism is and forever must be rooted in economic motive, professing only the doctrine of profit: for neither Indo-China nor Algeria were ever essential to the economic stability and security of the French Republic. But the French Army, driven back into its *champ d'honneur* as into a redoubt, could not forever act as a political agent and came at the last to a dry and bitter defeat. It was finally made plain that if empires could not be held together by physical force, there was nothing else to keep them in being.

Here again the British were to prove the most pragmatic in their work of imperial demolition, carried out with only one last nostalgic salute to empire and unilateral power (made, not wholly unfittingly, at the Suez Canal, "the swing-door of the British Empire,"[9] in November 1956). Decolonization was only a larger pattern of demobilization: it admitted that another course for the national life had to be plotted and set. All British power had to be concentrated, if any of it was to be conserved. Imperialism, like other things, begins at home. Accordingly, since it was not a practicable proposition to preserve the British Empire, it was not preserved. An old, tory view of "British interests" here obtained. Nothing was sensibly to be defined as a British interest which Britain in an emergency did not have the power to assert as such. To be able to declare an "interest" at all, and to have it respected at large, is itself a symbol of power. To declare as such what cannot be upheld is to be exposed to contempt, and thus to find whatever influence remains weakened further still. It was in accordance with this reasoning that the business of decolonization, begun by the Labour government in Asia, was continued by the Conservative Party at an accelerating pace throughout the 1950's and 1960's. Labour quit Palestine, India, Pakistan, Burma, and Ceylon (1947–48); the Conservatives retired from the Sudan (1952), from Egypt (1954), from Ghana and Malaya (1957), even from Sierra Leone (1962) and the Gambia (1964). They added North Borneo and Sarawak to a Malaysian emporium they did not control (1963). They asserted, and later reversed themselves, in Cyprus (1961) and Kenya (1963). Their last imperial structure was a federation in Central Africa (1953); but, when mined from within by black nationalism, white nationalism in Rhodes' own kingdoms found no support in London, and the structure was allowed to collapse after a ten years' existence. In the West Indies another federation, half-built in 1958, fell apart after four. The Colonial Office itself, long the

[9] This phrase was apparently coined, again not unfittingly, by Captain Anthony Eden when a young M. P. in 1929.

arbiter of half the world, was absorbed (1962) into the Commonwealth Relations Office; and although many dependencies still exist (1965) they arouse little enthusiasm among their paternal governors, since they are plainly more a legacy from the past than an investment in the future.

All this proved that the Second World War had placed a time bomb beneath all the imperial structures and all the doctrines that supported them.

For the nature of that war, engaging the children of the tired survivors of the earlier battle, made any case for imperialism look even worse than it had after the earlier armistice. The major justification of the imperialist doctrine of civilization had been that imperial control opened up for a subject race greater possibilities of life: wider horizons, the blessings of a superior culture, a world filled not only with better mousetraps but with higher thought. This argument could not make sense to the educated among the subject races, as they assessed the results of this new civil war that their masters had indulged in. Embarrassed memories of African fetish and *juju* paled before a thunderstruck confrontation of gas chambers and genocide. The glamour of the European image faded in the fiercer glow of high-explosive bombs on London and on Hamburg; while the atomic bomb, dropped on Japanese cities, served only to prove to Asians and to Africans that "the West" thought there were some things too dangerous to be used in a civil war, yet which well might be experimented with in areas that *Herrenvolk* deemed less important to the continuance of civilization.

For what, anyway, had the war been fought?

It had begun as a war against "Hitlerism." This was an ominous definition at best, for what, if one looked for a category, was Hitlerism? Bred in the heart of Europe, in a Christian society famed for its philosophy and learning, what was it but the extension of power over the unwilling and the fearful, by means of a jackboot tyranny? And what was this, but imperialism: no doubt of a kind better known in the ancient world than in the modern, but imperialism nonetheless? What was it, simultaneously, that the Chinese were defending themselves from? The imperialism of the Japanese, bent on exploiting what did not belong to them. What was it that Benito Mussolini was trying to set up in the

Mediterranean and in Africa? A new Roman Empire, combining no doubt a Carthaginian pursuit of monopoly with the *sacro egoismo* of Italian fascism. What was it that lay inert along the great chain of the East Indies, binding that tropical world to a small country in Europe, the Netherlands—a country that lacked the physical power to defend even its own borders, let alone a swathe of land and water some three thousand miles in length some ten thousand miles away? The prestige of imperialism: the accolade of vanished generations, granted to an Empire won long since and never called in question until this latter day. How came the French to be in residence in Algeria, in Syria, and in Indo-China? It was by force they had come, for to be sure no one who lived there had asked for their presence. And what was it that the Hindus of the Congress movement so railed against, but the stolid and unimaginative governance of the British *Raj*, its back set hard against the wall of the future? Certainly, the Führer of the thousand-year Third Reich and His Britannic Majesty ruled Empires of very different kinds: but were they not both *empires*, and although their manners were distinctive were their ideologies really so? Did not imperialism supply their motive force and their continuing purpose? Did they not both take for granted the doctrine of a master-race, a superior order, a greater efficiency, a truer reading of the map of life?

The war was also fought for freedom, as the Atlantic Charter of August 1941 took pains to underline. It was not supposed that the kinds of freedom it listed as essential would ever be got beneath anyone's imperial rule, however malevolent or benevolent a doctrine its rulers laid claim to. Once again a voice came from the wings of this stage, this time in a tone stronger than President Wilson's, since able to call on support from an audience such as Wilson could never assemble. Publicists in the United States made emphatic announcement that American forces had not entered the war in order to restore the British Empire to its accustomed place in the sun; and it was a particularly harassing campaign on that ground that brought Winston Churchill in November 1942 to his feet at the Guildhall to proclaim that he had not become the king's first Minister so that he might preside over the liquidation of the British Empire. But indeed that was to be his fate. His ejection from office spared him the decision in

1947 of abdicating power in India; but he was again Prime Minister in 1954 when British troops left India's anteroom, the Suez Canal Zone in Egypt, after a sojourn in that country of seventy-two years.

The tide of anti-imperialism had indeed been rising before the war broke out. Its height was measured by the British government itself, which saw to it that the report of the Moyne Commission on the condition of the colonies in the West Indies, although ready for publication in 1939, was not published until 1945 for fear of providing the Nazis with some very welcome propaganda —so shocking a state of social and economic life did it reveal, in an area the greater part of which had belonged to the paternalist Empire of England for three centuries. In these interwar years, the British Labour Party, never in real power but steadily increasing its influence, had taken care that the Leninist view of imperialism was never lost to public sight. Socialism was "opposed to the very principle of foreign domination of coloured races," one pamphlet announced;[10] while another stated that the Labour Party

viewed with great concern the appalling evils produced by capitalist exploitation in certain of the tropical and sub-tropical parts of the British Commonwealth of Nations.[11]

When war began, Labour's leader Clement Attlee emphasized in *Labour's Peace Aims* that the Labour Party repudiated imperialism and that it had "always been conscious of the wrongs done by the white races to the races with darker skins."[12] Given such a lead, those with darker skins were very anxious to increase the degree of this consciousness in the white man's world and felt sure they could rely on the white man's liberalism to help them do so.

This anti-imperialism, if natural to Englishmen who were also socialists, was of course even more natural to Americans who were nothing of the sort. (For it was an editorial in *Life* magazine

[10] British Labour Party, *The Colonial Problem* (Brussels, 1928), p. 174. (Material submitted to the Third Congress of the Labour and Socialist Internationals.)
[11] *Labour and the Nation* (Birmingham, 1928), p. 48.
[12] *Daily Herald*, London, 14 August 1941.

which stated, on 12 October 1942, that "one thing we are sure we are *not* fighting for is to hold the British Empire together.") The third article of the Atlantic Charter declared its respect for the right of all peoples to choose the form of government under which they would live. Now this was a quite a separate problem, Churchill later assured the House of Commons, from the progressive evolution of self-governing institutions in the regions and peoples which owed allegiance to the British Crown.[13] But Americans knew very little about any such process and continued to issue directives about the nature of the world that was to be born once the evil forces of fascism had been put to flight. Their Vice-President Henry Wallace insisted that no nation, when that time came, would have the God-given right to exploit other nations: "There must be neither military nor economic imperialism in the people's century which is now about to begin."[14] The Republican presidential candidate Wendell Willkie reported on his arrival home after a world tour that he had found everywhere the dread of imperialism.[15] President Roosevelt himself, in company with his Secretary of State Cordell Hull, insisted that the Atlantic Charter "applied to all humanity." He had not moved from his earlier conviction that "there never has been, there isn't now, and there never will be any race of people on earth fit to serve as masters over their fellow-men."[16] In 1942, after the failure of Stafford Cripps' mission to India to pacify the Congress, Roosevelt sent Churchill a thoughtful excursus comparing the aspirations of the thirteen American colonies with those of the subjected Hindus; to which Churchill replied that his communication was of high interest, "because it illustrates the difficulty of comparing situations in various centuries and scenes where almost every material fact is totally different."[17]

But if the nature of the war made it inevitable that anti-imperialism should increase in volume, with the cordial approval

[13] 9 September 1941: *Hansard's Parliamentary Debates,* fifth series, vol. 374, pp. 68–69.
[14] *The Times,* London, 23 May 1942.
[15] *The Times,* New York, 27 October 1942.
[16] F. R. Dulles and G. E. Ridinger, "The Anti-Colonialist Policies of Franklin D. Roosevelt," *Political Science Quarterly,* lxx (March 1955), p. 4.
[17] Winston S. Churchill, "The Grand Alliance," *The Second World War* (London, 1950), III, p. 214.

of its most powerful participant, so too did its course. For Japan was not forcibly displaced, by the valor of armed men confident in the justice of their cause, from the Co-Prosperity Sphere she had mapped out and occupied: an area that by 1945 included not only a great swathe of China but Southeast Asia and the Dutch East Indies as well. No Allied soldier forced her back at bayonet point into her home islands. When in August 1945 the Japanese retired from their imperial holdings, they did so quietly, folding their tents and disappearing over the horizon, apparently at their leisure and in their own time. The local inhabitants, lately their subjects, witnessed no heroic expulsion of their overlords by the triumphant Allied Powers. Malays and Burmese could see no good reason why the British, who had had to cut and run in 1942 (having put down no roots into the life of the people of the country, as *The Times* itself remarked) should walk back into their respective peninsulas and take up where they had left off, since they could hardly say they had earned the right to do so.

Since the white man's prestige, and with it the power, the *mana* of the empires he had built, was thus unrestored by any display of the warrior virtues, it evaporated. That process of growth in self-governing institutions, to which Churchill had referred, now seemed too painfully slow to the ambitious colonial nationalist, who wanted his own generation, not that of his children, to inhale the sweet smell of success. In 1938 a British Colonial Secretary had been able to assure the House of Commons that it might take generations or even centuries for the peoples in some parts of the colonial Empire to achieve self-government,[18] without arousing cries either of outrage or of ridicule; but ten years later no one who valued his political career would venture any such prediction. One unfortunate official who declared his opinion in 1954 that Cyprus was still just such a place was never to be heard of again.[19]

But the type and style of the Japanese achievement, even

[18] Malcolm MacDonald, 7 December 1938: *Hansard's Parliamentary Debates*, fifth series, vol. 332, pp. 1246–47.
[19] Henry Hopkinson (now Lord Colyton, then Minister of State for Colonial Affairs), 28 July 1954: *Hansard's Parliamentary Debates*, vol. 531, pp. 504–14.

though Japan herself was compelled to quit the world scene for an indefinite period, could not be forgotten. She enjoyed the prestige of the pioneer. She could claim a historic role as the torchbearer of progress amid a chaos of stagnant cultures and alien imperialisms. "Asia for the Asians" was blazoned on the banners she took with her into Burma in 1942; and, although the exigency of war demanded that the Japanese Army (no instrument of culture) should continue to control Burma's affairs, Japan encouraged the nationalists and promoted those ideas among them that she thought best fitted to survive into the world that was to come:

The Burmese government and its officers *should be put in a position* to convince the people that they are not just tools but have real power and prestige.[20]

On nationalism itself, the promoter of the Greater East Asia Co-Prosperity Sphere could not be expected to throw a blanket approval. Nationalist movements in Burma, in Indonesia, and in the Philippines had obvious social value, in that they could be used as weapons to turn against the imperialism of the enemy. But Singapore and the Straits Settlements of Malaya were too strategically important to be allowed autonomy, and their direct annexation was planned. In November 1943 Sukarno was in Tokyo, vainly asking the Tojo government for a Declaration of Independence for Indonesia. And some peoples, like the Annamese of Indo-China, were definitely inferior, with ideas to match, for

when independence movements are based on narrow-minded racialism or what tends to be racial egoism, it [*sic*] shall be corrected and guidance given to turn it into Oriental moralism.[21]

The Japanese had been sitting too long at the feet of confident European mentors not to have copied them in this too and to have developed a doctrine of civilization of their own, with its corresponding sense of mission. Fired by a schoolmaster's zeal, they were alike contemptuous of European imperialism, of American liberalism, and of Russian communism. All, all were spurious, self-

20 Elsbree, *Japan's Role,* p. 63.
21 *Ibid.,* p. 26.

interested dogmas, ill-fitted to Asian conditions, the nature of which only an Asian nation could truly know. To this situation the Japanese alone held the key; and since heaven had entrusted them with so noble a destiny, they deserved a loyalty and a respect, even a sympathy, in circumstances of such great difficulty. *Kodo*, "the imperial way," above all things required an understanding; and it was always one of Japan's chief grievances that her aims and purposes had never been and were never to be properly understood. That the West should misunderstand her was perhaps excusable; but even in the East Japan could never find, in her short heyday among her new subjects, the "sincerity" she sought.

Japan's wartime trials and errors served also another purpose for those who came after. Although the course of empire had taken her down an impasse, the impulse that had driven her onward came to be well understood by the "emerging" nations in Asia and in Africa during the next two decades. Was it possible to build a nation without at the same time laying the foundations for imperialism? Could any nation survive that was not prepared to reinforce and strengthen its power? This had long been the pattern of security in Europe: was it also to be true of Asia and Africa? Were the hundred years spanning 1950 to 2050 merely to repeat on those continents the nationalist record of the European continent in the previous century? Must the world wait while those who had at last inherited their own part of it learned at long last the lesson of coexistence that had become, at long last, a commonplace among their late masters? It was not a prospect that pleased anyone either in Europe or in Asia who was able to look down it.

An early sympathizer with the Arab struggle to find identity in the modern world had remarked that Asia, in order to survive, was obliged to remodel itself according to European standards, although in doing so it sacrifices half the value of its traditional ideas.[22]

In India, Gandhi, forever pursuing that same sense of identity, and seeking how best to express that unique Hindu contribution wherever it could be made, complained how mean were the aims

[22] Wilfrid Scawen Blunt, *My Diaries* (London, 1920), II, p. 390.

of a merely political nationalism and despaired of the Congress and its methods almost as often as the Congress despaired of him and his. Was India's fate to be made over into a false copy of a European nation, taking everything, including her own thoughts, at secondhand? Was Japan and her nervous schizophrenia a model really worthy to be repeated all over the globe? Of what value would India be to herself or to anyone else in such a guise? These were ringing questions: and when Jawaharlal Nehru, whose bewilderment with Gandhi was closely paralleled by his affection for him, became an independent India's Prime Minister in the 1950's he showed that he had recognized the force of the lessons they sought to teach, even though they were not such as the nationalists could have afforded to follow while actually engaged in the struggle for power. India became a State, and a state of mind, apart.

For Nehru stressed the otherness, the professional Asianhood of India by building her a platform of independence in foreign policy. It was one of nonalignment, commonly called neutralism, from whose moral pulpit India could from time to time call down anathemas on the scuffling craftinesses of the two ideologies whose forces stared at one another across the dry arenas of the Cold War. In the Indian view, the Cold War itself was merely the solidification of two imperialisms which would certainly have been in fluid movement had either dared break its own mold. This position of deadlock commanded no prestige. It even invited exasperated comment, that men who were supposed to be the masters of technology and progress should have so entrapped themselves. Of this there was a great deal forthcoming, from the Afro-Asian zone of protest, with Nehru's voice leading its chorus. But he was lucky in his time and generation, for even before he died it was made plain to him that this policy of neutralism was protected less by its own innate virtue than by its permissive acceptance by others, who knew that India was a vital power vacuum between the two worlds and were content to keep it so. It was an Asian neighbor, the People's Republic of China, which by its imperialist thrust into Tibet in 1962 made it clear to a discomfited Nehru that Asians, like other races of men, might sometimes hold the opinion that war had its victories no less renowned than peace.

For the disappearance of the empires of Europe from the continents of Asia and Africa, a process that was nearly complete twenty years after the end of the war, did not signify that imperialism itself, with all its doctrines and all their seductions, had disappeared either from the world's map or from the hopes and consciousness of those who, having now joined the ranks of the world's leaders, wanted to plot its future course. These new men took their places in a world already made, with assumptions already established. India's moral stature, to which a general consensus agreed she was entitled, shed luster on other ex-dependencies but could communicate to them neither the entitlement nor the stature itself. They had to draw their political weapons from armories already in existence. Tunisia's President Bourguiba tells us how complex is the world scene upon which a "new nation" is compelled to look. Bruised by its long struggles to free itself from the typical European bonds of colonialism, it finds itself, when at last emancipated,

faced with another form of imperialism, an imperialism which under the outward semblance of a popular regeneration—the rights of the proletariat, equality, prosperity, happiness—aimed at imposing on the world its own conception of the road to happiness.[23]

The goal was clear, but the way to it mined and wired. Nations that resolve to pursue happiness, whether along the American way or with the help of the dialectical process of history, are likely to be equally determined to arrange that their own nationals will enjoy the kind of happiness they know best. What guarantee has a Tunisian, or anyone else, that the view from either Washington or Moscow will be to his taste?

The British power in India, wrote a convinced imperialist of the nineteenth century,

is like a vast bridge over which an enormous multitude of human beings are passing . . . from a dreary land.[24]

Since the day he watched, multitudes had passed in procession, both over this bridge and over others similarly made. Yet west-

---

[23] Bourguiba, *op. cit.*, p. 426.
[24] Sir James Fitzroy Stephen, in a letter to *The Times*, London, 4 January 1878; quoted in Stokes, *Utilitarians and India*, p. 300.

ward, look—was the land any brighter? Eastward—might it not turn out to be even drearier? Had Asia, then, "sacrificed half its standards" for nothing of value in return? Must it forever find itself standing on the sidelines of two worlds to which it was equally antipathetic? Had those "claims and expectations," which Lytton had said could never be met, now been met indeed, but only in a context of finality, which denied them any further life? Had Cecil Rhodes' "back country," that grey area where men did not stir and hope did not move, turned out to be a larger region even than he knew—one that had grown, rather than diminished, since his time? In what Henry Wallace had hailed as "the people's century," the century of the common man, were common men commonly to find that happiness, in whatever guise it came, was attainable only in proportion to the size of the number that went looking for it? "The greatest happiness of the greatest number" had once been an excellent nostrum for successful social policy, according to the English philosophic radical Jeremy Bentham (1748–1832): but in a world that contained but did not nourish over three thousand million people, how *many* could expect how *much?*

As the twentieth century began to wane, no one could answer these questions. Many disliked their being put. Nevertheless the primary-producing colonies, become primary-producing nations, small "powers" with their desks at the United Nations' Organization, had to cope with the issues they set. They could still accuse the affluent powers, those ex-imperialists who had quit the field of territorial conquest but who still kept the keys of power and profit, of not only taking the advantage but of monopolizing it. The palace of the nations at Lake Success indeed rang with such charges. To get any advantage at all for themselves, the newcomers had to tread what soon became a wellworn path. It often took them back to the doorstep of their onetime "mother country," or to that of the State Department in Washington. And when they asked for a loan the new nations inclined to do so in the tone of one asking for the repayment of a debt, since it was only right (surely?) that the past misdeeds of the imperialists should be paid for and the imperialists themselves kept conscious of the extent of the reckoning. The borrowed money was then used to lessen the degree of economic dependence in the new nation.

Emphasis was everywhere placed on industrialization, and the prestige that had once attached to intangibles of empire now belonged to hydroelectric projects and colossal barrage dams.

For the new nations wish to make themselves as much like the old nations as possible. The imperialism of western technology knows no frontiers and few resistance movements whose history will be long. Money is its music. Everyone knows what money cannot buy; but only those who can afford to, forget what it can. It commands one thing at least; it can buy time; and it is time, in turn, that creates a context for culture and the experience of privilege. The man who has time is the man to envy: and the entire concept of colonialism—imperialism judged not from the sidelines but experienced from beneath—is owed to the universality of this Deadly Sin.

The primary-producing countries must deal in conditions of the market and with terms of trade which they do not control. In these circumstances a charge of exploitation is not only easily made but genuinely felt. Colony or ex-colony, the local economy is magnetized to a greater, and the emancipated nationalist, his political victories becoming stale, finds himself back in the shadow of "them," the machinators, the arrangers, the men who deal in "futures" not only of crops but of currencies. The United Africa Company in Ghana, *l'Union Minière* in the Congo, the oil empires of the Middle East, the banana and sugar corporations of the Caribbean—all of these have impacted heavily on the freedom of movement of new nations. The brand-new flag whose design has been the subject of popular competition may wave over a territory whose future is already mortgaged. The states of Latin America, which have enjoyed a political independence for over one hundred forty years, have also a longer experience of this problem than any: consequently, in the United Nations' Assembly, they have normally supported and have sometimes led the cause of anti-colonialism. Somewhere there is a conspiracy, somewhere a plot. Somewhere powerful agencies are suborning their dupes and keeping free peoples from being free. The Soviet propaganda that strikes this note, strikes hard.

The new nations have accordingly insisted that any grants-in-aid made shall be free of "strings"; that no condition shall be laid down that the recipient country align itself with a particular

political *bloc*. In the postwar era the Russians, beyond the immediate bounds of their Empire in Europe, have behaved circum-
spectly in this regard. They have left their *protégés* free to assert
themselves: not against their satellite position or against the fact
of Russian aid, but against the chorus of alarmed indignation
that is the inevitable reaction in the West. More colonialism is
found in the chorus than in the aid. I will shop in what market
I please, is the retort. It is one bred from the experience of con-
tributing to someone else's doctrine of profit.

Thus, although the style in imperialism may have changed, as
has the identity of those who follow it, the doctrines that underly
it remain what they have always been—moving men to envy and
to action. There is no lack of men in the political world who, if
they attain authority, will apply the lessons of the grim school
from which they graduated. Depending on what sphere of action
is open to them, they will still set out to westernize, to commu-
nize, to democratize, to industrialize, to modernize, perhaps even
to baptize, on the assumption that to do these things is also to
civilize. President Sukarno's description of the "unclassic" forms
which imperialism and colonialism take in the modern age is
indeed fast becoming classic itself: recent Indonesian imperialism
directed against another of the new states, Malaysia (1965),
argues that although the wish to establish a context of life for
others, whatever their views on the matter, may indeed be something that was learned from Dutch masters, it may also have its
source somewhere in that unmapped country of which Dr. Mannoni is a geographer, the country of instinct and impulse. If this
need for self-assertion becomes strong enough, a doctrine will
soon be produced that explains its motivation and outlines its
field of action. Aggression is anyway a form of therapy. It relieves
internal pressures and tensions. Is there not something exciting,
something truly emancipating, in the very act of throwing down
a gauntlet, of declaring, amid shocked surprise and flutters of
agitation, that one's patience is exhausted? Is not this in the very
best style of all those European nations who have made the map
of the world what it is?

Yet this emphasizes not a present condition of power but a
yearning to attain it. The last trophy—one yet to be seized from

the hands of the imperialists, the powerful, the affluent, the liberals, the whites, or whomsoever—is the initiative.

"A people of inheritance, as ye are to this day,"[25] says the book of *Deuteronomy*, of the Jews. It is true of all of us, but of ex-colonial countries more than most. What initiatives can they devise? What equipment will provide these? What standards of their own, ascertainable as such, do the "emergent" nations display? Twenty years have now passed without this becoming clear; and a new generation of men who were never put in jail or even told to get out of a white man's way has to face these questions. It is natural that the barrage against imperialism and all its works should have continued. The language of nationalism follows strict rules of political grammar: its chief danger is that a man who learns its semantics too diligently will never find time to learn anything else.

Yet the nationalist historians of Asia have found a means of escape from this. They are able to summon up the past in order to ease any pain their countrymen may feel in the present. To classify five centuries as "the Age of Vasco da Gama" is to use category as a salve for the wounds of colonialism, to write it off as a passing phase, an aberration, an interruption in the natural order. It is to see it, fatalistically, as but part of that cycle of change no race of men can escape: "there were others," as an English audience was reminded, "who a thousand years ago were stronger and more civilized than France or Britain or Holland, but who have suffered the same fate as many others before them—a fall, a decline, a regression."[26] It is likely enough that in Asia we will see a renaissance in arts and learning, a recrudescence of the culture that faded and withered beneath the baleful eye of da Gama and all his tribe. This initiative is certainly open to a man of the East. The same way was also open, in imperialist days ancient and modern, to Irishmen and Poles, to Jews and Slavs, who kept within themselves areas of life the alien proconsul could never pervade. To the African, however, this way is not open. These resources are not there. No communication

---

[25] *Deuteronomy*, IV: 20.
[26] Bourguiba, *op. cit.*, p. 428.

brings him light and help from the past. He can look only to the future. Ideas of Pan-Africanism, the sense of what has been called *négritude,* may help him reconcile what he does not know of the past with what he cannot know of the future. But in the meantime, the tenant of a country owing its political existence and even its name to the force of imperialism, he faces a formidable task.

Freedom and respect are neither owed nor issued. Everyone has to go into the world to look for them: they are not found on trees. The story of European imperialism records one such voyage of discovery: da Gama's striding, strident tribe had many strange encounters along the way. To the doctrines that supported them one can add one other: the doctrine of success. In western society the man who does not succeed in his quest can expect little sympathy if he blames others more than himself. This standard of achievement, and the degree of self-criticism that accompanies it, does not easily translate into other people's terms or relate to their experience. It is the product of a competitive tradition that the tropics do not know, where the very idea of a quest, the pursuit of happiness or the pursuit of anything, is incomprehensible.

Europeans when they first come in contact with that cheerful readiness to give up, since something is too hard; or with promises made without the intention of keeping them; or with engagements kept, but an hour late; or with professions promoted more because of their assonance than their actuality, have always been startled and taken aback. This was the factor that made them write off "the natives" as incorrigible and incapable, imitators who would never grasp the essence of what they were trying to copy. "You never know where you are with them": and both parties to the encounter can make the same complaint. When the explorer H. M. Stanley noted how some brawny Kavirondo porters in Central Africa laid down and actually died after meeting with a rainstorm in what was supposed to be the dry season, he was delineating one area of that context of bewilderment which spans between the expatriate who thinks he has much to teach and the native who does not understand what it is he is expected to know. Success is thus an alien standard, a curious way to judge things. To project oneself into a habit of mind that will accept it as *the* standard for every public action is immensely difficult, but this is what is being attempted, and very bravely. The struggle of the poorer nations, says Barbara Ward,

is to get through all the sound-barriers of their life at once: the economic barrier, the social barrier, the political barrier.[27]

The sound-barrier: it is a striking image. Anti-colonialism, too, is best described as a band of pressure. What techniques are needed to break it have not yet been discovered.

President Senghor of Senegal has remarked that "colonialism is a transitory stage—like feudalism, like capitalism."[28] Yet for practical purposes times of transition are unconscionably long in passing. If feudalism has gone, there are today Persians and Iraqis, Hindus and Siamese who have not been told of it. Capitalism in its turn has, these past hundred years, lain under a sentence of death not yet executed: Nikita Khrushchev's threat, "We will bury you," is rightly famous. (And its venom betrays the colonialist mentality that yet inhibits and embitters the Russians, kept outcast from western society for close on fifty years.) Moreover, to talk of transitory stages is to argue that there is available for consultation a map that marks the route on which these stages lie. President Senghor does not have such a map. Nor does anyone else. The only prediction safely to be made is that the world will continue to have *weather,* weather of a kind it has experienced before. It will rain on the just and on the unjust, on the rich and on the poor, on the agents and on the patients; and if a "Golden Age" of progress ever arrives, that may well be because men have resolved to deal with themselves as they are, not as they feel they should be.

But colonialism, that barrier to civilized intercourse, is perhaps transitory in this sense: the memory of old injury will fade, the memory of former dominance will evaporate (even in the dominant), and when these memories go so too will the complexes, inferior and superior, that attach to them. When that time comes the new nations will have made a mark in the world, will have

[27] Barbara Ward, *The Rich Nations and the Poor Nations* (Toronto, 1961), p. 69.
[28] *International Affairs,* vol. 38, no. 2 (April 1962), p. 189.

standards of their own making, and will therefore be able to measure their importance and have it measured by something better than nuisance-value. In creative action the self-contempt of the oppressed and of those who did not win their freedom but had it given to them will be interred. Less will be heard of nationalism, more of nationhood. The arts are there, ever a blessing to mankind, to be explored: when men agree on the dimensions of life and the proportion of things in it, they will be far on their way to that brotherhood the Utopians have so long sung. When these things have been achieved, the barrier of colonialism, like the sound-barrier itself, will be seen to have been broken.

Power is transient, too, but only in the sense that it changes hands. It does not change its nature, nor will that imperialism which epitomizes its public action and concentrates its force. The dominant, whoever is playing the part, will always be on stage. The doctrines that support imperialism will find their disciples in every generation. The indictments which have to date been brought against these were the products of an age that put its faith in liberalism and supposed that it was this which would continue as guide and mentor of their posterity. All their arguments, so self-evidently just, were set out by these men of goodwill in the conviction that, since their audience was also of that persuasion, it was only a matter of time before "the Great Illusions" of their time—such as war itself, imperialism, national sovereignty—would be exposed for the fraudulent things they were.

These progressives, staffing every school of thought and happy to promote an intercollegiate rivalry, did not question their own right to map the world's future, or foresee any wry Tunisian comment on the mysteries of such political cartography. Da Gama's age has ended, and its successor still lacks a name: but it is not the age that seers of the nineteenth century saw waiting in the wings of their future. The old illusions are the new illusions, the old rules are read, the old routes to security still clearly signposted. Multitudes still wait, in their dreary lands, to cross the old bridges. The action that men of action, still our heroes, can take—is the action that men of action took in the past.

For the only known road to survival, let alone security, takes the well-traveled imperialist route. Western technology owns the

greatest empire of all, and there is no nation that does not want
to become its satellite. It is because of this desire that nationalism
itself, invented in Europe but not intended for export, was so
eagerly seized on. All the world wants to climb up on to the
same wagon that took the Europeans to success, to promised
lands ruled by science and engineering and power. A country
that was never officially part of any European empire still pro-
vides the best example of this. The Japanese, pioneers in westerni-
zation, disguise themselves in western clothes during their working
day, and downtown Tokyo could be downtown anywhere: it is
at home that they follow the customs in dress and behavior of
their fathers and grandfathers. Outside, the world is mapped:
and although the newcomers can make their impact upon it, their
chances of greatly altering it seem small. Educated to western
techniques, they will certainly bring in ever larger numbers their
best energies to what it is they do, and their natural inventiveness
and capacities will find new methods of doing these things—but
they are the *same* things that will be done. Indeed they may
build a "better mousetrap," so that the world will beat a path
to their door: but they cannot now invent the idea of the mousetrap itself.

The valued political leader in a new state, the one who sur-
vives, is he who compels his people, often ruthlessly, to graduate
into the world's society, to follow along the lines that are already
laid down. His task is to see to it that they assimilate, and by
assimilation that they become equal to those who have gone
before and are still ahead of them. The modern "father of his
country," who hopes to earn that title, is determined on this: and
the degree of his determination is itself the best evidence of the
success of the imperialism of western technology, and of that
kind of political structure which best promotes the advance of
that technology. European political terms have everywhere had
to be grafted on to the native language, since nothing in that
language could be used to describe the arrangements that a
society bent on "progress" has to adopt. This invisible imperialism, growing daily in strength, is more encompassing than any
form of economic exploitation, and certainly more far-reaching
than the passing governance of someone with pretensions to be a
master-race.

Its areas of action have perhaps already been sketched out. Pan-Arabism and Pan-Africanism, for example, are two forms of imperialism which have not yet admitted to the name, nor produced leaders able to command success. Chinese power still lies latent in the world. The American democracy, in the throes of applying the democratic principle to those of its own citizens who have been denied it, has still to arrive at its full potential. The nations of Europe are experimenting with the idea of dissolving national sovereignty—an experiment which, even if never totally successful, will throw its shadow far. Industrialization is still at the beginning of its road. The force of religion, an absentee from the control of public affairs during the heyday of liberalism, may move spectacularly into some territory it has abandoned. The secular western institutions that the retreating empires left behind them are still on trial, and if in Asia and Africa parliamentary democracy has a struggle on its hands, this is not surprising, since the concept is essentially alien, and was brought to these continents as part of their mental baggage by imperialists who supposed that power and responsibility were mutually interchangeable terms. The imperialism that does not suppose so is as magnetic as ever. The imperialism that likes power for its own sake, profit for its own sake; that has the confidence to believe that its own values, and thus its own civilization, are superior to everyone else's, will continue to find its enthusiasts.

The extension of power by the establishment of "spheres of influence"—whether in political, social, economic, cultural, or religious affairs—is a natural habit of mankind. But we are beginning, perhaps, to know ourselves and our habits better than we did: and if the principle that politics is still fundamentally "the art of the possible" can find enough imperialists to respect it, even to make a doctrine of it, we will do well enough.

INDEX